ENGLISH Pressed Glass

1830-1900

RAYMOND SLACK

BARRIE & JENKINS

LONDON

First published in Great Britain in 1987 by
Barrie & Jenkins Ltd
289 Westbourne Grove, London W11 2QA

British Library Cataloguing in Publication Data
Slack, Raymond
English pressed glass, 1830-1900.
1. Pressed glass — England — History
    — 19th century
I. Title
748.292   NK5143

ISBN 0-7126-1871-6

Designed by Nigel Partridge
Typeset by SX Composing, Rayleigh, Essex
Printed in England by
Butler and Tanner Ltd, Frome

This book is dedicated to
Shirley Warren
whose continued support and
encouragement made the whole project possible.

ACKNOWLEDGEMENTS

I would like to express my gratitude to all those who gave assistance and encouragement in the writing of this book, and to those who have helped with inquiries where necessary. In particular, thanks of a special nature are due to Roger Dodsworth, Keeper of Glass, Broadfield House Glass Museum for supplying a photostat of the Thomas Webb II letter mentioned on page 22, Simon Cottle for helping to arrange transparencies from the Laing Art Gallery, Newcastle upon Tyne, Mr C. Mason for permission to view the collection of children's books at West Hill Library, Wandsworth, Mr Gordon Morrison for his help in locating material in the Library of the Institute of Mechanical Engineers, London, Gateshead Central Library (Local Studies) for information received, the Staff of the British Newspaper Library, Colindale, who were most helpful when difficulties arose with reproductions from contemporary journals, and the Staff of the Public Record Office, Kew.

My thanks go to Pauline Dickins for allowing me to photograph items in her collection (Plates 10, 48, 69, 70, 73, 74, 91 and 100, and Colour Plate XXVII); and to Jean Braid for allowing me to photograph the candlestick in Plate 50. Plate 8 is reproduced by permission of the Tyne and Wear Museums Service and Plates 9 and 11 by courtesy of Gateshead Central Library. Plate 59 is Crown copyright, Victoria & Albert Museum; Plate 88 is reproduced by courtesy of the Public Record Office, Kew, Plate 94 by courtesy of Broadfield House Glass Museum, Kingswinford, Colour Plates II-IV by courtesy of the Laing Art Gallery, Newcastle-on-Tyne, and Colour Plate XXIII by courtesy of the Libby Yalom collection, Maryland, USA.

Extra special thanks must go to Jack Davis, Director of the Suntex Group of Companies, for allowing me to see documents in his possession and helping personally; to Barbara Morris for reading the manuscript and making constructive comments; to Shirley Warren, who did a marvellous job, despite adverse circumstances, in typing out the registration numbers after accompanying me to the Public Record Office and helping me read through many lengthy documents; and to Neil Booth who kindly assisted in correcting the proofs.

CONTENTS

◆ ◆

LIST OF ILLUSTRATIONS

9

INTRODUCTION

Pressed glass in the nineteenth century had two main functions. The first, and the most important, was to satisfy the need of the people for good quality utilitarian glassware for everyday use at a reasonable cost, and the second was to supply functional objects that would adorn a household with a taste for the aesthetic and blend in with the Victorian fashions of the time. The latter was achieved admirably by the mould-makers who created designs in relief on their pressed glass inspired by classical architecture, wood carvings, paintings and illustrations, oriental designs and events of the day, to name but a few. Coloured glass, both opaque and translucent, was introduced and experiments in blending one colour into another were undertaken with outstanding success. Ornaments were made in a variety of shapes and sizes using all manner of designs and patterns, but most if not all had a useful purpose and were produced with considerable care and skill, the designer always combining practicality with ornamentation.

Catalogues and pattern books were produced to advertise the wares, and fortunately some of these are still extant to furnish us with some idea of the tremendous range of designs produced in the nineteenth century. Also, from 1877, we have descriptions of many of the wares in the main trade journal of the time, the *Pottery Gazette and Glass Trades Review*, hereafter referred to as the *Pottery Gazette*. With the aid of these, the design registry mark and sometimes a maker's trade mark, we can identify a great many of the pieces that are still in existence today.

The information in this book will, I hope, throw new light on a fascinating collector's field and help those whose collections have become a little static. Much research has been done, but it is by no means complete, and I hope that *English Pressed Glass 1830-1900* will open the way to further work and a still deeper understanding of the subject.

R.M.S.
1987

11

CHAPTER ONE

EARLY HISTORY

GLASS FOR THE PEOPLE

A hundred and fifty years ago, only the comparatively rich in England possessed glass in any quantity. The costly hand-made and cut crystal so often seen in stately homes and London auction rooms was simply too expensive for most people. The manufacture of this 'hand-blown' glass was a slow and costly operation: the glass-maker took a molten blob of glass from one of the 'pots' in the furnace of the glass house on the end of a blowpipe, and blew it into a bubble; this was then shaped into an article by 'free-blowing' the molten glass and manipulating it with special tools. Sometimes the blob of molten glass was blown into a wooden mould and the article given an initial shape before final finishing by the blowing method; these wooden moulds were known as 'dip moulds' and were used mainly to give a moulded decoration to an article without the costly addition of cutting. When cutting was used, this also required great skill, and it is not surprising that the finished articles were beyond the reach of the working and lower middle classes.

The invention of a process of shaping glass without the need for skilled hand-blowing and cutting made possible for the first time the production of glass in large quantities at a reasonable price. The glass thus produced – pressed glass – gave every householder a glass tumbler where before he had had a tin can or cup; it enabled a working-class family to aspire to the occasional luxury of an ornamental paperweight, a pair of candlesticks or a com-memorative plate. In terms of the improvements it brought to millions of people's lives, the invention of pressed glass was thus of enormous value. Certainly, the invention was in keeping with the paternalistic philanthropy of the day, as one contemporary comment shows:

> The manufacture of pressed glass has cheapened flint glass articles to such an extent that almost the poorest of the population may be supplied with elegant articles of domestic use, which a few years ago were far beyond their reach . . . It is to be hoped that the manufac-turers engaged in this important branch of our national commerce will energetically pursue the improvement of an art which most materially promotes the physical comfort and intellectual taste of the people – which has brought the costly crystal of antiquity to the tables of the poor, and has given, without stint, the light of heaven to the humblest of their habitations.[1]

THE ORIGINS OF THE TRADE

The process of pressing glass seems to have originated with the pressing of square feet of objects that were otherwise hand-blown, at the end of the eighteenth century. These square feet, also known as 'lemon-squeezer' feet because of their appearance from beneath, were attached to hand-blown goblets and other articles. The molten glass was shaped by being poured into a simple square mould and compressed with a plunger to give the concave 'lemon-squeezer' shape to the underside of the foot; the bowl of the goblet was then hand-blown and attached to the pressed foot while the glass was still hot.

There has been considerable controversy as to whether this process originated in America or Europe. The early days of pressed glass in America are rather difficult to assess, for, apart from a few obscure designs, most of the early patents were destroyed in a fire at the

American Patent Office in 1836, and the records that were kept from then on comprise little more than a few dates, with only occasional descriptions. However, the man often credited with the invention of pressed glass, the American Deming Jarves of the Boston and Sandwich Glass Company, himself acknowledged the European origins of the process in his *Reminiscences of Glass Making*, published in 1865:

> Although it is commonly believed here that the invention originated in this country, the claim cannot be fully sustained. Fifty years back the writer imported from Holland salts made by being pressed in metallic moulds and from England glass candlesticks and table centre-bowls, plain, with pressed square feet, rudely made, somewhat after the present mode of moulding glass.

That would put the date at *c.* 1815, and in fact we know that articles with pressed square feet were being manufactured in this country at the end of the eighteenth century.

1 Covered urn, *c.* 1800. An example of a lemon-squeezer foot on heavy luxury cut glassware before the advent of pressed domestic glass. Height 12 in (30.5 cm).

Indeed, an article on the origins of pressed glass written in 1881 recalled their popularity:

> Many in the English glass trade are living who remember the pressed square-footed ales and goblets; these are as old as the end of the last century, and were very fashionable with our ancestors . . .[2]

By the early part of the nineteenth century, glass of this type was produced in both Europe and America, but in England it was not until the 1830s that the first glass made solely by pressing rather than a combination of blowing and pressing was to appear and be produced on a commercial scale.

The Process of Pressing Glass

Pressing glass was, in essence, a simple process: instead of being blown by hand, and shaped either freely or in a wooden mould as described, the glass was shaped with a press and iron moulds. First, the glass was gathered from the crucible in the furnace by means of a blowing-

2 *Above* Lemon-squeezer foot on an early goblet, *c.* 1790-1800. Height 5¼ in (13.3 cm).

3 *Right* An early pressed-glass goblet made by Percival, Vickers of Manchester. Although this goblet was registered in October 1868, similar and rather cruder goblets of this type were made from the late 1840s on by the early pressed-glass manufacturers. Height 6⅛ in (15.6 cm).

iron and was dropped into the mould, a sufficient quantity being cut off from the rod with shears. Next, a plunger was used to press the plastic mass, so that after solidifying, by cooling slightly, the object would retain the form of the mould on one surface and that of the plunger on the other. After this, the article was removed from the mould and put briefly back into a hole in the furnace called the glory hole to melt away the imperfections on the surface caused by contact with the mould; this was known as fire-polishing. Finally, the finished article was cooled gradually – this process, known as annealing, was necessary because glass fractures if cooled too suddenly. The whole operation was so simple that unskilled labour could be used, and this, together with the speed at which glassware could be turned out, enabled manufacturers to sell the glass at prices most people could afford.

A contemporary account gives a good description of the basic process:

> The general use of glass vessels for domestic purposes has been developed by the partial substitution of mechanical pressure for manual labour. In the process of moulding glass the molten mass is forced to take the form of the mould, both on its inner and outer surface, by the pressure of the glass-blower's breath. In pressing glass, the molten glass takes the form of the mould upon its outer surface under the pressure of a metallic plunger, driven by mechanical means, whilst the form of the inner surface is modelled by the plunger itself. Pressed glass always requires to be polished by the re-melting of an outer film, roughened by contact with the metallic surface of the mould. The roughness is probably caused by the comparative coldness of the mould, which produces shrinkage upon the surface of the hot glass. It is found that the hotter the mould can be kept, the smoother and brighter is the surface of the glass. Hand pressure can be applied to the production of small articles by attaching a rubber or plunger, by hinges, to the mould, so that the hinges may form the fulcrum, and the resultant pressure may be obtained between the fulcrum and the handle attached to the plunger. For work on a larger scale, pressure is usually applied by a weighted lever, or a screw and fly-wheel.[3]

In the first of the two methods for applying the pressure described in this account, the mould was placed on a table directly beneath the plunger, which was supported in a frame that slid up and down on two uprights. The frame, together with the plunger, was lowered over the uprights by depressing a handle, which turned on a fixed axis at the side of the table. The handle, or lever, was restored to its original position by a counter-poise. This simple machine was known as the 'lever' press, and was supported on four small wheels for easy manoeuvrability. The 'screw' press was of similar construction, but instead of being operated by a handle, the plunger was depressed by means of a fly-wheel, which was rigidly connected with the screw and worked in a fixed cross-bar, being operated from above the machine. Both types of press are illustrated on page 16.

The same contemporary account goes on to describe the early moulds used:

> The moulds are usually made of iron, brass, or gun metal. The simplest form of mould is that employed for stamping flat diamond-shaped pieces of glass for 'Quarry' glazing (as

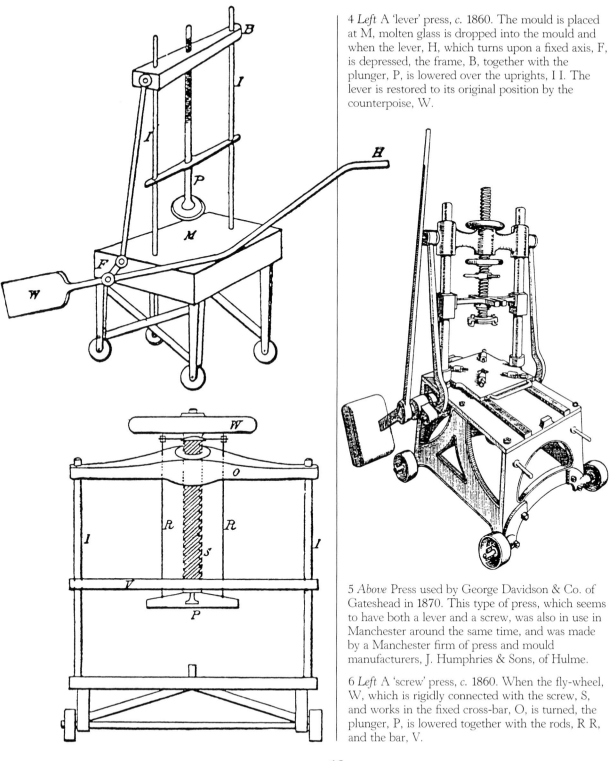

4 *Left* A 'lever' press, *c.* 1860. The mould is placed at M, molten glass is dropped into the mould and when the lever, H, which turns upon a fixed axis, F, is depressed, the frame, B, together with the plunger, P, is lowered over the uprights, I I. The lever is restored to its original position by the counterpoise, W.

5 *Above* Press used by George Davidson & Co. of Gateshead in 1870. This type of press, which seems to have both a lever and a screw, was also in use in Manchester around the same time, and was made by a Manchester firm of press and mould manufacturers, J. Humphries & Sons, of Hulme.

6 *Left* A 'screw' press, *c.* 1860. When the fly-wheel, W, which is rigidly connected with the screw, S, and works in the fixed cross-bar, O, is turned, the plunger, P, is lowered together with the rods, R R, and the bar, V.

used in lattice windows). In this case the mould merely consists of a flat slab of iron, with a slightly raised or depressed pattern, and of sufficient size to print two or more diamonds simultaneously. For articles of greater complexity, the moulds are made in two or more divisions, hinged together, and opening outwards by means of two handles, to facilitate the delivery of the glass. In the manufacture of a pressed ornamental salt-cellar the mould consists mainly of two pieces – viz a base and a collar. The collar is made up of three divisions hinged together. The several pieces are so hinged together that the article can be liberated with the greatest of ease, and the joints are so fitted that the new glass may be as little marked by them as possible. The bases of hollow vessels, after removal from the annealing kiln, require to be smoothed and polished.

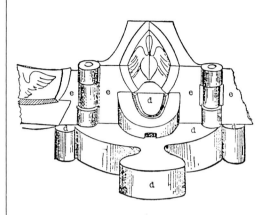

7 Mould for a pressed-glass salt cellar, c. 1860. The mould consists of two main pieces: the base, d and the collar, e.

At first, moulds and presses were fairly primitive both in form and function, and the glass produced was thick and uneven, but there were rapid improvements. One of the first – an American invention – was the use of a ring which fitted round the outer surface of the mould and the plunger. This ring enabled the plunger to be held exactly in position in the centre of the mould, so that the glass filled up the space between the mould and the plunger evenly. Another important development was the recognition of the principle that when the glass was flowing round the mould, it should not be forced into sharp angles – instead it should be made to flow round curves. This helped avoid wrinkling, and produced smooth, clear and even sur-faces, and was embodied in the use of the cup-shape given to the foot in the mould.

One of the defects of pressed glass, which showed its inferiority to cut glass, was the diffi-culty of producing and maintaining sharp angles in the finished object. If success was obtained with these angles in the mould, they were apt to be lost in re-heating and fire-polishing: the angles – being the thinnest parts – were the first to be affected by the heat, and were thus softened, and the sharpness was lost. To prevent this to a certain degree, the iron moulds were sometimes shaped so that the angles stood in bolder relief than necessary. If the heat softened them, they would still stand in relief. To solve the problem of the uneven surface of fluted articles, the moulds were constructed so as to make the flutes deeper in the middle, and with angles slanting towards this point. A flute composed of two angles slanting towards the centre was not as likely to show defects as a flute with a flat, plain surface.

Another defect of pressed glass was the marks left on the glass at points where the dif-ferent pieces of the mould were joined together. However skilfully the moulds were made, in the course of time the joints worked loose through the expansion and contraction of the metal,

8 Mould for a goblet. Sowerby's of Gateshead, late nineteenth or
early twentieth century.

and the glass was gradually pressed into the loose spaces of the joints; the surface of the articles was thus marred by ribs or sharp threads. To get round this problem, moulds were made to open at places on the article where they could scarcely be seen – in goblets, for instance, the marks were left on the edges of angles, or on the edge of the scallop made by the tops of the flutes.

Articles which were wider at the bottom than the top could not be pressed in the usual way, since the plunger, which was always a cone, had to be pushed into the mould and with-drawn. These pieces were pressed bottom up, and lips or projections sufficient to form the bottom were produced in the mould. The piece, after being pressed, was withdrawn from the mould, the bottom was heated, and the lips were closed together with a tool.

Presses and moulds quickly became more sophisticated – for instance presses were made with different mechanical devices that could operate a plunger below and another above, in order to form two cavities such as the cup-shaped foot and the bowl of a goblet. Moulds were made in several pieces, and were adapted to accommodate the introduction of lateral pieces with letters, monograms and so on. These pieces were movable – thus the same-shaped article could be produced decorated with several different emblems. This method was used to good effect, and considerable cost-saving, on certain commemorative pieces, especially on the issues of 1887 and 1897 for Queen Victoria's Gold and Diamond Jubilees respectively. Sliding lateral pieces were also used for moulding handles or forming holes in handles: the pieces were pushed through the side of the mould and then withdrawn before the articles were taken out. Handles were pressed in separate moulds, and the body of the object subsequently attached to them in another mould while the metal was still hot. Small hand-lamps were blown in ordinary iron moulds, and the handle formed by allowing hot molten glass to descend in a channel at the side of the mould until the two ends met the bowl of the lamp and became cemented to it.

Many articles, after being moulded, pressed or blown, had to be held by the foot for fire-polishing, or, in blown glass, to give them the final shape. It was customary, until about the 1870s, to do this by fixing the foot of the article to a piece of hot glass on the end of an iron rod known as a pontil rod. To detach the article from the pontil rod when finishing was complete,

9 Cutting a mould. Early twentieth century.

it was necessary to strike the latter with a sharp blow. This parted the two pieces, but the foot of the article frequently retained pieces of broken glass, which had to be removed by grinding. On some of the earlier pieces, the 'scar' was even left rough. To avoid leaving a scar when fire-polishing pressed glass, spring snaps were used. These consisted of a pair of jaws mounted on springs so that they could open and shut. These jaws were fastened at the end of an iron rod, like a blowpipe or pontil rod, and were clipped to the foot of the article being finished. Sometimes they were so arranged that they could be set forward and back and fastened by screws. This allowed them to be used to hold a variety of pieces of different sizes. This piece of apparatus became known as the 'gadget'. When it was first introduced into the trade in Lancashire in 1866, the glass-makers were reluctant to accept it on the ground that the coldness of the iron would crack the foot of the hot glass – they felt it would take a lot of practice to be able to judge the correct temperature at which the new invention could be employed. Because of this, the 'gadget' was not used for some years, but in the early 1870s it came to be used widely.

10 A pressed-glass commemorative plate made on the occasion of the death of Prince Albert in 1861. Diameter 4½ in (11.3 cm). Note the mis-spelling of the word 'EXALTETH'. Mistakes were often made on early pressings by inexperienced mould-makers, and were not corrected because of the high cost of making a new mould.

When in continuous use, the moulds often became overheated, and when this happened the glass would stick to them. This problem was eventually solved by the use of a cooling system which blew air into the moulds. By means of a revolving fan or other device, and tin pipes arranged round the furnace, a continuous stream of air was provided. India-rubber pipes were attached to the tin pipes at suitable places. By means of these pipes, a stream of air was sent into the mould after each pressing. The air circulating in the pipes could also be used for ventilation and for cooling the glass house, something that was of immense value considering the fierce heat produced by the furnaces.

It can be seen, then, that the pressing of glass in iron moulds presented many difficulties in the early days. The finished article tended to be rough, or at any rate to lack the polish of blown work. Improvements in presses and moulds held part of the key to the success of pressed glass in the second half of the nineteenth century; other developments, particularly the adaptation of the composition of the glass, and the use of suitable fancy designs in imitation of cut glass, were to set the seal on the establishment of the new industry; the latter will be discussed in the chapters on the individual manufacturers.

The First Manufacturers

The first makers of pressed glass in England were Rice Harris, Bacchus and Green, and John Gold, all of Birmingham. They were quickly followed by the Manchester firms of Percival and Yates (later Percival, Vickers) and Molineux & Co. (eventually Molineaux, Webb); by Thomas Hawkes in Dudley; and by Richardson; and Wheeley and Davis, in Stourbridge. All these firms were engaged in the blown-glass trade many years before experimenting with pressed glass, and some returned to this after a relatively brief flirtation with the new invention.

The vital prerequisite for making pressed glass was of course a mould, and the earliest mould maker we know of was James Stevens, who worked for Rice Harris of Birmingham. Stevens, a die sinker by trade, was said to have previously made moulds for a glass manufacturer in America, although we do not know who this was. Stevens made the first slip-out tumbler mould in about 1836, but it took him several years to persuade Harris, who at first considered the idea useless, to test it. When eventually the tumbler was made, it was clumsy and heavy: pressing tumblers thin at the sides was difficult even with later improved machinery. However, this prototype was eventually put into production and sold at about 6s per dozen. The second tumbler produced by Rice Harris was much improved in design, having six flutes and splits and a star bottom. Then came fluted tumblers with a host of other patterns, and very soon other manufacturers were entering the field.

As well as having to deal with technical difficulties, the early manufacturers were faced with the additional problem of the glass tax. This tax had been imposed on the industry in 1745 and was in force for a hundred years. By the turn of the century the tax had more than doubled, and was a severe obstacle in the way of the early development of pressed glass, since the first articles produced, being much thicker and heavier than blown glass, attracted more duty. This outweighed any savings that might have resulted from mechanisation. However, much to the relief of the pressed-glass innovators, the glass tax was eventually abolished in 1845. At last the industry could expand, and experiment with a much wider variety of articles in both size and weight. Thanks to its low production costs and the repeal of the tax, pressed glass was now able to sell at an extremely low price, and this found favour with a completely new class of consumer. It remained poor in comparison with the blown and cut glass which it sought to imitate, but for the majority of its purchasers its cheapness more than compensated for its lower quality.

In 1839 the Patent Office Design Registry was introduced. This gave protection to designs of goods for up to twelve months so long as the design was registered by the designer or manufacturer with the Registrar of Designs, and so from this date on we have a clearer picture of who made what in pressed glass. The first registration was made by Rice Harris of Birmingham on 24 January 1840. This was for a method of decorating pressed drinking glasses, such as goblets, ales, and so on, with flutes and slits alternately placed within the design. The second registration was again made by Rice Harris and was dated 30 January 1840, only a few days after the first. Again, this applied to a design of flutes suitable for pressed drinking glasses, but this time the registration included tumblers and no doubt referred to that first tumbler made from the mould designed by James Stevens a few years earlier.

In 1842 the Designs Act came into force and this provided for classes of ornamental designs to be registered with a designated Roman numeral. The first four classes were: I for metal, II for wood, III for glass, and IV for earthenware; other groups mainly concerned fabrics. The protection of these ornamental goods was for three years, and in 1843 'useful' goods as distinct from 'ornamental' goods were also included in the protection, also for three years. When a design was registered it was given a class – III for glass – the day, month and year were noted, and also the 'parcel' in which the design was registered, together with the design number.

This information was then transposed into a coded system using a diamond-shaped mark to be used on the goods that were under protection. This system was used from September 1842 to December 1883 in two cycles, the first from 1842 to December 1867 and the second from 1868 to 1883. Thereafter, a new system was introduced which used a registered number only: this appeared on the goods as 'Rd. No.', beginning at No. 1 in 1884. A full explanation of this system and how to read the different cycles is given on pages 131-2.

Before the middle of the century pressed glass was being produced in considerable quantity and in 1849 it appeared at the Birmingham Exhibition where it featured in the exhibits of Rice Harris, George Bacchus and Sons (as Bacchus and Green were known after 1840) and Lloyd and Summerfield, all of Birmingham. Although pressed glass was becoming popular with manufacturers and the public, its next showing, at the Great Exhibition of 1851, was received with mixed feelings and in fact the only leading manufacturer mentioned in the catalogue was Rice Harris. One review, however, gave a favourable report:

> Rice Harris and Sons' pressed glass is of the greatest interest. By pressing into moulds this elegant material is produced to the public in useful and symmetrical forms, at prices considerably below those at which cut flint glass could possibly be offered. Many of the specimens of pressed glass exhibited have a degree of sharpness in all the ornamental parts . . .[4]

Manchester, too, was producing pressed glass before the middle of the century. An extant letter dated 1848 and written by the founder of one of Manchester's most important glass factories, Thomas Webb II of Molineaux, Webb & Co., to the Warrington firm of Robinson and Skinner, describes how the manufacture of pressed glass was carried on at Molineaux, Webb. The men worked a basic 66-hour week made up of eleven moves or shifts of six hours each. They operated in teams of six called a 'place', which consisted of a presser, melter and gatherer, and three boys, the sticker-up, taker-in and warmer-in. The pressers received 21-23s a week before overtime, the melters 21-24s, and the gatherers 14-16s. The melter had the important job of taking the newly-pressed article to the furnace mouth and manipulating it in the heat to soften rough edges and seam marks but without destroying the sharpness and detail of the design. The letter also includes a list of the products being manufactured: tumblers, salts, sugar basins, dishes and plates, mustards, pickles, and butters. Large dishes were the most difficult job: only about 80-100 could be made in six hours, whereas up to 500 half-pint tumblers could be produced in that time.

The second half of the nineteenth century was to see the heyday of pressed glass, with countless experiments in methods of manufacture, both with machinery and ingredients. The trade spread, and established itself most successfully in Lancashire and Tyneside, two regions where coal was available to fire the furnaces and the ingredients for glass-making easier to acquire. Here, machinery and moulds could be made in the existing industrial workshops and materials that were not available locally could be brought in by ship to Liverpool and New-castle. Knowledge of the techniques was passed on to these new centres by the pioneers – for instance James Stevens' sons, after working with their father at Rice Harris in Birmingham, went on to manage the mould department at the greatest Tyneside factory, Sowerby's Ellison Glass Works at Gateshead. Meanwhile, the joint founder of Sowerby's Ellison Glass Works, Samuel Neville, had previously worked at Bacchus and Green.

At first, the canal system was used for transport, and in fact this may have been one of the reasons why Birmingham had early success in making so many manufactured goods. Birmingham had excellent canal connections with many parts of the country – Gloucester, London, Hull, Liverpool and Manchester – and by canal, too, came the Staffordshire coal for the glass furnaces. As railways spread throughout the country, however, rail was increasingly used. As pressed glass grew more successful, the major manufacturers opened up showrooms in the major cities – London, Birmingham, Edinburgh and Glasgow – and later in Europe, particularly France and Germany. A flourishing export trade grew up – for example in 1882 Sowerby's Ellison Glass Works were advertising weekly shipments of their glass to Germany, Holland, Belgium, Italy and Russia, and fortnightly shipments to Denmark, Norway and Sweden. Exports were also very strong to the colonies, with some pieces and even whole sets of glassware being made specifically for colonial use. It was not until the turn of the century that, faced with changing fashion and foreign competition, English pressed glass went into decline.

CHAPTER TWO

MANUFACTURERS

IN THE

NORTH-EAST

In the second half of the nineteenth century there were, as has been said, two major areas producing pressed glass in England: one in the north-east, centred on Tyneside and Wearside, and the other in the north-west, centred on Lancashire, and in particular the Manchester area. Of these, the north-eastern manufacturers were the more prolific in their output and in the variety of their products.

The most important of these north-eastern firms were Sowerby's Ellison Glass Works (formerly Sowerby and Neville), Gateshead; Neville Glass Works, Gateshead; George Davidson & Co., Teams Glass Works, Gateshead; Henry Greener & Co., Wear Flint Glass Works, Millfield, Sunderland; Edward Moore & Co., Tyne Flint Glass Works, South Shields; and W. H. Heppell, Newcastle Flint Glass Works, Newcastle. It is to these manufacturers that we shall first turn our attention.

SOWERBY'S ELLISON GLASS WORKS LTD

Glass for architectural purposes was first manufactured on the banks of the Tyne and although, as we have seen, pressed glass originated in the Midlands, Gateshead was to earn a high reputation for its pressed-glass products in the second half of the nineteenth century. The Sowerby name had been connected with the glass-making industry from the beginning of the century. George Sowerby, the earliest member of the family to have been involved in glass-making that we know of, was a partner in and eventually owner of the New Stourbridge Glass Works in Pipewellgate, Gateshead, in the early 1800s, long before the invention of machinery for pressing glass, and also seems to have owned another glass works in the same area. His son, John, followed him as owner in 1844 and continued the family business until his death in 1879. It was during this period that the famous Ellison Glass Works, later to become 'the largest pressed glass manufactory in the kingdom', were founded at East Street, Gateshead.

John Sowerby laid the foundation of the pressed-glass industry in the north-east when he established in 1847 what was said to be the first glass house in England to be devoted entirely to pressed glass. This factory, the Gateshead Stamped Glass Works, was situated in Pipewellgate by the river. It had a very short life owing to many production and industrial problems, and John Sowerby was forced to close it down in March 1848 after only a year.

In 1850 Sowerby decided to begin afresh, and took on as a partner in trade his former manager at the Gateshead Stamped Glass Works, Samuel Neville, who, as has been mentioned, had served his apprenticeship at the firm of Bacchus and Green in Birmingham. In November of that year the new partners leased land in East Street, Gateshead, from one Cuthbert Ellison, a prominent landowner in the area, for the purpose of building a new glass house. Building work soon began, and the new glass factory was eventually established as Sowerby and Neville, Gateshead-on-Tyne, in the early 1850s. In 1854 and 1856 more land was acquired on lease at East Street and the factory enlarged, and eventually, in December 1864, John Sowerby and Samuel Neville bought the land outright for the sum of £3,390, thereby setting the seal on the continued production of one of the most important pressed-glass houses in the north-east of England for the next fifty years.

The firm continued under the title of Sowerby and Neville until 1871 and during this period pioneered many important technological developments and led the way in matters of quality and design, becoming, unquestionably, the most important pressed-glass factory in the area. To give some idea of the success of this venture and the conditions prevailing at the

11 Gateshead towards the end of the nineteenth century, with
Pipewellgate, the site of the first pressed-glass house established
by John Sowerby in 1847, in the foreground.

SOWERBY'S ELLISON GLASS WORKS, LIMITED,

Formerly SOWERBY & NEVILLE, and SOWERBY & CO., Gateshead-on-Tyne.

The Company especially call attention to their Address and Title, viz.—

SOWERBY'S ELLISON GLASS WORKS LIMITED, GATESHEAD-ON-TYNE.

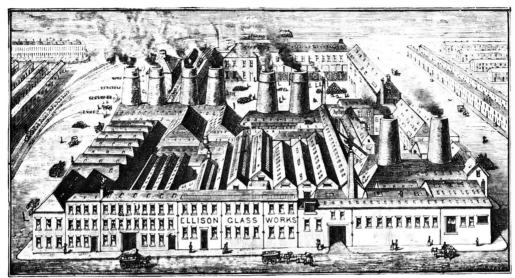

OFFICES & SHOW ROOMS:—

GATESHEAD-ON-TYNE.
LONDON : 19, Basinghall Street, E.C.
BIRMINGHAM: 10, Broad Street.

HAMBURG : 49, Gr. Reichenstr.
PARIS : 27, Rue de Paradis.
BRUSSELS : 56 & 60, Boulevard D'Anderlecht.

A **SPECIAL NEW SERVICE** including DISHES, BOWLS, BISCUITS, SUGARS, BUTTERS, PLATES, &c., OBSCURED AND PLAIN, just ready.—A Service entirely out of the hackneyed lines of those at present in the Market, and which will bring a paying profit to the SHIPPER and DEALER.   **PATTERNS FREE.**

New **Illustrated Book of Designs** publishing, free by post to **Home** and **Foreign.**

The Company, feeling that the Glass trade, **Home and Foreign,** require novelty, design, and freshness continuously, have decided upon publishing, periodically, Books of Illustrations, but their new things will be **enclosed free** to any of their Connection sending **Orders** or **Indents.**

They would also ask the indulgence of their Customers as to their **Cut Glass Orders,** which have greatly exceeded their arrangements of manufacture.   Extensions are in progress.

Their **Pressed and Moulded Varieties** include many new features, and their quality and variety are unapproachable.   Packages and packing a special feature.

☞ See that their **Trade Mark** and **Registered** number are upon each article.

Address—SOWERBY'S ELLISON GLASS WORKS, LIMITED, GATESHEAD-ON-TYNE

The old title of Sowerby & Co. (Limited) could not be registered from the circumstance that there was a Limited Company already by that title in Lincolnshire, so this change of title was insisted upon by the Registrar of Limited Companies.

time, it is interesting to cite some of the evidence given by Samuel Neville to the Children's Employment Commission in 1865:

> We are the largest manufacturers of pressed flint-glass in the kingdom. This manufacture has been very greatly developed in the last few years, and chiefly by our firm. This kind of glass differs from the blown in being made by machinery, and thus to a degree independent of skilled labour. We employ about 450 persons. The materials are mixed by machinery, which prevents the injury to health which results where they are mixed by hand, which I believe is almost universally the case. The materials are stored and prepared in a separate part of the building, and conveyed from thence straight to the furnaces in a way which secures the workers from any noxious dust or influence. Our glass houses are, I believe I may safely say, the best in the kingdom. It is not at all necessary for glass houses to be, as they are commonly supposed to be, and often are, hot, gloomy, and dirty work places. Ours is cool and well-ventilated, light, clean, and in every way as comfortable and healthy a workplace as can be desired.
>
> We have a different system of hours from that which prevails in blown flint-glass houses in this country. Our glass makers work in turns of eight hours instead of six. We were the first to introduce this plan about 12 years ago, to do away with the inconvenience of having the hands change in the middle of the night. It also saves time by diminishing the number of stoppages for changing. Work begins at 5 am on Monday, one turn beginning first one week, the other the next. By the middle of the week the metal is worked out, and an interval of 16 hours occurs for filling the pots with a fresh supply and founding. The second lot is always finished by Saturday morning at 5. Thus the hands in each turn get three clear nights sleep in the week, which is a great advantage to them.[5]

The firm continued to expand and develop under the partnership of Sowerby and Neville during the next few years, but in 1871 Neville left the company to establish his own glass works and the partnership was dissolved. The firm became a family business once again, with John Sowerby at its head, and its name was changed to Sowerby and Co. This title was short-lived, for when in 1882 the firm wished to register as a limited company under the Limited Liabilities Act, it was discovered that a Lincolnshire firm was already registered as a limited company under that name. The new title of Sowerby's Ellison Glass Works Limited was therefore decided upon and registered.

John Sowerby died in 1879. He can be regarded as the father of the pressed-glass trade and his fame was such that almost a decade later a writer was to submit a paper on him to the *Pottery Gazette*. The paper began by describing George Sowerby's work in the glass trade, and his factories in Pipewellgate, and showed how John served his apprenticeship to his father:

> . . . about 1820 . . . his son John, the subject of this paper, came upon the scene, as a boy to assist his father in the management of the works, as well as to travel to augment the sales, a

12 *Opposite* Advertisement from the *Pottery Gazette* of 1889 showing
an engraving of the Sowerby works and a selection of products.

difficult and trying matter at this early period, without a railway to assist his movements or to carry the goods which were sold.

Over his hospitable board at Benwell, we have heard him describe his early journeys by coach to London, near 300 miles, and heard him speak of many old glass dealers gone near half a century ago. How few present-day travellers can form any idea of 300 miles outside a coach! How few have the physique to endure it! How few would have the pluck to prosecute the calling of a commercial traveller as it was at this period!

The old Pipewellgate Works were given up forty years ago, and the present Ellison Works, situate on the North Eastern Railway, built at that period with every new invention and appliance possible, and even in this day they represent an unique feature in glass furnaces, for there are six eight-pot furnaces under one roof; these six furnaces were built to minimise cost, as well as for the comfort of the workmen. The other three furnaces, outside, were additions made at different periods . . .

Here at the new works were erected cupolas, turning and drilling machinery, casting, and every modern invention for the iron part of the business. Pressed glass is more the invention of the iron worker than the glass maker. Here they brought out such novelties as to bring about the fierce competition of Wright Brothers, and others long since dead and gone, while the Ellison Works still stand, a monument to the enterprise of John Sowerby, who, at a minimum calculation, has paid over a million sterling in wages for pressing glass – and this in a trade practically unknown until the first quarter of this century.

During the years he was at the head of the firm, nearly every improvement known in the pressed trade was perfected by him and his inventive staff, and his noble character and disinterestedness is evinced by the fact that not one of these inventions were patented, they were left to the world free as the air; and it was not until the Act for the Registration of Designs came into force that he protected himself against the numerous copies of his costly and clever designs.

All honour is due to the Ellison; the works have become historic as the nursery of the pressed glass trade, and where coal and civilisation exist, the freedom and simplicity of its inventions will be recognised, and posterity must feel their indebtedness. This paper would be incomplete without adding a word or two on pressed glass. It is generally thought this description of glass, being moulded, is of little value as an art production, for it is an artistic production, when taste and quality, in addition to utility, enter into its designs.

How is it that artistic and general goods in china and other products in clay do not rank as moulded articles like pressed glass? They are produced from the model in common plaster moulds, while moulded glass is produced from the most elaborate and costly iron moulds – indeed, every piece of iron used in these moulds are examples in ironwork, a study for the critic as well as the artisan. Truly pressed glass makers have never had the credit for their productions to which they are entitled. Probably had the pressed glass trade been recognised as it should have been, its inventors and designers would have ranked with such names as Wedgwood and Minton; but it must be left to another generation to do justice to the productions in artistic pressed glass – which emanated from the Ellison Glass

Works during the fifty years, or nearly so, John Sowerby conducted this and his early works in Pipewellgate.

The Ellison Glass Works is now worked by a company, the shares of which are almost entirely held by the Sowerby family.[6]

John Sowerby's son, John George Sowerby, was born in 1850, and from an early age he was groomed for eventual control of the family business. He managed the Ellison Glass Works from the early 1870s onwards, and when his father died the works passed automatically to him. His contribution to the firm was in some respects less impressive than his father's but was still very important. During his directorship, which included periods of severe depression in the trade, the firm did not expand in size, but John George Sowerby succeeded in consolidating the company's position at the head of the pressed-glass trade, mainly by making considerable improvements in the quality of the glass it produced. He was well equipped to do this since he possessed both a thorough technical knowledge of pressed glass and an aesthetic sensibility in design. It was this combination that enabled the firm to meet the demands of the high Victorian market with more success than any of its rivals.

Such were John George Sowerby's achievements at the Ellison Works that we can find plenty of reference to him in the trade journals and local newspapers of the time. A report on an exhibition he staged in Manchester in 1882 with his free blown art glass (for the firm continued to make this type of glass as well) gave a detailed account of the pressed-glass side of the business and an interesting description of the factory:

The Ellison Street Works[7] are the largest pressed glass manufactory in the world. They cover an area of five and a half acres of ground and from 700 to 1,000 hands are employed in them. They were established at Redheugh about a hundred years ago by the grandfather of the present managing partner, Mr J. G. Sowerby, but for many years the entire operations of the factory have been conducted at Ellison Street.

The production at the present time is about 150 tons per week of finished manufactured glass goods, and the materials necessary to make such an immense quantity of the substance may be said to be brought to Gateshead from the ends of the earth. The cryolite spar, used for the manufacture of opal glass, comes from Iceland; the nitre from Peru; the pearl ash from North America; the barytes from Germany; the manganese from Greece; and the fine silicious sand from Fontainebleau, in France. The soda, oxide of lead, and arsenic used in the processes are, of course, obtained at home.

The factory works continually, day and night, all the year round, the hands employed being divided into three shifts of eight hours each. One hour of each shift may be deducted for meals, so that the work-people labour for no more than seven hours per diem. The staple articles of production are drinking glasses of various kinds, decanters, salt cellars, cake and fruit dishes and plates, and various objects in opaque glass. To the production of these goods in the manufactory there is practically no limit but the demand, and the rate at which they can be turned out of hand, may be guessed from the fact that each man working at the moulds can make from 1,100 to 1,200 tumblers during his seven hours work. In the melting room are nine furnaces, containing in all 78 pots more or less constantly in use. Each pot holds from twelve to fifteen hundredweight of molten glass.[8]

Much of the early pressed glass produced in the nineteenth century comprised rather heavy, low-priced utilitarian objects such as tumblers, glasses, dishes and salts, in clear flint glass. As the century progressed, however, there was increasing competition from pressed-glass makers abroad – mainly American, Belgian, French, German and Bohemian – and English manufacturers were forced into a more competitive position. Sowerby's were quick to recognise the danger and in the mid-1870s embarked on a policy of expansion with the accent on quality as opposed to cheapness – although they took care at the same time to keep prices within the reach of the working-class population. A report written in 1878 mentions the company's efforts to restore the trade in England:

> Some months back we drew attention to the quantity of light American pressed glass now in England, and pointed out the necessity of our manufacturers giving the matter their attention. The warning, we are happy to state, will have a good effect, not only on the present but on the future trade of England. By means of a new and beautiful metal and by instantaneous pressure, Messrs Sowerby and Sons have produced some tumblers the lightness of which (we speak advisedly) is astonishing. A well known Glasgow manufacturer remarked on seeing them that they were the most marvellous pieces of work produced since the invention of pressed glass, and with his observation we thoroughly concur. This invention will, we trust, go far to restore the trade which of late years has suffered so sadly, and enable glass buyers once more to deal in the productions of their own country.[9]

We also know that by 1889 the company had showrooms in Hamburg, Brussels and Paris in addition to those catering to the home market in London and Birmingham. This must have been another weapon to counter the incursions of foreign competitors.

The reports in the trade journals of the time show that Sowerby's were responsible for many innovations in the pressed-glass trade, and many of these were due to the creative imagination of John George Sowerby. An able and talented artist in his own right, he designed many of the moulds for the firm's most successful products. He was also responsible for the introduction of a new type of opaque glass which was to revolutionise the pressed-glass industry. This new glass, which first appeared in 1877, was called 'Vitro-Porcelain'. A report in the November issue of the *Pottery Gazette* gives an account of the invention:

> One of the features of our paper being to notice new inventions, we have much pleasure in directing attention to a novelty of Messrs Sowerby and Co., which they have wisely named

13 *Opposite above* Opal Vitro-Porcelain pierced basket-weave plate, *c.* 1877. Design registered by Sowerby's 18 August 1876. Trade marked. Diameter 8¾ in (22 cm).

14 *Opposite below* Opal Vitro-Porcelain two-piece comport, *c.* 1876. Sowerby trade mark. Height 4½ in (11.4 cm). Diameter of dish 8 in (20.3 cm).

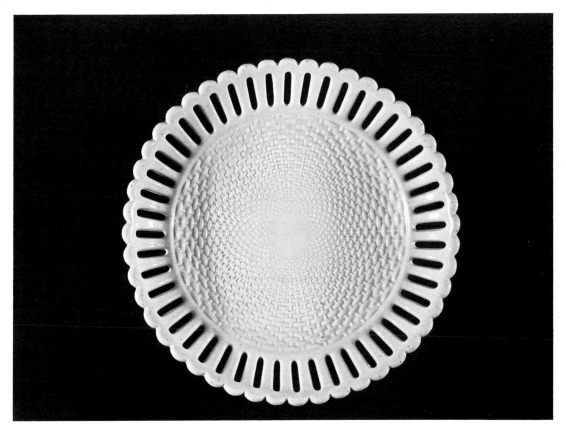

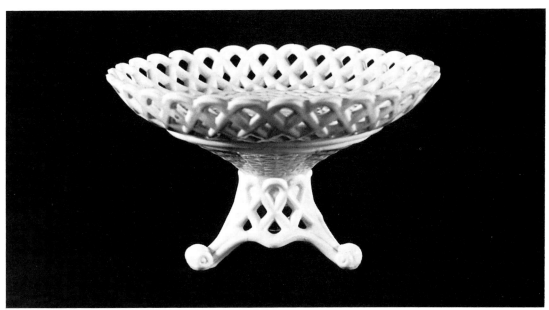

Vitro-Porcelain, since it appears to embrace both glass and china – the former in its mode of manufacture and the latter in its appearance and composition. The most difficult colours can be produced in this material, not, as is the case in porcelain, in the glaze only, but in the body. Some of the articles in turquoise are exquisite in design and colour, whilst their cheapness will, we hope, place them within the reach of those who at present draw their ideas of ceramic art from the contemplation of atrocious, highly-coloured specimens of dogs, cows, etc, which adorn their cottage mantel-shelves.

We believe that this substance has a great future before it, and that it is capable of very much in the hands of the ironworker, for it is to this handicraft that the design and make are indebted rather than the glass-maker. All we have said applies also to an article manufactured by the same firm, and of the same body, which they call 'Sorbini' or 'Malachite'. Perhaps the former name is the most suitable, for to manufacture Malachite in blue and brown, in addition to its natural colour green, is to 'add a perfume to the violet'. It is not often that art beats nature in variety, but it is so in this case, and very beautiful the varieties are. The designs in this body differ greatly from those in the 'Vitro-Porcelain', great care being taken that the exquisite lines in the Malachite are left unbroken – a precaution which adds greatly to the beauty, making the articles appear as though manufactured by the Malachite cutters of Russia.[10]

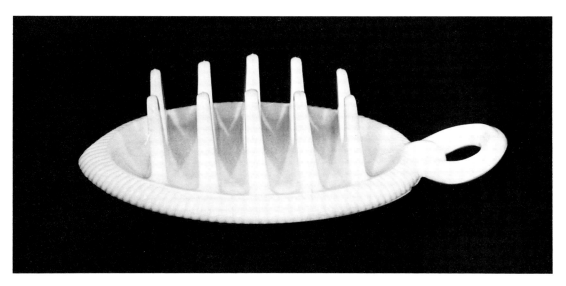

15 Opal Vitro-Porcelain toast rack bearing the Sowerby trade mark. Length 7¾ in (19.7 cm). Although it also bears the registration mark for 15 December 1877, the item does not appear to have been officially registered as it does not appear in the Registers at the Public Record Office. This occasionally happens in both cycles of registrations and can be misleading.

I *Opposite* Sample sheet of Sowerby's Patent Queen's Ivory Ware from the *Pottery Gazette*, 1 November 1879.

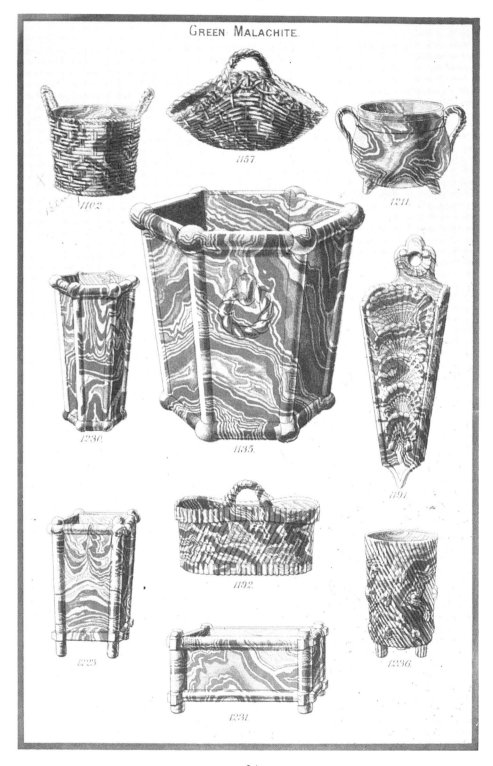

1157

1102

1211

1230

1135

1191

1225

1192

1236

1231

The main ingredient for the manufacture of this Vitro-Porcelain was cryolite, a compound of hydric fluoride, water, and the sodic and aluminic oxides. If four parts of cryolite were added to one of oxide of zinc and ten of sand, a milk-white opal was produced which was transparent for light rays, but cut off the red. If a smaller quantity of cryolite was added, a transparent white glass was the result, of greater brilliancy, strength, and refractive power. If, on the other hand, more than four parts of cryolite were used, an opaque mass, closely resembling china or glazed earthenware in appearance, was obtained. This opaque substance, either white or coloured, was then pressed into a variety of utilitarian and ornamental articles and marketed under the name Vitro-Porcelain by Sowerby's, and later under this and other names by most other manufacturers of pressed glass in the north-east. The first Vitro-Porcelain produced by Sowerby's was in plain colours: white, which they called Opal, and blue, which they called Turquoise. Other colours, all based on the original recipe for Opal with the addition of other raw materials to produce differing colours and effects, followed later. Thus copper scale was added to the Opal mix to produce Turquoise, and uranium to produce an ivory version called 'Patent Queen's Ivory Ware'.

Queen's Ivory Ware was, apparently, a special line introduced by the firm, and in 1878

II *Opposite* Page showing articles in Green Malachite Vitro-Porcelain from Sowerby's Pattern Book VIII, published in 1880.

16 *Above* Turquoise Vitro-Porcelain pin tray showing the Sowerby trade mark in relief as part of the moulded decoration, *c.* 1876. Diameter 3⅛ in (7.9 cm).

John George Sowerby took out a patent to protect his invention. Entitled 'Manufacture of Glass of a Novel Colour', the provisional specification was submitted to the Office of the Commissioners of Patents on 29 May 1878. Letters Patent were filed in the Great Seal Patent Office on 28 November 1878, the specification being as follows:

My Invention relates to the production of a description of glass of a peculiar yellowish colour or body, termed 'Ivory'.

An approximation to this colour or body has been obtained by adding to the usual ingredients of common flint glass, arsenic to make the glass opaque; and uranium, to give it the yellow tint.

I obtain a much finer body than can be obtained by the above combination, in fact, a china body, by dispensing with the arsenic and substituting cryolite spar.

My combination of cryolite and uranium may be added to any ordinary batch for flint glass, and I find a batch composed as follows answers very well:

Sand	12 cwt
58% Soda	1 cwt
Baryta (Carb)	1 cwt 1 qrs
Nitrate of Soda	1 cwt 1 qrs
Manganese	14 lbs

19 *Below* Advertisement from the *Pottery Gazette* of 2 February 1880 showing the Sowerby trade mark and announcing Patent Queen's Ivory Ware (sometimes, as here, called Patent Ivory Queen's Ware). The advertisement also shows the decline of the earlier colours in Vitro-Porcelain, Opal and Turquoise, mentioning that goods in these colours have been reduced in price.

SOWERBY & CO., Ellison Works, Gateshead.

ESTABLISHED IN 1786.

TRADE MARK.

OFFICES:
6, COLEMAN STREET, BANK, LONDON, E.C.
10, BROAD STREET, BIRMINGHAM.

Manufacturers of CRYSTAL.

PRESSED, CUT, AND COLOURED GLASS.

MAKERS OF VITRO-PORCELAIN AND PATENT IVORY QUEEN'S WARE.

S. & Co. *CONTINUE TO PAY THE GREATEST ATTENTION TO THEIR SHIPPING TRADE.*

New Book of Flint Patterns now ready, comprising their latest Designs to the date of publication.——Book VII., "Vitro-Porcelain," on application.

ALL DESIGNS REGISTERED.—S. & Co. will esteem it a favour by being informed of any infringement of their DESIGNS or TRADE MARK.

REDUCED PRICE LIST OF TURQUOISE AND OPAL GOODS JUST READY.

17 *Opposite above* Turquoise Vitro-Porcelain sugar bowl and cream jug with high-relief moulded floral emblems, and the jug with a rustic handle, *c.* 1880. Sowerby trade mark. Height of bowl 4 in (10.2 cm), diameter of bowl 5 in (12.7 cm), height of jug 3¼ in (8.2 cm).

18 *Opposite below* Sugar bowl and cream jug in Enamelled Opaque Glass, *c.* 1882. This variation on plain Vitro-Porcelain appeared in many colours. Design registered by Sowerby's 2 December 1879. Height of bowl 3 in (7.6 cm), diameter of bowl 4½ in (11.4 cm), height of jug 2⅞ in (7.4 cm).

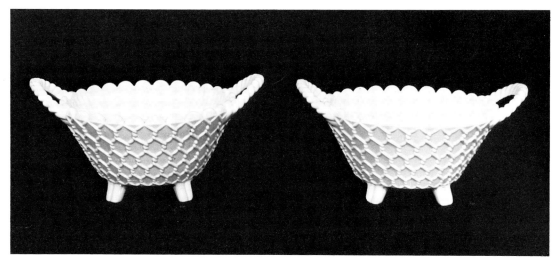

20 Above Pair of Queen's Ivory Ware salt cellars with moulded wire netting decoration. Design registered by Sowerby's 2 December 1879. Trade marked. Height 2⅛ in (5.4 cm), diameter 3⅜ in (8.4 cm).

21 Below Fruit bowl in Queen's Ivory Ware, with moulded sunflower decoration and standing on dolphin feet, *c.* 1880. Sowerby trade mark. Height 4¾ in (12 cm), diameter 7 in (17.8 cm).

To every 12 cwt of this batch I add 24 lbs of uranium, and 1 cwt 3 quarters 8 lbs of cryolite, and operate as in making ordinary flint glass.

I am aware that cryolite is largely used in glass making, but not in conjunction with uranium or for the object of my Invention. Having now described and ascertained the nature of my said Invention, and in what manner the same is or may be performed, I desire it to be understood that I do not restrict myself to the proportions above given, nor to any particular relative proportion of the cryolite to the uranium, or to any other of the ingredients above enumerated, or which may be used in the manufacture of glass, as such may be varied according to the quality of the ingredients used and otherwise, and that what I claim as secured to me by the herein-before in part recited Letters Patent is, the use in the manufacture of glass, of cryolite in combination with uranium, and the usual ingredients of glass making, substantially as and for the purpose above specified.[11]

A report printed in the *Pottery Gazette* of 1 January 1880, which was written late in 1879, gives an account of this 'ivory' version of opaque glass along with other colours in production at the time:

Messrs Sowerby and Co., Ellison Glass Works, Gateshead-on-Tyne, are making a speciality of their Patent Queen's Ivory examples. It is also made from original models by Eminent Artists, comprising Jardinières, Rose Baskets, Table Decoration, Vases, Specimen Vases, Toilet Table Requisites, Dessert Ware, Tea Cups and saucers, Tiles for Cabi-

22 Left: Blue Malachite flower trough. Right: Turquoise Vitro-Porcelain spill vase. Both *c*. 1876-80, and bearing the Sowerby trade mark. Length of trough 4½ in (11.4 cm), height of vase 5¾ in (14.5 cm).

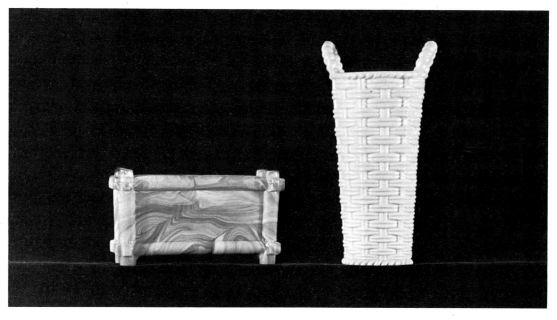

net Work and Stoves, Card Trays, &c. This well-known firm are also manufacturing General Domestic Glass in Butters, Honeys, Sugars, Celeries, Biscuits, &c, in original and registered designs, Zephyr Pressed Tumblers and Light Elegant Glass in great variety. They have a wide reputation for Vitro-Porcelain Dessert Ware, Vases, &c, in Turquoise and Opal colours, Malachite, Agate and Sorbini, in fancy Vases, Flower Pots, &c.[12]

By January 1880 it appears that Sowerby's were having great success with their more striking colours, including Malachite; and an 'Aesthetic Green' was advertised extensively during the 1880s along with a very pleasant yellow called Giallo. Other colours included Gold and Blue Nugget. By this time the original colours of Turquoise and Opal were on the wane, and most advertisements were declaring that a reduced price list of Turquoise and Opal goods was 'just ready'. In July 1882 a summer novelty was introduced under the name of Tortoise-shell Glass, and was reported as 'very pretty and attractive. Its imitation of the real shell is striking, and being brought out at a popular price it must have a large sale.' The same year saw the introduction of a deep red translucent glass called Rubine. Another new colour appeared in the advertisements at about this time which closely resembled the Brown Malachite of earlier manufacture; this was called New Marble Glass.

In the early years of opaque glass, Sowerby's advertised, along with the more popular

23 Posy vase in Blue Malachite, c. 1885. Sowerby trade mark.
Height 2½ in (6.4 cm), diameter 3½ in (8.9 cm).

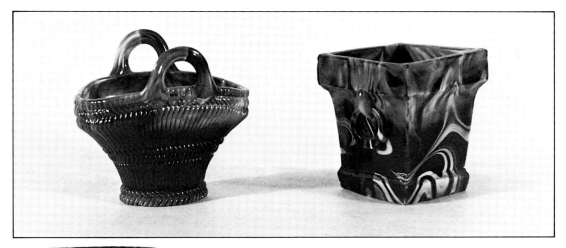

24 *Above* Novelty posy holders in Brown Malachite, *c.* 1880-5. Sowerby trade mark. Height of both items 2½ in (6.4 cm).

25 *Left* Candlestick of classical type in Brown Malachite, *c.* 1885. Sowerby trade mark. Height 9 in (22.8 cm).

26 *Below* Spill vase in New Marble Glass with three moulded swans in the aesthetic style, *c.* 1885. Sowerby trade mark. Height 3¾ in (9.5 cm). New Marble Glass superseded Brown Malachite and shows an amethyst hue.

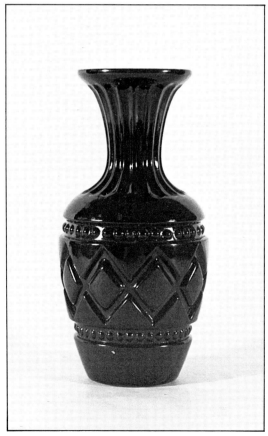

27 *Above* Two posy holders, both *c.* 1885 and bearing the Sowerby trade mark. The one on the left is in Jet, and the one on the right is in 'slag' glass. Height of both items 3¼ in (8.2 cm). The opaque glass of various colours known as Vitro-Porcelain is often erroneously referred to as 'slag' glass.

28 *Left* Vase in Jet, *c.* 1885. Sowerby trade mark. Height 5¾ in (14.6 cm).

29 *Below* Jardinière in Jet, 1880s. Design registered by Sowerby's 6 March 1876. Trade marked. Height 6¼ in (15.9 cm), diameter 7¼ in (18.4 cm).

colours such as Opal, Turquoise and Malachite, a glass called 'slag'. This was a type of glass which was black by reflected light, and either a bottle-green or dark purple colour by transmitted light. As far as is ascertainable this was the only coloured glass that was termed 'slag glass', and it always appeared semi-opaque, being made in the same manner as cheap bottle glass. It was a short-lived product and was superseded by a dense black opaque glass which was advertised throughout the 1880s as Jet.

On 1 May 1880 a new glass was announced and a report of that date in the *Pottery Gazette* gave the following appraisal:

> Amongst the latest novelties in glass is an article called Blanc-de-Lait ware by Sowerby and Co. We begin to look every spring for something new in the fancy line by this firm, and this year they certainly introduced a very cheap, pretty, and charming novelty, and they deserve great praise for putting into the hands of the people of slender means an article of fine and undoubted taste.[13]

30 Visiting-card tray in Blanc-de-Lait, *c.* 1880. Sowerby trade mark.
Diameter 5¼ in (13.3 cm). These card trays in various shapes and
sizes were placed on small tables in the hallways of well-to-do homes.

This 'new' glass was a beautiful opalescent material which Sowerby's had been perfecting for some time, and was based on an original recipe for the production of their free-blown art glass:

> Three years have been spent in experiments on the opalescent product by Mr Sowerby and his art workmen, with the result that they can manufacture the most beautiful varieties of the glass of a consistency that will enable them to press and mould it after the fashion of the ordinary flint glass. This discovery will enable them to work the glass into the everyday service of the public – that is, to make objects of household use and ornament in the beautiful material, and to sell them at a cheap rate.[14]

Production of this opalescent glass by means of press-moulding began in earnest in May 1880 and within a very short time the added novelty of decorating it with opaque-coloured staining was to become a popular feature of production. Sowerby's advertisements of the time show 'Decorated Opaque Stained Blanc-de-Lait' being prominently displayed alongside Opal, Turquoise, Gold, Jet, Giallo, Patent Queen's Ivory Ware and Malachite. An interesting article which appeared in the *Pottery Gazette* gives a vivid description of this new glass in its opening paragraph:

> During a visit to Paris a Newcastle tradesman distinguished for his good taste in household decoration, was attracted to a shop window by a new form of ornamental glass. It was of a rich, lustrous, milky colour, verging in the thinner portions into that 'sky-blue' which milk

31 Salt cellar in Blanc-de-lait, *c.* 1880. Sowerby trade mark.
Height 2 in (5.1 cm), length 4⅝ in (11.8 cm).

assumes when its vendor has had dealings with 'the cow with the iron tail'. Held up to the light, it shone like opal, in a hundred delicate hues, chief amongst which was a glowing yet tawny gold, that suggested the sun shining through a purple mist in evening. This beautiful glass was made into graceful objects intended for decoration, and our tradesman bought several samples, imagining that he was thus securing examples of the most recent development of the art workmanship of France. It was not until he had returned to Tyneside, and had admiringly pointed out his new acquisition to his acquaintances that he learned that the new glass had not been produced in Paris, but in Gateshead, and that, in bringing specimens of it over the Channel, he had, in fact, been 'carrying coals to Newcastle'.

The article goes on to describe in detail the production of pressed glass within the Sowerby works and in particular Patent Queen's Ivory Ware and Blanc-de-Lait, which it compares with the products of two important potteries of the day, Vallaurie and Dunmore:

The Gateshead Glass Works, appropriately situated at no great distance from Bottle Bank, turn out a greater quantity of fancy goods than any similar place in England.

One enters them through a great warehouse, with long racks, reaching from floor to ceiling, and each rack full of table glass-decanters, salt-cellars, wine glasses, butter coolers, spirit bottles, and innumerable other articles - all arranged in a sort of order in which the stranger can only find confusion. This first warehouse is chiefly devoted to the older kinds of ornamental glass. Here one recognises the patterns that were peculiar fifty years ago, and

32 Rare butter dish bearing the word 'DEPOSE'. Design registered by
Sowerby's 31 August 1877. Trade marked. Length 6⅝ in (16.9 cm).
Manufactured in Gateshead for the continental market.

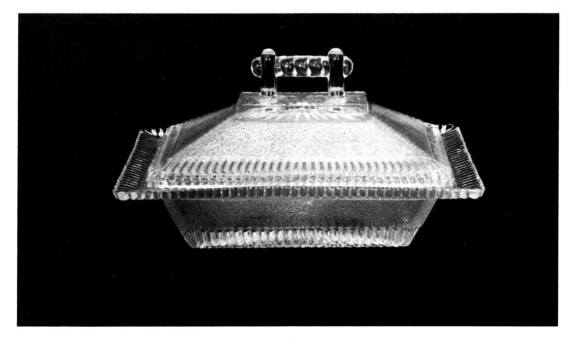

that are still in demand, though their glory has been eclipsed by newer fashions and more aesthetic shapes.

The 'Specialities' of the Gateshead Works, the newer and finer developments of glass manufacture, have a warehouse to themselves. One ascends a flight of wide stairs, and finds a large well-lighted room, its ample shelving filled with Blanc-de-Lait and 'Queen's Ware', the two latest triumphs of the Gateshead manufactory. In these one perceives at once to what beautiful uses glass may be put. The Blanc-de-Lait was described at the beginning of this article. The 'Queen's Ware' is of a delicious cream colour, with about the transparency of porcelain, for which it has before this been mistaken. Moulded into all beautiful shapes, it is taking its place alongside the productions of our art potters, and it may well vie as an ornament with the exquisite objects manufactured at Vallaurie and Dunmore. Besides its rich and permanent colour, it has the further attractions of beauty of shape and choiceness of ornamentation. Yet it is not merely valuable for decoration. It is made into dessert services as well as into ornamental objects, and it is already beginning to supersede the 'china sets' which are the pride of so many middle-class households. Whilst we stand admiring it, the process of packing is busily going forward, for the Gateshead Glass Works are daily despatching large quantities of their new specialities to all parts of England and the Continent.

To see ornamental glass in the process of manufacture is a strange and amazing thing. Imagine a huge shed, with half-a-dozen huge round chimneys at about twenty yards from each other. The bottom of each chimney is a furnace. One sees the fire blazing through great openings, each of which indicates the locality of a 'pot'. A pot is a mighty jar constructed after the fashion of those which are made to do duty in the pantomime of 'The Forty Thieves'. Some three or four of these, filled with the components of glass, are placed in each furnace before the fires are lighted. Then the men in the 'caves' down below – every glasshouse is built over a series of 'caves' or subterranean gangways – 'light up', and the material in the pots is fused until it becomes a white-hot liquid, capable of being moulded into any shape whatever. And then the work of manufacturing glasses and decanters begins. A man stands ready with a mould and a pair of scissors. To him comes a boy with a piece of molten glass gleaming on the end of a rod. A portion of it is dropped into the mould, the workman cutting off with his scissors just as much as he needs, then the mould is closed, and a moment afterwards you have a complete object, whether it be a 'tot glass' or 'a Queen Ann candlestick'. Immediately after being pressed in the mould, the glass is again attached to a rod and carried to a furnace. From thence it is removed to a place of slightly lower temperature, and so on until it is cooled, glass being liable to explosion if it cools too suddenly. Whatever object is to be made, the process is much the same as I have described.

The construction of moulds is a very important department of the art of glass manufacture. At the Gateshead Works, everything of that kind is done on the premises. The mould shop might easily be mistaken for a work-room in an engineering establishment. Here some twenty men are continually employed in making new moulds or in altering old ones. There are implements at once elaborate and expensive. As fashion changes the mould becomes obsolete. There is striking evidence of this in one of the departments of the works at Gateshead. One of the rooms is full of old moulds, thousands of them, piled on each other, rusty, unused for years past. Perhaps one or another is wanted now and then, when a demand arises for old-fashioned articles such as our grandmothers used; but the stock is being continually added to, and new ones, as I said, are as continually being made.

Mould making is a slow business, demanding much skill and requiring the services of the most experienced draughtsmen. The engraver on steel, working at some great picture, is no more careful in his labour than the mere workman who is engaged on making a mould for ornamental glass. The latter has to work on a hollow instead of a level surface, and he may have to produce the configuration of a leaf, or the head of a swan, or some rushes by a river's brim. Done carefully, as it is at Gateshead, work of this kind produces a clear, sharp image on the glass, satisfactory at once to the eye and to the touch.

To attempt a description of all the departments and products of the Gateshead Glass Works would be to bewilder without greatly enlightening the reader. Many are a secret as is the manufacture of the 'Queen's Ware', and the Blanc-de-Lait. There are, indeed, many secrets at the Gateshead Works, where, amongst other things, there has been discovered a method of making glass as cheaply as our cousins of the American continent.[15]

Flint glass was used exclusively for pressed work until 1864, when William Leighton, an American glass-maker, discovered the value of using a glass prepared with soda and lime as a flux. This glass was a clear, lighter and less resonant glass, ideal for pressing and much cheaper than flint glass. It is recognised by its light weight and its dull note, and by the fact that it does not fluoresce under the modern-day ultra-violet lamp as does lead glass. An article written in 1888 explains the difference between the two types of glass and shows how the English pressed-glass manufacturers, and in particular Sowerby's, adopted the idea of the cheaper glass but improved upon it by retaining a small amount of lead in the mix:

Fifty years ago common glass for domestic purposes was made from the cullet or broken glass of this country, and this being entirely lead metal, for the duty prevented imported glass of this description, the quality was often very good, and it had the ring of crystal. It should be understood that glass made from the lead body, often fluxed, may lose its brilliancy; still it rings, for the lead in it is the only part which never burns out. This will explain that the ring in glass is no warranty of its quality without judging it by its colour also. This was the only known glass body in England at this time.

The Ellison Glass Works, Gateshead, many years ago introduced the cheaper metal into the glass trade of this country, a metal in which there was only a small proportion of lead, and to this fact must be attributed the increase of this class of common glass, now known as pressed glass, then called stamped glass. This glass is now known as lime metal by our competitors in the States; but it would not be just to call it by this name in England, for it is really as worked by the best English pressed houses a semi-lead glass, embracing the cheapness of the one with the brilliancy of the other.

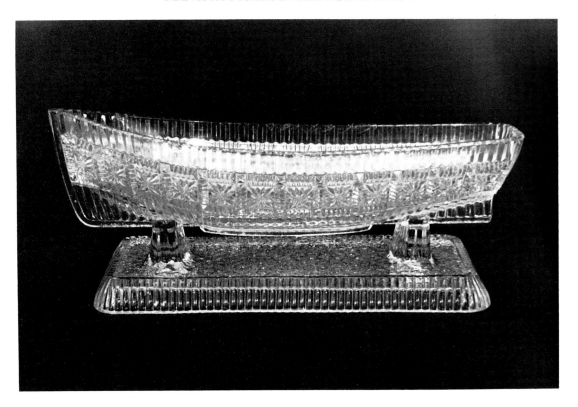

33 *Above* Flint glass flower holder in the shape of a boat on a stand, intended for table decoration. Design registered by Sowerby's 10 February 1886, Rd. No. 42947. Trade marked. Length of boat 10¼ in (26 cm).

34 *Left* Flint glass pin tray in the form of a font. Design registered by Sowerby's 13 February 1877. Trade marked. Height 3¾ in (9.5 cm).

35 *Opposite above* Flint glass two-piece comport with 'jewel' decoration, *c.* 1885-90. Sowerby trade mark. Height 4½ in (10.8 cm), diameter of dish 9 in (22.8 cm).

36 *Opposite below* Flint glass flower holder in the form of a shoe, 1880s. Sowerby trade mark. Length 8 in (20.3 cm).

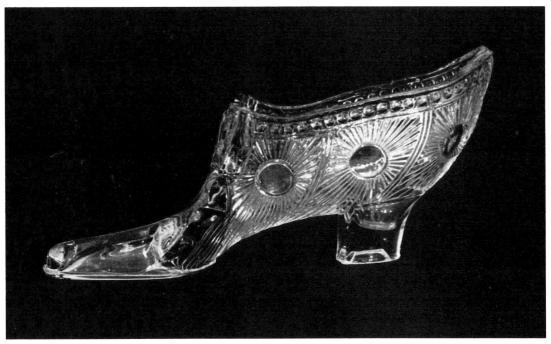

Our object in explaining this class of glass to our readers is to call attention and also to explain the present quality of glass of this description made in England, compared with similar class of glass imported, which is understood as lime glass, a matter of justice to our English manufacturers.

Perhaps the greatest assistance the chemist has afforded the glass mixer has been rendered by the patented inventions of alkali manufacturers: this, with the pure sand imported from France, has much improved, of late, the glass of the best houses in the pressed glass trade. But this is not all; the quality of coal in the north – the fields of Durham and Northumberland in particular – has had much to do with the improvement here indicated, for without great heat in the furnaces it is impossible to produce it; therefore it is clear that the imported glass cannot be of the quality, even if it contained the ingredients the English glass does; their want of our fuel completely prevents them making it.

This will account for the gradual increase of the pressed glass businesses in the north; and when we see the beautiful productions now being produced, we do not wonder at the increased and increasing shipments, as well as the home trade.

Good pressed glass is a requirement in every household, and we think the manufacturers see the necessity of producing pretty and classical designs in this industry, and to eschew the vulgarity which too often mars articles in pressed glass. It is a trade as yet only in its infancy, for it is capable of being improved by taste and design into a much higher position than it has occupied. The word moulded should be no detriment to it, for this word might also be used for all china, earthenware, majolica, yes, and bronzes too, for all are moulded in very inferior and easier-made moulds than is pressed or moulded glass.[16]

John George Sowerby's foresight in keeping ahead technologically enabled him to make further improvements in methods of manufacture, and in 1881, with the new 'metal' already in production, he patented an idea for 'an Improvement in the Manufacture of Pressed Glass':

My invention relates to the use of the process of pressing glass for the production of patterns hitherto only obtained by the blowing process, and consists in adapting to what are known as deep cylinder moulds a pillar or corrugated plunger, which produces a pattern inside the article manufactured, thereby increasing the brilliancy thereof.[17]

The invention must have been effective for in November 1881 the *Pottery Gazette* made the following comment:

Messrs Sowerby & Co. have just introduced a new idea in pressed glass, by which a brilliant effect is produced by pressing. It has been patented. We pronounce a large sale for this quaint idea.[18]

Apart from the pioneering of Vitro-Porcelain and the introduction of many varied colours, both in opaque and translucent glass, John George Sowerby's own artistic achieve-

III *Opposite* Page showing articles in Brown Malachite Vitro-Porcelain from Sowerby's Pattern Book VIII, published in 1880.

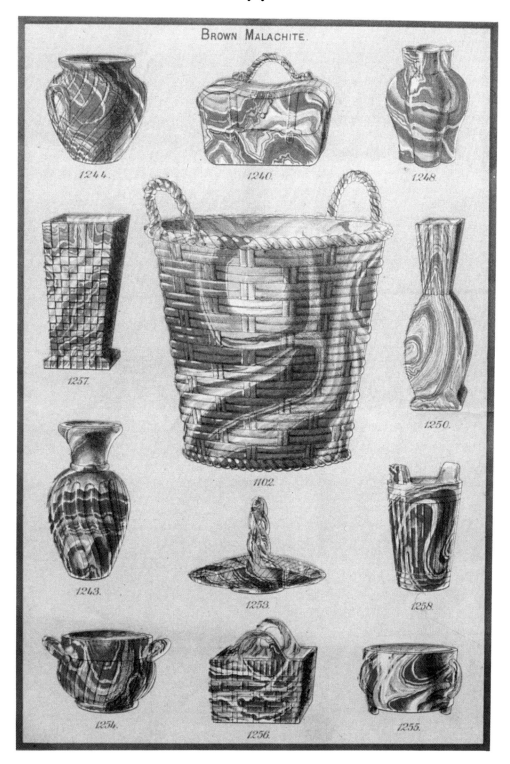

BROWN MALACHITE.

1244.   1240.   1248.

1257.   1102.   1250.

1243.   1253.   1258.

1254.   1256.   1255.

1157

1192

1152

1197½

1196

1199½

1209

1160

1173

1239

1193

1159

1271

1174

1232

1219

IV *Opposite* Page showing articles in Gold from Sowerby's Pattern Book VIII, published in 1880.

V *Right* Illustration showing 'Jack and Jill' from *The Baby's Opera* by Walter Crane (1877).

VI *Right* Flower holder in Opal Vitro-Porcelain, *c.* 1880, showing the nursery-rhyme characters 'Jack and Jill'. Sowerby trade mark. Height 3½ in (8.9 cm).

VII *Above* Flower holder in Turquoise Vitro-Porcelain, *c.* 1880, showing the nursery-rhyme character 'Cross Patch'. Sowerby trade mark. Height 3⅜ in (8.6 cm).

VIII *Right* Illustration showing 'Cross Patch' from *An Alphabet of Old Friends* by Walter Crane (1874).

ments and connections enabled the company to bring out many novel designs in pressed glass. Although perhaps less important than his technological innovations, his activities in this field are equally interesting for being, arguably, one of the few successful attempts to marry the Aesthetic movement of the 1870s and 1880s with manufacturing industry.

Pressed glass was in every respect an unlikely medium for up-to-date concepts of art and design. Whatever its virtues in bringing glass to the poor at a cheap price, pressed glass had always been considered as lacking artistic merit; it was considered of poor quality and, despite efforts by the manufacturers to make it otherwise, a badly finished glass. Pressed glass, in the eyes of its critics, failed in artistic merit without the properties of ductility and transparency. It was considered vulgar, for not only did it have a solid rather than a fluid appearance but, more damningly, it was formed by a machine rather than by the artistic hand of the craftsman. However, this view was not shared by everyone, as a report on the Great Exhibition of 1862 shows:

> It is obvious that the rules of art which apply to blown glass generally cannot be applied, or can only partially be applied, to cast, moulded, or cut glass, and it has been assumed by critics of high standing that all glass except blown is essentially inartistic. That such an assumption is perfectly gratuitous can, we think, be easily shown. In the case of pressed glass, cheapness of production is an element of primary importance and a perfectly mechanical similarity in all the wares from the same dies is unavoidable. The same, however, can be said of our coinage and other manufactures in which these conditions are by no means held to exclude even high artistic treatment.
>
> Pressed glass is further capable of producing effects quite distinct in kind from those productible in glass under other conditions or in any other material. There would thus appear to be a legitimate field for the artist even in this department of the manufacture, and although in all probability the taste of the general purchasers of such wares, who prefer bad imitations of more costly articles to wares good in themselves but manifestly uncostly, will for a long time retard its artistic development, there is no *a priori* reason why it should not hereafter produce really artistic shapes treated in a style peculiarly and legitimately its own.[19]

This plea for pressed glass to be treated in a style 'peculiarly and legitimately its own' was not realised until Sowerby's 'aesthetic' designs appeared in the 1870s and 1880s.

John George Sowerby was, as stated earlier, an able and talented artist in his own right. He was a well-known illustrator of children's books and collaborated with Thomas Crane, the elder brother of Walter Crane, to produce an illustrated children's book, *At Home*, in 1882. Before this, in November 1881, he had himself published *Afternoon Tea*, very much after the style

IX *Opposite below* Pair of spill vases in Turquoise and Opal Vitro-Porcelain, *c.* 1880, showing a character from the nursery rhyme 'Multiplication' which appears in Walter Crane's *Baby's Own Alphabet* (1875). The Opal vase has a gilt rim. Sowerby trade mark on both items. Height of both 4¼ in (10.8 cm).

of Kate Greenaway. In fact a review in the *Pottery Gazette*, which was admittedly biased, had commented that 'Miss Greenaway is beaten very easily at her own game. There is nothing half so sweet in life as the young folk whom Mr Sowerby pictures.' Indeed, his talents as an illustrator of children's books were without question, and in 1886, with the pending publication of a sequel to *At Home*, the journal of the glass trade was prompted to recognise his standing in this branch of the arts with the following review:

37 Advertisement from the *Pottery Gazette* of 1882 showing
Sowerby's range of colours in opaque glass.

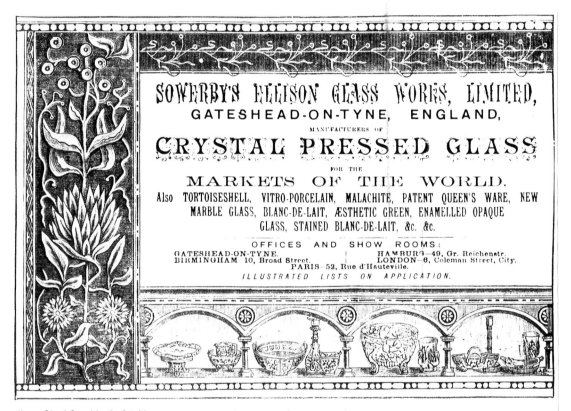

We learn that the author and illustrator of *At Home*, Mr Sowerby, has another book in the press, which is to be called *At Home Again*. Marcus Ward & Co. are charged with its publication, a guarantee that it will be well done and perfect in colour printing as was their last work by the same author. We claim this clever illustrator as one of our trade, for Mr J. G. Sowerby has large works to manage, and books are only an amusement. Yet he has given us in his former two books genuine amusement as well as artistic treatment in a line which few can successfully follow. He, of all others, is destined to take the field poor Randolph Caldicot has left open. We say this without intending to say anything disparaging of Walter Crane or Miss Greenaway – they are great in their way – very great – but Mr Sowerby has marked out a line of his own, which has led to fame, and this new effort is, we hear, likely to increase it. The book is in a new form and greatly in advance artistically of books of its class.[20]

Although John George Sowerby's books were considered in the glass trade as 'only an amusement', his talents as an illustrator were also turned towards producing some of the finest designs in pressed glass using the 'aesthetic' symbols that were ever manufactured in nineteenth-century England. Sowerby's association with Thomas Crane must have brought him into contact with his brother, the celebrated Walter Crane, for it is to this man that he turned

38. Opal Vitro-Porcelain flower holder, *c.* 1880, showing the nursery-
rhyme character 'Old King Cole' after a design by Walter Crane.
Sowerby trade mark. Height 3¼ in (8.2 cm), length 5 in (12.7 cm).

for his most ambitious creations in pressed glass. He began to produce in about 1877 a range of fancy goods in Vitro-Porcelain with moulded relief decoration depicting nursery rhyme themes, classical figures and aesthetic motifs, all based on designs by Walter Crane. Whether Sowerby had permission to copy and use the drawings of Walter Crane to design the moulds for his glass, or whether he commissioned him to design for him, is not known for certain. Looking at the activities of Walter Crane at the time and given that he worked in a variety of media as a freelance designer, the latter is the more likely.

Crane is primarily known for his imaginative illustrations of children's books and among these illustrations we can discover many designs that appear on John George Sowerby's glass. Most of these illustrations can be found in *The Baby's Opera*, which was engraved and printed by Edmund Evans from the drawings of Walter Crane and published by George Routledge and Sons in 1877. A few examples taken at random reveal that 'Little Jack Horner' illustrated

40 *Below* 'Old King Cole' from *An Alphabet of Old Friends* by Walter Crane (1874).

39 *Above* Opal Vitro-Porcelain flower trough depicting 'Oranges and Lemons', *c.* 1880, after a design from *The Baby's Opera* by Walter Crane (1877). Sowerby trade mark. Height 1¾ in (4.4 cm), length 4¼ in (10.8 cm).

41 *Opposite above* Turquoise Vitro-Porcelain flower holder showing 'Dance a Baby', *c.* 1880, after a design from *The Baby's Opera* by Walter Crane (1877). Sowerby trade mark. Height 3⅛ in (7.9 cm), length 4½ in (11.4 cm).

42 *Opposite below* Opal Vitro-Porcelain flower holder showing 'Skaters', *c.* 1880, after a design from *Baby's Own Alphabet* by Walter Crane (1875). Sowerby trade mark. Height 2¼ in (5.7 cm), length 4⅛ in (10.5 cm).

43 Turquoise Vitro-Porcelain flower holder showing the nursery
rhyme characters 'Elizabeth, Elspeth, Betsy and Bess' ('They all
went together to seek a bird's nest . . .'), *c.* 1880, after a design
from *An Alphabet of Old Friends* by Walter Crane (1874). Sowerby
trade mark. Length 6¼ in (15.8 cm), height 2⅜ in (6 cm).

on page 31 of *The Baby's Opera* is depicted on a hair-tidy in the shape of a bellows shown as
pattern No. 1285 on page 5 of the Sowerby *Pattern Book of Fancy Goods*, Book IX, June 1882.
On the same page of the Sowerby pattern book are 'Little Bo-Peep' (No. 1263), 'Jack and Jill'
(No. 1281), 'Oranges and Lemons' (No. 1293), and 'Dance-a-Baby' (No. 1294); all these designs
are taken from illustrations accompanying the respective nursery rhymes in *The Baby's Opera*.
Many more designs were used as shown in the pattern book, and most if not all can be traced
to a particular design by Walter Crane; they can be encountered in all the Sowerby colours in
Vitro-Porcelain as well as in clear flint glass. Moreover, *The Baby's Opera* is not the only book
where designs can be discovered that appear on Sowerby products. *An Alphabet of Old Friends*
(1874) and *The Baby's Own Alphabet* (1875) give some idea of the great influence Walter Crane
had on the designing of moulds for Sowerby's pressed glass.

Three children skating on ice is a good example of how a design was used both in Vitro-
Porcelain and ceramics, for a tile produced by one of the major ceramic tile manufacturers of
the time, Maw & Co. of Jackfield, Shropshire, shows the same subject, and an engraving illustrated in the *Art Journal* edition of the catalogue to the International Exhibition, Paris, 1878,
showing more tiles produced by this firm, depicts 'The Seasons' and 'Times of Day', a Walter
Crane design that also appears on a vase in the Sowerby pattern book: No. 1404, on page 8.
Walter Crane had been commissioned by Maw & Co. to design some tiles for them in about

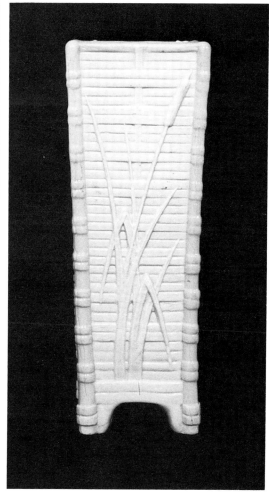

44 *Above* Miniature tea caddy in Queen's Ivory Ware in the Japanese style with a pagoda-type lid. Design registered by Sowerby's 10 March 1879. Trade marked. Height 3½ in (8.9 cm).

45 *Right* Turquoise Vitro-Porcelain spill vase with bamboo and bullrushes relief-moulded decoration in the Japanese style, *c.* 1876-80. Sowerby trade mark. Height 4½ in (11.4 cm).

46 *Below* Fruit bowl in Queen's Ivory Ware in the oriental style. Design registered by Sowerby's 6 June 1879. Trade marked. Length 8½ in (21.6 cm).

1874, and the designs he used were obviously very suitable for the new Vitro-Porcelain invented by John Sowerby, for he, too, was manufacturing tiles for stoves and fireplaces and in a material that closely resembled those made in ceramic.

Not all of the designs necessarily depicted nursery rhymes. Instead, themes and aesthetic motifs were used to blend in with a particular design being modelled. For instance, the swan trough vase, No. 1328 on page 6 of the pattern book, has an affinity with the swan, rush and iris wallpaper dado designed by Walter Crane. Meanwhile, Japanese influence was apparent in some of the designs made; the miniature tea-caddy shown as No. 1388 on page 7 of the pattern book is typical. The hair-tidy, No. 1216, on page 3, portraying Japanese figures, was perhaps influenced by another of Walter Crane's picture books, *Aladdin* (1875). Candlesticks appeared in the neo-classical style, copied from eighteenth-century designs in silver and porcelain. One such candlestick was the 'Queen Ann', made exclusively by Sowerby's for J. Mortlock & Co. of Oxford Street and Orchard Street, London, and clearly inspired by eighteenth-century designs in architecture. It is interesting to note that the Royal Worcester Porcelain

47 Right: Classical candlestick in Royal Worcester porcelain, 1875.
Left: Identical candlestick in Sowerby's Queen's Ivory Ware, *c.* 1876.
Height of both 10¼ in (26 cm). Sowerby's produced this candlestick,
inscribed 'Queen Ann Candlestick' and trade marked, exclusively
for a London merchant, J. Mortlock & Co.

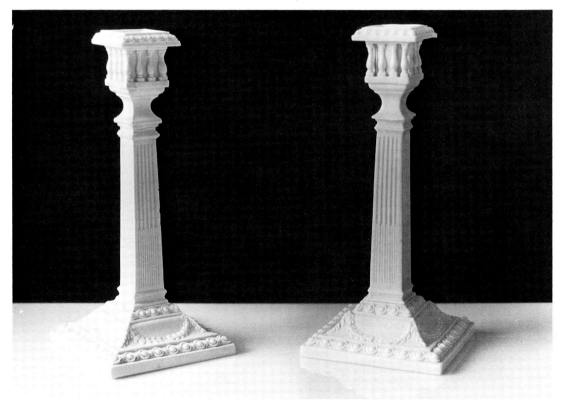

Company produced a porcelain candlestick in the same design at about the same time, 1875-6.

Peacocks, frogs, geese, swans, rushes and irises, sunflowers and daisies were all used in designs by Walter Crane, and these motifs can be seen frequently on Sowerby's products. Practically all of them can be termed 'aesthetic', and it is, perhaps, significant that John George Sowerby used the family crest, a peacock's head, as his trade mark, for it blended in well with the other aesthetic motifs appearing on his glass. He registered the trade mark on 26 January 1876 (see pages 133-4).

There can be little doubt as to the popularity of Sowerby's pressed glass in the latter half of the nineteenth century, and the numerous items produced in the 'aesthetic' style were among the most attractive pieces manufactured at the time. Queen Victoria made several purchases and Sowerby's glass was featured at the International Health Exhibition of 1884 as being both artistically appealing and conducive to health and cleanliness. The *Pottery Gazette* remarked at the time:

48 Commemorative plate for the Diamond Jubilee of Queen Victoria in 1897. Design registered by Sowerby's 1 May 1895, Rd. No. 254027, but adapted for the Jubilee in 1897 by the addition of the official portrait photograph issued at the time. Diameter 9 in (22.7 cm). Most pressed-glass houses produced their own versions of Jubilee commemorative plates, but pieces bearing the official portrait photograph are quite rare.

. . . their fancy glass should have been in the art gallery, but being of such a cheap and popular character, we suppose they were inadmissible. Still in taste and aesthetic treatment they rank as art goods, notwithstanding their cheapness. We may call it 'Art for the million'.[21]

The year 1887 marked the Golden Jubilee of Queen Victoria, and many glass houses produced commemorative pressed-glass pieces in a variety of designs. Sowerby's contribution was a pressed-glass plate and bowl with a medallion portrait of the Queen which was described in the *Pottery Gazette* at the time as 'really a likeness'. The plates and bowls were used again for the Diamond Jubilee in 1897, with the appropriate inscription altered. These articles, along with many domestic wares, were produced in clear and coloured flint glass only: Vitro-Porcelain was beginning to lose its popularity in the last few years of the century.

As the century came to a close, foreign goods began to flood the English market. Always technologically advanced, Sowerby's countered the threat by replacing the old hand-operated press with the newly developed, more powerful steam press. A report in the *Pottery Gazette* on 1 November 1900 described the other technical improvements that had helped the firm become the leading pressed-glass house in the country. The photograph which accompanied this report was one of the first photographs of Sowerby's pressed glass to be published, and is of great help to the collector who wishes to identify pieces. In particular, the photograph proves that Opal glass was opaque white – there has been some controversy as to whether Blanc-de-Lait, rather than Opal, was Sowerby's opaque white glass, whereas in fact Opal was the name given to the opaque white glass, and Blanc-de-Lait was, as has been stated, opalescent.

Sowerby's Ellison Glass Works, Limited, Gateshead-on-Tyne, and 19 Basinghall Street, London E.C. – We called at the London showrooms of the company a few days ago and met their London representative, Mr J. H. George . . . Mr George is just now showing a very large collection of samples of the company's productions. It needed but a cursory inspection of these, with the vivid recollection of the North Country pressed glass of thirty years ago which we happen to possess, to realise the great improvements that have been made in pressed glass in that period. But younger men than ourselves will recognise and appreciate the remarkable improvements in the goods the company are now showing. The greatest improvements have been made within the last year or two – improvements in every detail, more artistic designs, a marked sharpness in the pressed work, and more brilliant metal. We remember the time when North of England glass was noted for more or less pronounced green and pink tints. The samples we have just seen are in bright, clear metal. This, however (and Messrs Sowerby's would be the first to admit it), is characteristic of all North Country glass of today. It has none of the dull, cloudy, lifeless appearance which was at one time inseparable from it. The quality of North Country glass is many grades better than it used to be.

But there are special features in the improvements noticeable in Messrs Sowerby's samples that do not pertain to others. They have introduced special moulding machinery

49 *Above* One of the first photographs of Sowerby
products, taken at the end of the nineteenth century,
showing flint glass domestic wares and 'specimens of Opal
glass' (two tall candlesticks) with 'three specimens of
Messrs Sowerby's well-known Queen's Ware'. This
photograph appeared in the *Pottery Gazette* on 1
November 1900 with a report which included the above
quotations.

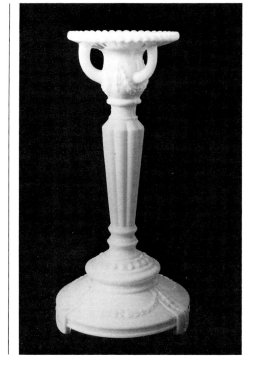

50 *Right* Opal Vitro-Porcelain candlestick, *c.* 1890-1900, as
seen in the photograph above. Height 9 in (22.8 cm). The
candlestick can also be seen on the pattern sheet of
Queen's Ivory Ware shown in Colour Plate I.

which enables them to produce fine pressed patterns that have a close resemblance to hand work. But perhaps Messrs Sowerby's greatest achievement is in their method of oil-fire polishing. The effect of this is self-evident. There is a beautifully clear skin on all glass treated in this way that cannot be produced by any other means. It is this clear brilliancy which gives the company's productions such pre-eminence at the present time. They are showing samples of pressed glass suitable for all the markets of the world. There are some excellent shapes in celery vases, cake stands, oval and round dishes, sugars and creams, and butters and covers to match.

We give an illustration of some of their selling lines. We show some round dishes with crimped edges, and sharp star bottom, that look very well on a white table-cloth. The bright glass does not lend itself well to photography, so that our illustration does not do justice to these patterns, which are shown en suite at the rooms. In these, and many other patterns of dishes, the beautiful skin to which we have alluded is very effective. We saw a number of good coloured and nicely cut and engraved water-jugs. The company show specimens of opal glass. We include two tall candlesticks of this make in our illustration. We also show three specimens of Messrs Sowerby's well-known 'Queen's Ware'. This is not a new production, though, as it is many years since it was made, it will be new to many retailers, and may well be again stocked as a novelty. It has a pretty ivory body, and the beauties of the very fine embossed designs are enhanced by the improved methods of production now adopted. The company make an enormous number of different pattern tumblers, and these especially bear witness to the advantages of the oil-firing. There is a greater contrast between the pressed tumblers of today and those of twenty years ago than is seen in any other glass goods.[22]

In Sowerby's glass, then, one finds a blend of innovative genius, talented design and glass-making skill that renders it among the most attractive and collectable of pressed glass today. John George Sowerby died on 14 December 1914, after retiring to Herefordshire. The firm remained in existence until 1972, and the glass works were demolished in 1982.

GEORGE DAVIDSON & CO.

The second major glass house on Tyneside was another Gateshead firm, George Davidson & Co., of the Teams Glass Works. Founded in 1867, the firm quickly became famous for its manufacture of pressed glass, and the credit for its success must go in no small measure to its enterprising founder who entered the glass trade with no glass-making experience and at a time of growing competition amongst larger concerns in the same area. George Davidson's early life and business career bear witness to his eventual success in the glass industry.

George Davidson was born on 29 September 1822 at Cow Close Mill, Gateshead, near Ravensworth Castle. His father was a miller there, and George was one of a family of twelve. He went to Lamesley school, and then to Anchorage school at Gateshead, before joining the building trade, where, in 1841, he worked on the completion of Ravensworth Castle. He later set up as a butcher in Low Fell, Gateshead, where he stayed for about twenty-seven years.

Davidson was evidently a pillar of the community, singing Tyneside songs in a fine tenor voice at local concerts, and becoming famous for his rare fund of old Tyneside stories. Moreover, in 1856 he was elected uncontested to the council for the south ward of Gateshead. He was a shareholder in several factories, a director of the Northern Accident Insurance Company, and a director of the Newcastle and Gateshead Boiler Insurance Company from its foundation. He was also chairman of the branch of the Federal Fire Insurance Company established in Gateshead, a tax commissioner, and a large property owner in the west ward of Gateshead.

In 1867 George Davidson decided upon an entirely new speculation. He bought four acres of land at the Teams, Gateshead, and on this he determined to build a glass works. Starting with only a handful of men, he gradually enlarged the works over the next twenty years so that by 1887 they employed a workforce of some 350 hands and had a monthly output of between 200 and 250 tons of glassware.

An early success for George Davidson had been glass chimneys. At this time, the paraffin lamp was becoming increasingly popular as a means of internal house lighting, but when the lamps were first introduced they had a naked flame which was dangerous and smelt unpleasant. The introduction of a glass chimney to cover the flame was a big improvement in this respect with the added bonus of far more efficient light emission. The popularity of this new light source grew and demand quickly outdid supply, since the bulk of these glass chimneys were manufactured in Belgium and had to be imported. George Davidson saw the potential of these chimneys and decided to try to make them in his new glass house in Gateshead. He was successful, and soon developed a good trade with the hawkers, who would come to the glass house overnight, sleep outside, and buy the lamp chimneys in the morning as soon as they were cold. To begin with there were no annealing facilities, and the glasses were simply put on the floor to cool, in the hope (often unfounded) that not too many would shatter.

As soon as George Davidson found he was successful with his lamp chimneys, he extended the range of products to include articles such as wine glasses and small bottles, and for these coal-fired lehrs, or annealing ovens, were installed. These ovens were shaped like tunnels, and were heated to a very high temperature at one end, while at the other they were kept only at room temperature. The glass passed slowly from the hot to the cool end of the tunnel on a conveyor belt, and thus was allowed to lose heat only very gradually.

The business expanded, and by the end of the first decade four furnaces were in production. The furnaces were circular in shape and had a small brick cone. They housed six or eight covered pots, each with a capacity of about six or seven hundredweight of glass, and were direct coal-fired. Eventually commercial changes rendered the production of lamp chimneys comparatively unprofitable and that branch of the trade was abandoned in favour of pressed glass. This took off quickly, and by the early 1870s biscuit barrels, tumblers, dishes, plates, jugs, mustard pots, salt cellars, comports, and so on were in production – a line of domestic ware that was to make George Davidson's glass house one of the most prolific in its output in the north-east.

The foundations of an export trade in glass were established by George Davidson in a rather curious way. His brother, Joseph, emigrated to Australia, and the records of the com-

GOLD MEDAL.

NEWCASTLE EXHIBITION, 1887.

SPECIMEN PAGES

OF

1889 Catalogue

OF

GOLD MEDAL.

NEWCASTLE EXHIBITION, 1887.

PRESSED GLASS

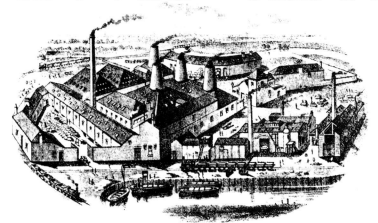

MANUFACTURED BY

GEO. DAVIDSON & CO.,

Teams Glass Works,

GATESHEAD-ON-TYNE.

OFFICES WHERE SAMPLES MAY BE SEEN:—

LONDON:—

23, Thavies Inn, Holborn, E.C.

MANCHESTER:—

15, Booth Street, Piccadilly.

pany show that a considerable barter trade was established between the two brothers in about 1878-9. In exchange for glassware sent to him by George, Joseph was exporting from Australia butter, wheat, flour, tallow, bicarbonate of soda and salt pork, and by 1881 George was exporting to Australia not only glass but herrings and salad oil. It was recorded that shipping space had to be carefully conserved at the time and orders from Australia contained such curious requests as 'biscuits stuffed with mustards'.[23] It seems probable that, in common with the other major pressed-glass houses, Davidson's trade with Australia grew, and extended to other colonies and to Europe – we know, for instance, that the company had an office in Paris.

One of the hazards which the glass industry faces is that of fire. This was much greater in former times, when the safeguards of today were lacking. Most of the glass houses in nineteenth-century England suffered loss by fire at some stage in their lives, and George Davidson's was no exception. Early in January 1881, a serious fire occurred at the Teams Glass Works, destroying most of the warehouse and processing departments. Although the furnaces themselves were not damaged, production was stopped as it was impossible to cope with the glassware produced. In February 1881 it was reported that 'The disastrous fire at Messrs Davidson's Teams Glass Works has caused 300 people to lose their employment, and this, added to the depressed state of the trade, has told seriously on the glass-makers. There are several reports as to the future of the Teams Works.'[24] However, despite these rumours, a report in the April issue of the *Pottery Gazette* shows that re-building was soon begun. This report also mentioned the fact that the company had acquired the moulds of the Neville Glass Works, which had itself been destroyed by fire the year before:

> Messrs Davidson & Co., Gateshead, whose works were destroyed by fire early in January, have begun re-building and, with the energy these gentlemen possess, no doubt they will soon be in the field again. Messrs Davidson & Co., I hear, have bought all the patterns and moulds of the Neville Glass Works, Limited (whose place is still lying idle), and this acquisition must prove a great benefit to the firm.[25]

By June the works had commenced production again with one furnace, and by August the second furnace was alight and there was increased activity in the workshops. On 1 October it was reported that 'Messrs Davidson, Teams, have commenced in earnest to recover lost ground. The Firm have three furnaces going at present, and will turn out a lot of work weekly.'[26] The firm was now well on the way to full recovery and was once again producing 'every description of pressed glass including Vitro-Porcelain'. On 1 December 1884 it was announced that 'Messrs G. Davidson and Co., of the Teams Glass Works, Gateshead-on-Tyne, have purchased from Messrs W. H. Heppell & Co., Newcastle-on-Tyne, the extensive stock of moulds lately used by that firm, and will be able to supply buyers with patterns, matchings, &c.'[27] This purchase was advertised extensively along with other, similar, purchases of moulds and was aimed at enhancing the company's products and making available a

51 *Opposite* Advertisement from the *Pottery Gazette* of 1 April
1889 showing an engraving of the glass works of George
Davidson & Co.

much wider variety to both the trade and the public. An advertisement in the *Pottery Gazette* at the time stated:

> We have just purchased from Messrs W. H. Heppell & Co., of Newcastle-on-Tyne, their extensive Stock of Moulds; also recently those of the late Messrs Thos Gray & Co., of Carr's Hill Glass Works, Gateshead-on-Tyne. We also take this opportunity of reminding buyers that we purchased, some time ago, the whole of the Moulds of the Neville Glass Works (Ltd), Gateshead-on-Tyne. These valuable additions to our own numerous stock of patterns make it one of the most extensive and complete in the trade.[28]

The same advertisement also showed that the company had offices and showrooms in London at 23 Thavies Inn, Holborn, in Manchester at 15 Booth Street, Piccadilly, and at the works, 'where new showrooms have recently been fitted up'. It also informed the readers that 'Trams run from Gateshead station to the Works every twenty minutes.'

The year 1886 saw a full range of domestic tableware being manufactured comprising jugs, dishes, comports, salad bowls, salvers, butter dishes, sweets and water sets in both flint glass and Vitro-Porcelain. Old Davidson catalogues show that water sets then consisted of a

52 Flint glass cream jug, *c.* 1885. Davidson trade mark. Height 4¾ in (12.1 cm).

X *Above* Four-piece table decoration in Opal Vitro-Porcelain, made up of rectangular and semi-circular flower troughs moulded with characters from the nursery rhyme 'Oranges and Lemons', *c.* 1880, after a design by Walter Crane. These table decorations could be added to in order to make any length. Sowerby trade marks.

XI *Below* Swan flower-holder with relief moulded water lilies and bullrushes in the attractive Aesthetic Green produced by Sowerby's in the early 1880s. Sowerby trade mark. Height 3⅛ in (7.9 cm), length 5¼ in (13.3 cm).

XII *Below* Wall-hanging hair-tidy in Turquoise Vitro-Porcelain, *c.* 1880, with figures resembling designs by Walter Crane in the book *Aladdin* (1875). Sowerby trade mark. Length 6 in (15.2 cm).

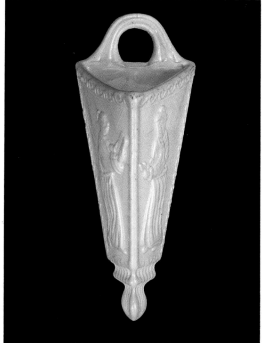

XIII *Left* Water jug in Brown Malachite. Design registered by Sowerby's 17 December 1877. Trade marked. Height 4½ in (11.4 cm).

XIV *Left* Salt cellar in Blanc-de-Lait, *c.* 1880. Registration mark illegible. Sowerby trade mark. Length 3¼ in (8.3 cm).

XV *Below* Ornamental basket posy holder with pinched in sides in Blanc-de-Lait, *c.* 1880. Design registered by Sowerby's 18 February 1879. Trade marked. Length 5¾ in (14.6 cm).

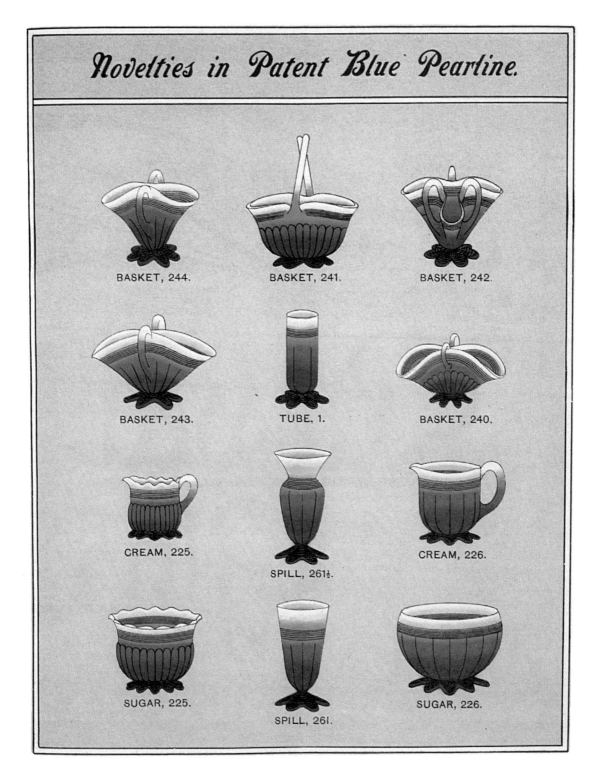

Novelties in Patent Blue Pearline.

BASKET, 244.

BASKET, 241.

BASKET, 242.

BASKET, 243.

TUBE, 1.

BASKET, 240.

CREAM, 225.

SPILL, 261½.

CREAM, 226.

SUGAR, 225.

SPILL, 261.

SUGAR, 226.

XVI Sample sheet showing Davidson's Patent Blue Pearline from
the *Pottery Gazette*, 1 July 1891.

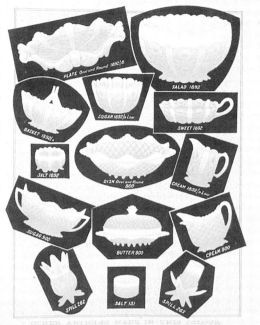

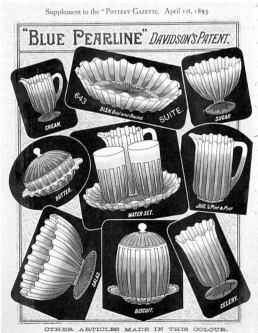

XVII *Top* Pattern sheets showing Davidson's Primrose Pearline from the *Pottery Gazette*, 1 April 1893.

XVIII *Above* Pattern sheets showing Blue Pearline from the *Pottery Gazette*, same issue.

jug and two tumblers on a glass tray, compared with the present-day standard set of a jug and six tumblers without a tray. In 1887 a range of products was produced for Queen Victoria's Golden Jubilee and samples were sent to the *Pottery Gazette* for comment:

> Messrs George Davidson & Co., Teams Glass Works, Gateshead-on-Tyne, have sent us samples of some Jubilee ware which they are producing. These are pressed plates and bowls of an attractive character. In the centre is a crown with 1837 at the top and 1887 at the bottom, and round the side 'The Queen's Jubilee'. The lettering is sharp and clear, and the whole neatly executed.[29]

In the same year the company was awarded a gold medal at the Newcastle Exhibition, thus enhancing its reputation. The firm had now begun producing suites of tableware each year in a different design. The 'Hob Nail Suite' appeared in 1885 and the 'Daisy Suite' in 1886. In 1887 production was geared to Jubilee ware, and in 1888 to commemoratives for the Silver

54 *Above* 'Dolphin' pedestal salt cellar in Blue Vitro-Porcelain, *c*. 1885. Height 3⅝ in (9.2 cm). Unmarked. This design, and that in Plate 55, appears in an undated Davidson catalogue and was probably made from moulds bought from W. H. Heppell, the latter being famous for their fish designs.

53 *Left* Celery vase with neo-classical relief decoration in Brown Marble Vitro-Porcelain, *c*. 1885. Davidson trade mark. Height 10⅜ in (26.3 cm).

Wedding of the Prince and Princess of Wales, but thereafter 'suites' were named after the year: the '1889 Suite', the '1890 Suite', and so on. A report at the time describes the 1889 Suite:

> This is made in oval and round shapes. The oval with a fluted rim has a capital appearance, and the water sets are especially striking. The whole of the ware has a good 'skin' on the inside of the pieces, and the quality of the metal is all that could be desired. Pressed glass is in fact making great advances. A full line of these goods can be seen at the showrooms (Mr J. J. M. Laidler) 23 Thavies-inn, Holborn-circus, E.C.[30]

The year 1889 also saw the introduction of perhaps the most famous of the company's lines. This was the Blue and Primrose 'Pearline' glass which was patented by George Davidson's son, Thomas, as patent no. 2641 on 7 December 1889, under the title 'Improvements in the Manufacture of Articles of Pressed Glass'. In the specification for this, Thomas Davidson gave a description of the composition and appearance of his invention:

> According to my invention I manufacture articles such for example as ornamental dishes, vases, jugs, tumblers, and the like of pressed glass in such a manner that at the base they are composed of clear glass or glass of any transparent colour whilst towards the top they gradually become milky and at their upper edge opaque. This I effect in the following manner: I take phosphate of lime, arsenic and limespar and mix them well with the ordinary materials used for making flint glass, and expose the mixture thus obtained in the usual way in a crucible until ready for working. The glass is then moulded in the usual way for making pressed glass. The moulded article which at this stage is transparent I allow to cool for a short time and then expose it on a punty or rod in a strong heat, it then assumes the effect described; the parts most heated being most opaque, and the parts not heated so much remaining clear which is regulated by the workmen according to the length of time the article is kept in the flame. I find the following batch suitable but I do not confine myself to any particular batch.
>
> Sand ....:..560 pounds
> Alkali ....210 pounds
> Nitrate of Soda ....84 pounds
> to this I add
> Phosphate of lime ....70 pounds
> Lime spar ....84 pounds
> Arsenic ....35 pounds

55 *Right* 'Dolphin' candlestick in Black Vitro-Porcelain, *c.* 1885. Unmarked. Height 6¾ in (17.1 cm).

56 *Opposite* Page from George Davidson & Co.'s advertisement in the *Pottery Gazette* of 1 October 1890 showing examples of their 1890 suite. This suite was produced in flint glass and the popular Blue and Primrose Pearline.

1890 SUITE.

CRIMPED PLATE, 1890 8.
Oval, 7, 8½, 10½, and 12 Inch.
Round, 7, 8½, 10½, and 12 Inch.

CRIMPED DISH, 1890 S.
Oval, 6, 7½, 9, and 10½ Inch.
Round, 6, 7½, 9, and 10½ Inch.

JUG, ½-pint and pint.

BUTTER.

BISCUIT, 2 or 3 pieces.

SUGAR.

WATER SET.

CREAM.

DISH, 1890.
Oval, 6, 7½, 9, and 10½ Inch.
Round, 6, 7½, 9, and 10½ Inch.

SALAD BOWL

Having now particularly described and ascertained the nature of my said invention and in what manner the same is to be performed I declare that what I claim is:

1. The manufacture of pressed glass, by adding phosphate of lime, lime spar and arsenic to the ordinary materials, moulding the article in the usual manner from the mixture, allowing the article to cool slightly and then reheating it in such a manner that it becomes hotter in some places than in others.

2. The manufacture of pressed glass by adding phosphate of lime, lime spar and arsenic to the ordinary materials in about the proportions specified, moulding the article in the usual manner from the mixture, allowing the article to cool slightly and then reheating it in such manner that it becomes hotter in some places than in others.[31]

Although the patent was not officially accepted at the Patent Office until 7 December 1889, Thomas Davidson had secured protection for his invention early in the year, his first advertisement appearing in a supplement in the *Pottery Gazette* of 1 June 1889. In fact as early as 1 March that year a report in the *Pottery Gazette* gave the first account of it:

Messrs George Davidson & Co . . . have just secured provisional protection for a new fancy glass to which they have given the name of 'Pearline'. The base is in a rich blue and the edge is of a paler colour, to which the name 'Pearline' is most appropriate. The shape is excellent and the effect altogether is striking. Both the colour and shapes are the production of Mr

57 Sugar bowl and cream jug in Primrose Pearline. Design registered by George Davidson & Co. 2 October 1896, Rd. No. 285342. Height of bowl 2¾ in (7 cm), diameter 4¾ in (12.1 cm), height of jug 3¼ in (8.2 cm).

Tom Davidson. There is no reason whatever why we should not have a long series of novelties in pressed glass.[32]

By 1890 this new glass, which had been produced first in Blue and later in Primrose, was very successful and proved to be one of Davidson's most popular products. Reports at the time were very favourable and advertising extensive, culminating in excellent sales throughout the 1890s. A few of those reports give some idea of the impact Pearline was having:

Messrs George Davidson & Co., Teams Glass Works, Gateshead-on-Tyne, are finding an excellent sale for their blue 'Pearline'. The new shapes in this electric blue are really very pretty, and for artistic inexpensive tableware there is no wonder that it should be greatly in favour. It is made in a variety of goods, comprising dishes, sugars and creams, baskets, oval and round, and other leading lines. Samples can be seen at the London offices, 23 Thavies-inn, E.C. [1 April, 1890].[33]

We give illustrations of a Blue Pearline suite patented by Messrs Geo. Davidson & Co., of the Teams Glass Works, Gateshead-on-Tyne, in pressed glass. Novelties are always in demand, and manufacturers must be frequently perplexed to know what to bring out next. Their 1890 suite is a very good pattern, and the metal is bright and clear. Their designs are usually well received, because they display an amount of artistic merit combined with utility of purpose. [1 October, 1890][34]

Messrs George Davidson are pushing their 'Primrose' and 'Blue' Pearline glass. [1 April, 1895].[35]

Messrs George Davidson & Co., like many other of our pressed glass houses, are very busy just now. Their 'Primrose' set is still selling well and the samples of it now on show leave nothing to be desired. [1 October 1896].[36]

Thus it can be seen the Pearline series was a very successful part of the output of the Teams Glass Works and many thousands of items were produced in the last decade of the nineteenth century. But fashions changed quickly in Victorian England, especially towards the close of the century when 'brilliant-cut' glass was back in fashion, and as the Edwardian era dawned so the demand for Davidson's Pearline faded away and manufacture eventually ceased. Collectors today can be grateful to those who cherished the Pearline of the past and left extant pieces for a new generation to collect, a legacy of the inventiveness of Thomas Davidson.

The success of Pearline glass prompted Thomas Davidson to bring out a new colour in translucent glass, and in 1896 he launched it using the patterns and shapes in which he previously issued his Blue and Primrose Pearline. He named the new colour 'Patent Rose' and the *Pottery Gazette* reported favourably on it:

Their latest novelty is what they call their Patent Rose Glass. This is a very delicate colour – something like a pale ruby. They make it *en suite* and we were struck with the remarkable uniformity of shade in all the samples in their showrooms. When there are such a number of pieces – necessarily made at different times – it is not unusual, in this class of goods, for some of the pieces to be a shade darker or lighter than others. But in the 'Patent Rose' there is not the least apparent difference. This glass looks remarkably well in the new strawberry diamond pattern.[37]

This new colour in pressed glass was produced using the same moulds as the Pearline series and therefore will be found, in some cases, bearing registration numbers giving a date earlier than the introduction of the colour. This happened often with pressed glass, for moulds, being costly to produce, were made to last as long as possible and often outlived the fashionable colour of the time.

On the morning of Sunday 22 February 1891, George Davidson died suddenly, probably as a result of a fall from his horse the previous day. The control of the firm passed to his son Thomas, who had entered the business in 1878 to be groomed for eventual takeover. During

58 Flint glass dog paperweight, *c.* 1895. George Davidson & Co. were advertising pressed-glass dogs in the 1890s, and dogs like this one were probably from the Davidson glass house. They are unmarked, but this could be because either they were manufactured after the death of George Davidson, when Thomas took control and discontinued the trade mark, or because the moulds were bought from another glass manufacturer. Dogs like this also appear in Vitro-Porcelain, mainly in Brown Marble and Black, although examples in Opal have also been noted. Length 7 in (17.8 cm).

the later years of George Davidson's life, Thomas had already taken charge of most of the firm's affairs and he was to be responsible for many important improvements. It was he who prepared all the designs, and this occupied a large portion of his time, as he was almost weekly issuing new patterns and new articles. Under Thomas Davidson's guidance and able administration the firm increased its range of products, and quite a number of specialities were produced, including baskets, dogs, paperweights, piano insulators, and candlesticks.

The works themselves were a model of convenience and compactness. A report in the *Pottery Gazette* of 1 December 1888 gives a graphic account of them. According to this report, the first room reached on entering was the designing room – Thomas Davidson's sanctum – which was plentifully strewn with designs and drawings of all descriptions. Beyond this was the sample room, in which was a beautiful assortment of finely finished glass of every shade and pattern. Beyond this was the packing room, which was arranged on a plan designed by George and which probably differed from that adopted in any other glass warehouse. It was filled with a series of shelves from floor to ceiling, into which an enormous number of boxes could be pushed and drawn out again like drawers. Thus, though many tons of glassware were stored there, every piece could be easily reached. There was also a steam engine, which provided power for the various glass-making processes, in this room.

59 Flint glass tea caddy in the shape of a house, the roof forming the lid. Design registered by George Davidson & Co. 20 February 1893, Rd. No. 207909. Height 4¾ in (12.1 cm).

Wherever practicable George Davidson used concrete for both floors and ceilings. He was a great believer in concrete, and his experience as a builder stood him in good stead when designing and planning his glass works. Dryness is absolutely essential in glass manufacture, and concrete helps to keep out damp. The floor of the packing room was of concrete, and below was an extensive cellar, where an immense quantity of packing paper and straw was stored. The ceiling of this room was also of concrete, slightly arched to give it strength; this roof would also help prevent fire spreading if it broke out here. The galleries leading between the furnaces were also laid with concrete, which added greatly to their cleanliness and warmth. Beyond the packing room was the cutting shop, and then the wash house and finishing room, where the glass goods were put through the last stages, wrapped up and passed on to the packing room to be made ready for export. Overhead was the mould room, where about twenty hands were engaged, the work performed here being the most difficult and delicate in the whole glass-making process.

The works were never idle, the hands working in shifts day and night from 6 am-2 pm, 2 pm-10 pm, and 10 pm-6 am. All the furnaces were under one roof, so that while there was ample space for working, they were conveniently close to each other. Here, as elsewhere, could be seen Thomas Davidson's attention to detail, which was directed both at improving the efficiency of the work and ensuring the comfort of the workers. Although working close to a source of enormous heat, the workers were kept comparatively cool by a current of cold air that was pumped into the works by steam power; this also helped cool the moulds. Salt cellars, milk jugs, candlesticks, sugar basins, glasses, plates, dishes and other articles in a great variety of colours and designs were produced.

The process of pressing glass had been greatly improved by the late 1880s and the Davidson factory was technologically advanced. The lehrs were said to be 'unique in glassware manufacture', although we do not know in what way, and the mechanical process of mixing the coal for the furnaces had also been perfected. The furnaces were worked by the Frisbie Feeder, and were fired from below. The coal was tipped into a receptacle, and then, by mechanical means, forced through the bottom of the furnace into the middle of the fire. The smoke had thus to pass right through the fire, and the carbon consumed added enormously to the heat obtained; only a minimum of smoke, barely noticeable, escaped by the chimney.

Frisbie's Patent Feeder (see illustration below) was a hopper which was charged below the furnace and was raised into the centre of the grate by means of a lever. The bottom of the

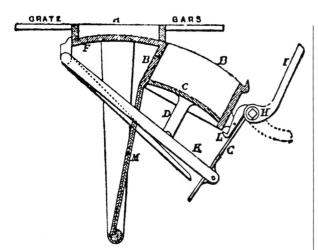

60 *Above* The Frisbie Feeder as used by George Davidson. The hopper, B, was charged with coal; it was then raised into the grate opening, A, by moving the lever, I. The movable bottom of the hopper, C, was thus pushed forwards, forcing the coal out into the furnace. When the hopper was moved back to starting position to be refilled, the apron, F, filled the opening in the grate.

61 *Above* Top hat in Brown Marble Vitro-Porcelain, *c.* 1885. Davidson trade mark. Height 3½ in (8.9 cm).
62 *Opposite* Page from the 1885 trade catalogue of Silber & Fleming, a firm of London glass and china merchants. Identical wares can be seen in the catalogue of George Davidson & Co. of *c.* 1885, thus showing that Davidson supplied Silber & Fleming with pressed glass.

SUPERIOR PRESSED, ENGRAVED, AND CUT GLASS.

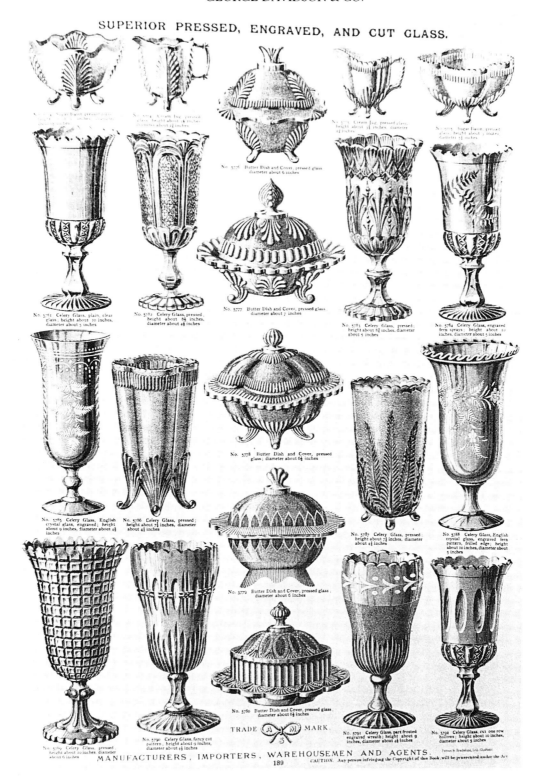

No. 5771 Sugar Basin pressed glass, height about 5 inches, diameter about 5 inches

No. 5774 Cream Jug, pressed glass, height about 4 inches, diameter about 2½ inches

No. 5776 Butter Dish and Cover, pressed glass diameter about 6 inches

No. 5775 Cream Jug, pressed glass, height about 3½ inches, diameter 2½ inches

No. 5773 Sugar Basin, pressed glass, height about 3 inches, diameter 5½ inches

No. 5781 Celery Glass, plain, clear glass; height about 10 inches, diameter about 5 inches

No. 5782 Celery Glass, pressed; height about 8½ inches, diameter about 4½ inches

No. 5777 Butter Dish and Cover, pressed glass diameter about 7 inches

No. 5783 Celery Glass, pressed; height about 8½ inches, diameter about 5 inches

No. 5784 Celery Glass, engraved fern sprays; height about 10 inches, diameter about 5 inches

No. 5785 Celery Glass, English crystal glass, engraved; height about 9 inches, diameter about 4½ inches

No. 5786 Celery Glass, pressed; height about 7½ inches, diameter about 4½ inches

No. 5778 Butter Dish and Cover, pressed glass; diameter about 6½ inches

No. 5787 Celery Glass, pressed; height about 7½ inches, diameter about 4½ inches

No. 5788 Celery Glass, English crystal glass, engraved fern pattern, frilled edge; height about 10 inches, diameter about 5 inches

No. 5789 Celery Glass, pressed; height about 10 inches diameter about 6 inches

No. 5790 Celery Glass, fancy cut pattern; height about 9 inches, diameter about 4½ inches

No. 5779 Butter Dish and Cover, pressed glass; diameter about 6 inches

No. 5780 Butter Dish and Cover, pressed glass, diameter about 6½ inches

No. 5791 Celery Glass, part frosted engraved wreath; height about 9 inches, diameter about 4½ inches

No. 5792 Celery Glass, cut one row hollows; height about 10 inches, diameter about 5 inches

TRADE MARK

MANUFACTURERS, IMPORTERS, WAREHOUSEMEN AND AGENTS.

hopper could be forced upwards, so as to introduce the fuel into the furnace, and when the hopper was removed an apron attached to it filled the opening left by its withdrawal. By this principle of feeding from below the fire, the igniting of the fresh coal was a gradual process, and all volatilised coal, combustible gas, and carbonaceous matter passed from below through the live coals above, and broke at once into flame; thus, perfect combustion and great intensity of heat were secured. The heat of the surface of the fire was not abated, nor was cold air admitted into the furnace while supplying fresh fuel, so that a perfectly uniform heat was maintained, and, as the hottest part of the fire was constantly at the top, all the heat was utilised, and the grate-bars were preserved from burning and from clinker. The coal was pushed up and outwards equally from the centre of the grate, and the whole fire was stirred and broken up at each fresh supply of fuel, so that no raking was required, and the coal was evenly consumed, leaving little refuse, except fine ashes which dropped down through the grate-bars without raking.

Because George Davidson built his glass works almost on the banks of the river Team, he was faced with the constant danger of flooding: in the early years the water used to reach nearly to the furnace door. A two-foot cement wall was therefore built in front of this door to keep the tide out. To transport the glass, George Davidson laid lines of rails, connected with the North-Eastern Railway, around the works.

It was a proud tradition of George Davidson & Co. that theirs was a family business, not only at the top, but throughout the works. In some cases three or four generations worked at the glass works, and their descendants continued well into the twentieth century. The firm, which now makes industrial glass, still exists today.

The identification of Davidson products today is no mean feat. The trade mark of a demi-lion issuing from a mural crown was apparently not registered under the Trade Marks Registration Act of 1875 and appears not to have been adopted by the company until about 1880 when it first appeared in the *Pottery Gazette*. It disappears in about 1890, probably because it had been used by George Davidson, and his son, Thomas, discontinued it after his father's death in February 1891. It is interesting to note that it was revived in a different format in the moulds of the 1920s and also on a sticky label in use even later.

63 Vase in the form of a bugle in Brown Marble Vitro-Porcelain. Unmarked but showing mould marks as seen on registered items from the Davidson factory during the 1890s. Height 5½ in (14 cm).

During George Davidson's lifetime the company bought huge stocks of moulds from other companies which, for one reason or another, had gone out of business. These were incorporated into Davidson's own stock, which was made on the premises and obviously bore the Davidson trade mark (see pages 133-4). The majority of the moulds bought did not have any identification on them, so the glassware produced by Davidson using them is unmarked.

A few pieces can be identified as coming from other companies, notably those bought from W. H. Heppell of Newcastle, who had registered some of their designs, and whose moulds therefore bore the diamond registration mark. After the purchase of the moulds by Davidson, the Heppell designs began to appear in the Davidson pattern books. Unfortunately, since W. H. Heppell was producing articles in the same type of glass – Vitro-Porcelain – as Davidson, long before they sold the moulds, it is impossible to determine which factory produced which articles. Little help can be got from catalogues, either, since only two survive from the Davidson factory, and we have no catalogues from the factories which sold their moulds. There is no doubt that a great many articles of glassware that left the Davidson factory were unmarked, and a careful comparison of hundreds of unmarked pieces in Vitro-Porcelain with the designs that appear in the Davidson catalogues in existence prompts the conclusion that a large quantity of the unmarked specimens we see today emanated from the glass works of George Davidson.

HENRY GREENER & CO.

Sunderland was already an old-established glass-making centre when, at the beginning of 1820, Henry Greener was born in a house directly opposite the gates of the flint-glass house of Vent, White & Tuer at Deptford. His father, Robert Greener, was an established glass-engraver, and his mother was the daughter of Robert Elliott, a flint-glass maker of considerable local repute. At the age of twelve Henry was apprenticed to John Price, a glass manufacturer of Pipewellgate, Gateshead. He was evidently successful, for at the age of nineteen he was promoted to travelling salesman. He subsequently accepted a similar appointment under John Sowerby at the Ellison Glass Works, and stayed in Gateshead for some years.

In 1858 he returned to Sunderland, and in partnership with James Angus, a former glass merchant, he took over a business in Trimdon Street known as the Wear Flint Glass Works. The partnership lasted for almost twelve years until the death of James Angus, after which Henry Greener moved and built a large new glass works with five furnaces on a site in Back Alfred Street, Millfield, Sunderland. Between 1858 and 1869 the company traded as Angus and Greener and registered its first design on 21 December 1858, subsequent designs being registered at intervals thereafter until the death of James Angus in 1869. Henry Greener continued to register designs himself and began to expand the range, from common table ware to fancy glass and commemorative articles. When the firm moved to Millfield, production expanded rapidly and during the 1870s the number of designs registered indicates that the glass works were an outstanding success. In 1876 Henry Greener decided to take advantage of the Trade Marks Registration Act of 1875 and registered his own trade mark to protect his

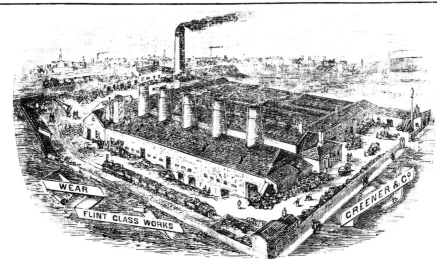

GREENER & CO.,
WEAR FLINT GLASS WORKS, MILLFIELD,
SUNDERLAND,
MANUFACTURERS OF EVERY DESCRIPTION OF
Pressed ✦ Table ✦ Glass
For HOME and EXPORTATION.

SPECIAL LINES in NEW JUBILEE SUGARS and CREAMS, BUTTERS, DISHES, &c.

A GOOD ASSORTMENT OF PATTERNS OF SUGARS AND COVERS, BUTTERS AND COVERS, DISHES, TUMBLERS, &c., SUITABLE FOR THE FOREIGN AND COLONIAL MARKETS.

WE BEG TO DRAW SPECIAL ATTENTION TO THE SUPERIOR FINISH OF OUR TUMBLERS, WHICH ARE BEING MADE UNDER A NEW PROCESS.

BIRMINGHAM:	HAMBURG:
41, Cherry Street.	39, Grosse Reichenstrasse.
Mr. E. I. GREENER, Agent.	Messrs. OTTO, WICK, & CO., Agents.

LONDON OFFICES AND SHOW ROOMS—
5, THAVIES INN, HOLBORN CIRCUS, E.C.

REPRESENTATIVES { Mr. FRANK O. THOMPSON.
Mr. ARTHUR B. HERITAGE.

goods. This was in the form of a heraldic crest: a demi-lion rampant facing left and holding a five-pointed star in its right paw (see page 134).

By the end of the decade things were going less well, however. Although an active business with a wide range of domestic pressed ware, the company fell into debt and in 1877 the glass works were mortgaged for £9,000. This was a considerable amount in those days, but, undeterred, Henry Greener cleared his debts and began once more to issue new patterns to add to his already vast range. He also branched out in the composition of the glass, and introduced coloured opaque glass in the form of Vitro-Porcelain, in imitation of that already produced by the firms of Sowerby and Davidson.

In 1879 a successful line in ornamental glass was introduced, which Henry Greener termed 'Roman Tiles, or Glass Mosaics'. They were suitable for general, ecclesiastical and domestic decorations, but were specially adapted for window boxes, conservatories, sanatoriums, dados, fireplace jambs and hearths. The *Pottery Gazette* gives a description of them:

> Each tile is made in one solid body throughout, and thus there is no enamel surface to craze. They are not in the least degree porous, and therefore never retain any of the atmospheric impurities by which they may be influenced. The tiles are capable of beautiful combinations of colours, giving them a most effective appearance. There is every reason to believe that these tiles will soon become as general as they are now novel.[38]

These tiles were produced in the new opaque glass lately introduced and were advertised in the following colours: Light Malachite, Dark Malachite, Opal, Black, Salmon, Dark Turquoise, Opaque Green, Blue and Black Majolica – Light and Dark, and Light Turquoise. They were put on show in the firm's London showroom, at 16 Thavies Inn, Holborn Circus.

By 1881 the company had expanded its range of goods once more and by this time had showrooms not only in London but also in Birmingham and Hamburg. It advertised itself in that year as a manufacturer of 'Pressed and Blown Table Glass, Cut and Engraved, Flint and Coloured, Blue, Green, Amber, Puce, Blue and Black Majolica, and Malachite . . . A large assortment always on hand of Sugars and Covers, Butters and Covers, Plates, Bowls, and Dishes, suitable for Exportation.'[39]

In 1882 Henry Greener died. He had appointed as his executors the three men who had for some years been most actively involved in the business. They were his son, Edwin Greener, who had been his manager, Frank Ord Thompson, his confidential clerk for fifteen years, and his nephew, Thomas Scurr, who had acted as his principal accountant for some years. Under the conditions of the will the executors would carry on the business as hitherto in the interests of the family. For the next three years Frank Thompson, in conjunction with his co-executors, ran the business for the benefit of Henry Greener's widow. In 1885 it was reconstructed under the name of Greener & Co., but the company ran into debt again, and by 1886 was facing bankruptcy.

64 *Opposite* Advertisement from the *Pottery Gazette* of 1 July
1887 showing an engraving of the works of Henry Greener & Co.

James Augustus Jobling, who was a prominent industrialist from Newcastle-on-Tyne, the owner of the Tyne Oil and Grease Works, and one of the largest mineral merchants in the North of England, had been supplying Greener & Co. with glass-making materials and was its principal creditor at the time. He therefore decided to buy the business and reorganise it, building on the goodwill of the employees and the reputation of the products. Jobling retained the company name of Greener & Co., and the firm continued in business for the remainder of the century and well into the next, becoming a limited company in 1921. Interestingly, in 1922 it became the first company in England to make Pyrex glass, which it did under licence from the Corning Glass Works of New York; later it was taken over by Corning.

Jobling adopted a new trade mark, again in the form of a heraldic crest – this time that of the Jobling family: a demi-lion rampant holding a battle-axe (see page 134). Thus it will be seen that two trade marks were used to identify the products of the Greener firm in the nineteenth century: the first, a lion holding a five-pointed star, from 1876-85, and the second, a lion holding a battle-axe, from 1885-c. 1900, the date the trade mark began to disappear from references, no doubt due to the advent of new types of glassware being manufactured by Jobling for industrial use: trade marks were not usually put on industrial goods. Some of the moulds bearing the Greener marks lingered on into the twentieth century but when they wore out they were not replaced.

It is interesting to note that the word 'Flint' was dropped from the name of the works of Greener & Co. in 1896: from this date the company was known as Greener & Co., Wear Glass Works, Sunderland. The reason for this was that when Henry Greener had first taken over the business in Trimdon Street, it was known as the 'Wear Flint Glass Works' to differentiate it from another firm just opposite, which had been established in 1837 by James and John Hartley, and which had already taken the title 'Wear Glass Works'. In 1896, Hartley's works were closed and dismantled, thereby allowing the name 'Wear Glass Works' to be used by the remaining glass works, Greener & Co.

The output of the Greener works, from its establishment in 1858 through to the turn of the century, was not as prolific as that of its two main rivals twelve miles away in Gateshead, Sowerby and Davidson, but it equalled them in inventiveness and originality. One example of this originality was the issue of articles commemorating historic events, both in England and abroad. Pressed glass was ideally suited to this type of production, for the moulds could be fashioned to include various inscriptions, medallion portraits and their accompanying dates. Greener's ideas in fact set a fashion that was to continue throughout the century.

The first of these wares, and perhaps the most famous, was initiated by Henry Greener himself, and the design registered on 31 July 1869. Towards the end of 1868 a general election had swept the Liberal party to power, and its leader, Gladstone, became Prime Minister. Gladstone was already very popular throughout the country, and the next six years saw him at

65 *Opposite* Advertisement by Henry Greener & Co. from the *Pottery Gazette* of 1 October 1884 mentioning Opal, the name used by this firm and by Sowerby's for opaque white Vitro-Porcelain.

HENRY GREENER,

MANUFACTURER OF EVERY DESCRIPTION OF

PRESSED GLASS.

TABLE GLASS IN FLINT, OPAL, BROWN-MARBLE, AND OTHER COLOURS, FOR HOME USE AND EXPORTATION.

SHIPS' SIDE-LIGHTS AND DECK-LIGHTS,

And every other Description of

HEAVY PRESSED WORK.

INVENTORS AND PATENTEES ARE INVITED TO SUBMIT THEIR SPECIALITIES FOR QUOTATIONS.

Recent Alterations in the Works afford facilities for the rapid execution of large orders.

COVERED SUGARS, BUTTERS, TUMBLERS, BOWLS, DISHES, &c., in great variety, for Home and Foreign Markets.

WEAR FLINT GLASS WORKS, MILLFIELD, SUNDERLAND.

Samples may be seen and prices obtained at

THE WORKS,
MILLFIELD,
SUNDERLAND.

HAMBURG:

35, Grosse Reichenstrasse,

Messrs. OTTO, WICK, & CO., Agents.

LONDON SHOW ROOMS:

5, FARRINGDON ROAD, E.C.

Wm. Thomson, Agent.

Please Notice the Change of London Address.

the height of his powers. Henry Greener's commemorative articles, bearing the inscription 'Gladstone For The Million', echoed the feelings of many people and, since they were reproduced on domestic articles cheap enough for most of the poorer people to possess, were a huge success. Many of these pieces – plates, dishes, sugars and creams, cups and saucers – have survived today.

The second commemorative design registered by Henry Greener marked the death of George Peabody in November 1869 and was registered on 7 December that year. George Peabody was a wealthy American merchant distinguished for his philanthropy. Born at Danvers, Massachusetts, on 18 February, 1795, he ran a large company in Baltimore, before coming to London in 1843 and establishing a banking and mercantile business under the name of George Peabody and Co. During the next twenty years he made many generous contributions towards furthering education in America in the form of donations to fund libraries in various towns. In 1862 he placed £150,000 in the hands of trustees for the benefit of the poor of London, to be employed in building model dwelling-houses and letting them at moderate rents; he later added £200,000 more. Peabody dwellings were erected in numerous districts of London, and in 1866 George Peabody received the Freedom of the City of London. In his will he left another £150,000 to the London Peabody Fund, making in all £500,000. His buildings still stand in many parts of London, a fitting memorial to a man whose unremitting generosity did so much to house the poor in nineteenth-century London. His death was proclaimed throughout England, and Henry Greener's commemorative pressed glass, since it was cheap

66 Flint glass commemorative plate marking William Gladstone's first administration. Design registered by Henry Greener & Co. 31 July 1869. Diameter 8¼ in (21 cm).

67 Flint glass commemorative plate honouring George Peabody, the philanthropist. Design registered by Henry Greener & Co. 7 December 1869. Diameter 8¼ in (21 cm).

XIX *Right* Advertisement for the '1889 suite' in Davidson's Pearline from the *Pottery Gazette*, 1 June 1889.

XX *Below* Three tumblers in Blue Pearline. Designs registered by George Davidson & Co. 13 August 1889 (Rd. No. 130643), 31 March 1888 (Rd. No. 96945), and 6 September 1893 (Rd. No. 217752) from left to right respectively. Heights 5-5½ in (12.8-14 cm).

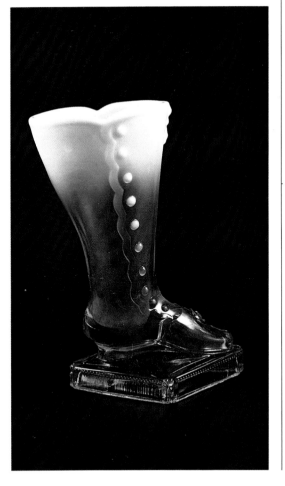

XXI *Above left* Butter dish in Primrose Pearline, *c.* 1890. This design appears in one of the Davidson pattern sheets shown in Colour Plate XVII. Height 4¾ in (12.1 cm).

XXII *Above* Small covered preserve pot with relief-moulded fish-scale decoration in Brown Marble Vitro-Porcelain, *c.* 1885. This design appears in the Davidson *c.* 1885 catalogue. Height 3½ in (8.9 cm).

XXIII *Left* Spill holder in the form of a lady's boot in Davidson's Blue Pearline, *c.* 1890. Height 6⅛ in (15.5 cm).

XXIV *Above* Vase in Blue Marble Vitro-Porcelain.
Design registered by George Davidson & Co. on
16 January 1877. Height 7¼ in (18.1 cm). This was
the first design registered by Davidson's and
appears in most colours produced by them.

XXV *Right* Spill holder in the form of a lady's boot
in Brown Marble Vitro-Porcelain, *c.* 1880-5. The
existence of this item in Blue Pearline (see Colour
Plate XXIII) proves that, although unmarked, it was
made by Davidson.

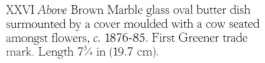

XXVI *Above* Brown Marble glass oval butter dish surmounted by a cover moulded with a cow seated amongst flowers, *c.* 1876-85. First Greener trade mark. Length 7¾ in (19.7 cm).

XXVII *Left* Lion paperweight in translucent green glass, *c.* 1890. Unmarked but almost identical to the marked lion paperweights by Henry Greener shown in the picture below. Lion paperweights like this were probably also made by Greener, but from a slightly larger mould, and are probably unmarked because they date from the period after Henry Greener & Co. was acquired by James Jobling. Height 6 in (15.2 cm).

XXVIII *Left* Pair of lion paperweights in Brown Marble glass by Henry Greener, *c.* 1880. The lions' front paws are resting on Britannia shields, a variation on the lion paperweights produced by other manufacturers. First Greener mark. Height 6 in (15.2 cm).

68 Flint glass commemorative cups and saucers. Left: George
Peabody. Right: William Gladstone. Designs registered by Henry
Greener & Co. on 7 December 1869 and 31 July 1869
respectively. Height of cups 2⅝ in (6.7 cm), diameter of saucers
5 in (12.7 cm).

enough to be afforded by the poorer classes, was much in demand. The design shows a crown within a heart and radiating concentric lines with three circles of stars representing the Stars and Stripes of America, together with Peabody's name, in large letters. It can often be seen today on plates, dishes, cups, and saucers.

The next commemorative line was brought out to celebrate the military prowess of Frederick III, King of Prussia, who had married, in 1858, the Princess Royal of Britain, eldest daughter of Queen Victoria. At the outbreak of the Franco-Prussian War in 1870, Frederick, as Crown Prince, commanded the Prussian army, and during the ensuing campaigns he scored many victories culminating in the defeat of Napoleon III at Sedan. This accomplished, he pushed on to Paris, and after surrounding the city established his headquarters at Versailles, where he remained until the capitulation in January 1871. In recognition of Frederick's successes, Henry Greener produced a commemorative sugar basin with the inscription 'Friedrich Wilhelm' around the top. The design was registered on 10 November 1870.

One of the most attractive designs in commemoratives to come from the Greener works was produced in 1878. This was the now-famous design commemorating the state visit to Canada of Princess Louise and her husband the Marquis of Lorne in November of that year, the Marquis having been made Governor-General in July. The extremely well-executed

95

design was especially made with the Canadian market in mind: it had British national floral emblems as its background and an inscription giving the date of the couple's landing in Halifax, Nova Scotia – 25 November 1878. The *Pottery Gazette* later described the goods brought out in this design and mentioned an improvement in the manufacture of the opaque coloured glass in which they were made:

> As an appropriate domestic memento of the attachment of all classes of our Canadian kinsmen to the Marquis of Lorne and the Princess Louise, Mr Henry Greener has specially prepared some neatly designed Glass Sugar Basins and Covers, Cream Jugs, Butter Dishes, and Spoonholders. Each article is embellished with finely executed medallion likenesses of Her Royal Highness and the Marquis, and an inscription containing the date of their landing at Halifax, N.S. There are also oval dishes in various sizes of a neat and suitable pattern. The sets are made in Flint Glass, Opal, Malachite, and Blue and Black Majolica.
>
> A special feature in these goods is the perfection of the annealing. This has been effected so thoroughly, that many of the casualties to which these coloured glass goods are ordinarily liable are entirely avoided. The sets are, therefore, admirably adapted for shipment to the Dominion on economic grounds, as well as by reason of their special reference to the popular Governor-General and his illustrious consort.[40]

Benjamin Disraeli was another prominent figure featured in the commemorative designs of Henry Greener. Born in London in 1804, Disraeli entered Parliament in 1837 as Conserva-

69 Opal glass sugar bowl celebrating the landing in Halifax, Nova Scotia, of the Marquis of Lorne and Princess Louise on 25 November 1878. First Greener trade mark. Height 5⅜ in (13.6 cm), diameter of bowl 5⅞ in (14.9 cm).

70 The same Opal glass sugar bowl showing the portrait medallion of Princess Louise.

71 *Above* Opal glass sugar bowl and cream jug celebrating the success of Benjamin Disraeli, Earl of Beaconsfield, at the Congress of Berlin in July 1878. Design registered by Henry Greener & Co. 31 August 1878. First Greener trade mark. Height of bowl 5⅝ in (14.3 cm), diameter of bowl 5½ in (13.3 cm), height of jug 4⅜ in (11.1 cm).

72 *Right* Detail of inscription on the above bowl.

tive Member for Maidstone and for the next fifty years was active in politics, including two terms – in 1868 and 1874-80 – as Prime Minister. In 1877 he entered the Upper House as Earl of Beaconsfield, and the following year attended the Congress of Berlin on the Eastern Question, from which he returned with Lord Salisbury bearing 'peace with honour'. Henry Greener's design to commemorate this can be found on sugar basins and cream jugs in both opaque and flint glass; both articles bear a medallion portrait of the Earl of Beaconsfield and the sugar basin has an inscription on the reverse side which reads 'Earl Beaconsfield the Hero of the Congress, Berlin, July 1878' surrounded, as is the portrait, by a wreath of laurel leaves. Both articles have the floral emblems of England, Scotland and Ireland. The design was registered on 31 August 1878.

The same design as the Earl of Beaconsfield commemorative was used again in 1880 when William Gladstone was once more elected Prime Minister. In September 1878 war had

73 Opal glass sugar bowl to celebrate Gladstone's second administration which began in May 1880. The same bowl was used for the earlier commemorative of the Earl of Beaconsfield, hence the registration mark on this article for 31 August 1878. First Greener trade mark. Height 5⅝ in (14.3 cm), diameter 5½ in (13.3 cm).

broken out with Afghanistan and had lasted for two years, during which time Gladstone continually attacked the government for its war-mongering policies. Within four months of his re-election, Gladstone successfully concluded negotiations for peace. Henry Greener produced a commemorative to celebrate this, and to hail the Liberal leader's election as Prime Minister. As with the Earl of Beaconsfield commemorative, the new Gladstone commemorative took the form of a sugar bowl and cream jug, with a medallion portrait of the Prime Minister within laurel leaves and showing the emblematic symbols of thistles, roses and shamrocks. The inscription reads: 'Gladstone the Liberal Champion. Peace. Retrenchment. and Reform' and below this, 'May 1st 1880 and Premier of England'. The article bears the diamond registration mark for 31 August 1878, which is the same as that first used for the Earl of Beaconsfield commemorative in 1878, and does not signify the date of manufacture of the new Gladstone commemorative, which did not occur until 1880. This is a good example of how the registration date mark does not necessarily denote the year of manufacture of an article.

74 Opal glass tankard to honour the oarsman Edward Hanlan. Design registered by Henry Greener & Co. 8 December 1880. Height 4¼ in (10.4 cm).

Events of national political importance and royal occasions were the most popular of Henry Greener's commemorative output, but other events did not escape his notice. For example, when one of the world's greatest oarsmen, the Canadian, Edward Hanlan, was matched to race Edward Trickett, the Australian champion, for the championship of the world, in England, Henry Greener produced a tankard to commemorate the event. This race has gone down in the annals of sculling races as the most sensational of all world championship meets. It was rowed on the championship course which is the same as that now used in the annual race between Oxford and Cambridge – from Putney for 4 miles 440 yards to the University Post at Mortlake. Hanlan won the race in 26 minutes 12 seconds. It was appropriate that Henry Greener should mark this event with a commemorative piece, for rowing was a popular pastime on the river Tyne and Hanlan had already beaten the English champion, William Elliott, in a championship race on that river in 1879. The design of the tankard Henry Greener produced shows a man in a rowing skiff on a clear ground surrounded by the inscription 'Edward Hanlan

Champion Of The World', and beneath 'Nov. 15th 1880 Beat Trickett of NSW'; on either side of the rustic handle is a pair of crossed oars on a stippled background. The design was registered on 8 December 1880, and each tankard bears the diamond registration mark.

In 1887 the Golden Jubilee of Queen Victoria was celebrated and Henry Greener & Co., along with other pressed-glass houses, brought out many articles to commemorate the event. These were mainly in the form of plates and sweetmeat dishes, which gave a good ground to show off the motifs and inscriptions, although other articles such as butter dishes were also produced. The Jubilee articles produced by Greener usually bear the second trade mark of a lion holding a battle-axe and the inscription incorporates the dates 1837-1887. The company presented the Queen herself with one of its Jubilee plates, and this was 'gracefully acknowledged'.[41] Other royal events followed in the range of Henry Greener's commemoratives. It is interesting to note here that in 1897, when the Queen's Diamond Jubilee was celebrated, the same designs were used for the commemorative ware, and the moulds used in 1887 were adapted for use with the inscriptions changed in the manner explained in Chapter 1.

Lastly, Henry Greener & Co. produced a novel commemorative piece to mark another well-known event of the day. This was the erection of the Eiffel Tower on the Champs de

75 Flint glass wheelbarrow and coal truck salt-cellar ornaments. Design registered by Henry Greener & Co. 20 September 1893, Rd. No. 218710. Height of wheelbarrow 2½ in (6.3 cm), length 4⅝ in (11.8 cm). Height of coal truck 2 in (5.1 cm), length 3⅛ in (7.9 cm). Larger versions were also made to be used as sugar bowls and were popular among mining communities in the area.

Mars in Paris in 1889. A report in the *Pottery Gazette* at the time gave the following account of this novelty:

> Messrs Greener & Co., of Sunderland, have some novelties in pressed glass ware, which their managing representative is now showing at their rooms, No. 5, Thavies-Inn, E.C. One article, very appropriate to the time, is the Eiffel Tower candlestick. The design is a good combination of the useful and the ornamental. The 'Tower' is made in flint and coloured glass. It looks very well in opalescent.[42]

After Henry Greener's death in 1882 the firm began to expand under the able direction of its new owner, James Augustus Jobling. A variety of pressed-glass articles, ornamental and utilitarian, and in both flint and opaque glass, was produced. In February 1887 it was reported that the company was producing some special lines in patterns called 'Colonial' and 'Starlight': sugars and creams, butters, and so on, but the identity of these patterns is difficult to establish. Novelty goods such as ash trays, vases and ornaments, costing a penny each, were being made in considerable variety and it was stated that the finish of the tumblers in this range was 'worthy of note'. Later in the year they brought out a new pattern which they called 'Royal Star': this was a complete set of tableware in pressed glass decorated with a diamond-cut star, encircled with smaller stars of different shape, available with either crimped or plain edges. It became a popular line and again enhanced the firm's reputation for good utilitarian glassware. Greener & Co., as the firm was still called, exhibited at the Newcastle Exhibition of 1887 and was awarded a silver medal for its pressed glass. Journalists from a local newspaper visited the company the same year and reported very favourably on their conducted tour. An account of this visit appeared in the *Pottery Gazette* later that year:

> Through the kindness of Mr J. A. Jobling, we had the pleasure of a visit to the extensive works of Messrs Greener & Co., and with Mr Frank O. Thompson, Mr Jobling's manager, as *cicerone*, we must confess to having been highly edified and instructed by the visit. It may here be observed that pressed and not cut glass is chiefly manufactured. The process of pressing opaque 'metal', by which term glass is technically called, was invented by Mr Sowerby some twenty years ago. Messrs Greener's establishment occupies a wide area of ground.
>
> Our townsman, Mr James A. Jobling, is the head of the Sunderland firm. As an athlete in his younger days, his dogged perseverance and courage pulled him through from 'scratch' in many a tough contest. It required no small amount of pluck, and still more intelligent supervision and ceaseless industry to restore to Sunderland, as he has done, an industry which, but for him, would have gone to another quarter.[43]

Thus it can be seen that the firm of Greener & Co. was held in high esteem in the pressed-glass trade in the north-east. It continued to produce new patterns throughout the last decade of the nineteenth century, and in 1897, the year of Queen Victoria's Diamond Jubilee, once again excelled in the commemorative line, producing 'a very pretty suite of dishes and plates with an inscription commemorative of the Queen's long reign'.[44]

In conclusion, the history of the pressed-glass house of Greener & Co. in the nineteenth century was a remarkable one. From its humble beginnings in 1858 it was beset with problems, and had it not been for the perseverance of its founder and its successive management, we could not now enjoy collecting some of the finest pressed glass produced in England. A report in the *Pottery Gazette* at the end of the nineteenth century contained a fitting tribute to the company:

> Messrs Greener pride themselves in supplying goods suitable for the million. They do not lay themselves out for what is known as a best-glass trade, but they none the less claim that they supply the best glass possible at their prices. Messrs Greener have for many years been producers of really good pressed glass tableware, but they are now showing specimens in every way superior to their best productions of a few years ago. We can safely say that we never saw finer pressed glass goods than our English makers of today are turning out, and Messrs Greener have some samples that cannot be surpassed. Our pressed glass manufacturers are certainly making strong efforts to wipe out the stigma of 'common' that was at one time freely applied to their productions. Messrs Greener & Co. have done their share in this advancement.[45]

NEVILLE GLASS WORKS

The Neville Glass Works, which stood at the end of Park Road, Gateshead, within sight of the town's famous chemical works, were established in 1871 by Samuel Neville after his departure from the Ellison Glass Works, where he had been John Sowerby's partner for more than twenty years. The new company immediately obtained a satisfactory measure of commercial success, but, despite Neville's expertise and reputation, the wares it produced were never of as high a standard of design and finish as those of the best houses in the north-east. Moreover, the firm fell victim to the effects of the depression, which began in 1877 and lasted, with occasional fluctuations, until 1885. The depression weighed upon the glass trade with exceptional severity. Money among all classes was scarce, but particularly among the working classes, and pressed glass had the double disadvantage of not being a necessity and of being targeted at those who were hardest hit by the depression. One consolation, however, was that glass was one of the trades to receive the greatest upward stimulus from the renewed prosperity that came after 1885.

The Neville Glass Works, although situated in a soot-encrusted back street and surrounded by chemical factories and the North-Eastern Railway Company, were large and well laid out. Not much is known about the products of this firm, but, despite their lack of distinguishing character in design, there must have been a very wide variety of them, since they aroused the interest of George Davidson who, as has been said, bought the moulds for his own use after Neville's closed down.

The moulds used by Samuel Neville in his pressed-glass manufacture were made on the premises in a section of the building housing twenty to thirty mould-makers. The moulds had to be taken out of the machines and cleaned very frequently; there was a room expressly for this work and a number of employees were exclusively engaged in it. The packing shop was very large, and there was also a well-stocked showroom. When working full the establishment employed 300-400 people, but as with many glass works in the uncertain economic climate of the 1870s, work stopped and started according to the number of orders.

On 1 January 1880 the Neville Glass Works came to an untimely end. At about ten o'clock in the evening a fire broke out in the pot-loft, which was to the south-east of the building, and in a very short time, there being a high wind, the whole building was in flames. Within half an hour of the discovery of the first indication of the fire, the building was ablaze from end to end. From the pot-loft the fire spread through the packing rooms to a straw loft on the opposite side of the building, and soon the store-rooms, moulding and cutting departments, cooperage and offices fell prey to it.

The only departments untouched by the fire included the places where the glass and mould-makers worked, that is the kiln house and the iron department. The rest of the buildings were completely destroyed, as well as all the appliances used in the manufacture of glass, besides a large amount of stock and fittings. A report of the fire in the local paper the next day contained the following extract:

> The works have been lying idle for some months past, and, so far as can be learned, the only person on the premises yesterday was the watchman. The calamity will fall with peculiar heaviness on Messrs Neville's workmen, 400 in number, as we understand there was a prospect of the works being speedily re-started. That prospect has now, of course, vanished, and instead of, as was hoped, there being shortly a busy hive of industry, there now stand gaunt, blackened, windowless walls – a hideous ruin in place of a cheerful workshop. It is impossible with any degree of accuracy to compute the damage, though we should imagine it will amount to between £10,000 and £20,000, but Messrs Neville have, we believe, the satisfaction of knowing that they were fully insured.[46]

The Neville Glass Works were never re-started, and three years later, on 14 January 1883, Samuel Neville died at Boulogne-sur-Mer in France. Despite the disastrous fire his designs in pressed glass lived on for, as has been said, George Davidson of the Teams Glass Works, Gateshead, bought the moulds and incorporated them into his own patterns.

W. H. HEPPELL & CO.

On the opposite banks of the Tyne from Gateshead, in Forth Street, just behind Newcastle's Central Railway Station, stood the glass house of William Henry Heppell. In the first half of the nineteenth century the works had belonged to the Wright Brothers, a well-known local glass-making partnership which at one time had had premises in Pipewellgate, Gateshead. The glass-making activities of the Wright Brothers came to an end in 1867, and after passing through two other ownerships the works were eventually taken over, in 1874, by W. H. Heppell & Co.

Not much is known about this glass-making venture, but the Heppell family were well

W. H. HEPPELL & CO.,

PRICES & SAMPLES

ON APPLICATION.

MANUFACTURERS

OF VARIOUS DESCRIPTIONS

OF

BLOWN, PRESSED FLINT, OPAL & MARBLE GLASS

TABLE GLASS.

Cut & Engraved Moons,

Confectionery Glass,

Fancy Glass.

KNOBS.

Lenses,

Lamps for Collieries

(Stephenson & Clanny Lamps).

STREET LIGHTS.

Street Lamps,

Deck Lights,

Masthead Lights,

Anchor Lights.

THE SPECIAL ATTENTION OF BUYERS IS CALLED TO OUR

CUT AND ENGRAVED MOONS.

NEWCASTLE FLINT GLASS WORKS,

NEWCASTLE-ON-TYNE.

London Offices:—26, ST. MARY AXE, E.C.

76 *Above* Advertisement from the *Pottery Gazette* of 1 December 1880 naming W. H. Heppell's two colours in Vitro-Porcelain: Opal and Marble Glass (opaque white and opaque brown marble).

77 *Below* Two Opal milk jugs and an Opal cream jug from the glass works of W. H. Heppell in their popular 'fish' designs. Designs for all three registered 24 November 1882. Heights: milk jug (left) 4⅛ in (10.4 cm), milk jug (centre) 5⅛ in (13 cm), cream jug (right) 5⅛ in (13 cm).

known and respected in the town of Gateshead as ironfounders, with business premises in Pipewellgate that had been in existence since the middle of the century. The Pipewellgate Foundry was principally confined to light castings, and particularly to glass-house mould castings, for which it had a high reputation. It is not surprising, therefore, that another member of the family should set up a pressed-glass factory near the family foundry where he could obtain his moulds.

Unfortunately, as far as I am aware, no pattern books or catalogues exist today from this firm to enable us to see the products that made up the company's main output. However, the firm did register some of its more unusual designs, and thus through these we can get some idea of its products. In 1880 the firm was advertising its pressed-glass products in Flint, Opal and Marble glass, the Flint appearing in coloured as well as plain glass, and the Opal and Marble being Heppell's version of the opaque introduced by Sowerby's as Vitro-Porcelain – Opal was opaque white, and Marble was the same as Sowerby's Brown Malachite. Heppell only produced these two colours in the opaque glass; if the collector should encounter any other opaque colour, such as Green Malachite, on articles bearing the registration mark for W. H. Heppell & Co., this will indicate that the piece was produced later at George Davidson & Co., who bought all the Heppell moulds when the business ceased in 1884.

Many of these designs appear in an extant Davidson catalogue of *c*. 1885: there are jugs and basins in the shape of fish in one series, and in another are interleaved sea-shells – these were registered in 1882 and 1881 respectively by Heppell. It is interesting to note here that the firm introduced into the design patterns two jugs in the shape of fish, one for milk and the other for cream, the difference being that the milk jug had a pinched-in lip whereas the cream jug had a wide mouth so as to enable the cream, which is of course of thicker consistency than

78 Butter dish and cover in Opal glass. Design registered by W. H. Heppell 24 November 1882. Height 3½ in (8.9 cm).

79 Unusual sugar bowl in Opal glass. Design registered by W. H. Heppell 24 November 1882. Height 5⅛ in (13 cm).

milk, to pour evenly. Once again we see ingenuity and practicality combined with novelty in the manufacture of pressed glass.

Other novel designs registered by Heppell included jugs and sugar basins in the form of coal scuttles, sugar containers and salts which were modelled on colliery coal trucks, and others in the form of wheelbarrows of various sizes. Although it was only a small glass works, and only in operation for ten years, W. H. Heppell produced articles that were original in design, had a novel appeal with their visual impact, and yet combined all this with practicality in use. It must have been these qualities that persuaded George Davidson of the Teams Glass Works to buy up all the moulds to enhance his own stock when the company shut down in 1884.

EDWARD MOORE & CO.

Another important manufacturer of pressed glass in the north-east, and one of the larger concerns, was that of Edward Moore of the Tyne Flint Glass Works, South Shields. Established in 1860 after the acquisition by Edward Moore of the business of Shortridge, Sawyer & Co., who were flint-glass manufacturers at West Holborn, South Shields, the firm had a very large home demand for its manufactures, which were distinguished for cheapness, durability, and beauty of design, and exported very largely to the Colonies and Europe. By 1865 the firm had two furnaces working and was in the process of adding a third. A description of some of the activities of the glass works was given by Edward Moore when he gave evidence to the Children's Employment Commission in 1865:

> We make pressed flint glass. We employ now upwards of 200 persons; about as many out of the glass-houses as in them. Of those not in the glass-houses some are men and women who are employed in the mixing room, where the materials are mixed with shovels, and others in the pot lofts making pots. A number of big girls and women wash the glass, others wrap it up in paper, or do warehouse work. There are a number of apprentice boys in the cutting shop, and a few boys who clean the moulds in which the glass is pressed, and which soon become dull and require rubbing with a rag and emery. This must be done very frequently to keep the moulds fit for use. All these hands out of the glass-houses work by day only, viz from 6 am to 6 pm with the usual hour and a half for meals.
>
> In the glass-houses the work is done by relays working eight hours each. There are eight chairs in each house, and on the average six persons to a chair, eg to take an average set, a taker-in, two stickers-up, a gatherer, a presser, and a melter. Work begins at 5 am on Mondays, and generally stops at 9 pm on Tuesday or 5 am on Wednesday for 16 hours; and generally also for a time between then and Saturday morning, when it finishes.[47]

Edward Moore's business seems to have flourished from the beginning, soon acquiring a reputation as a good quality pressed-glass manufacturer, with displays at major exhibitions. Moore was the only exhibitor of pressed glass at the International Exhibition held at the Crystal Palace in 1862, where his designs were praised as 'marvellously cheap and technically excellent' – although they were also criticised for being imitations of cut glass. In 1869 he exhibited at the Netherlands International Exhibition of Domestic Economy, which was held in Amsterdam, and won a silver medal. A report referring to Edward Moore & Co. at the time stated: 'Its collection of Glass at Amsterdam was much admired by the Dutch, and it is hoped that the firm will reap, in a practical shape, advantage from their appreciation.'[48] The firm opened showrooms and offices in Hamburg, but not, as far as we know, in Holland.

Edward Moore was obviously getting results from these showings at major exhibitions, for in 1879 he set out to capture the Australian market with exhibits at the Sydney International Exhibition. But a report sent back to England this time gave his pressed glass only lukewarm praise:

> This firm displays a collection of flint glass, table and ornamental glass ware. The coloured glass toilet sets are effective, and the patterns of the table glass are neat, but the goods are not of the highest quality.[49]

By the beginning of 1881, Moore, like other pressed-glass manufacturers in the north of England, was feeling the pinch of the depression, and he had to give notice to about forty hands as a result. On Sunday 28 August of that year the largest cone at the works fell 'with a

80 Blue Vitro-Porcelain sugar bowl, the double ogee bowl
moulded with elongated acanthus leaves on a stippled background,
c. 1885. Unmarked, but appears in the catalogue of Edward Moore,
c. 1885. Height 4½ in (11.4 cm), diameter 5½ in (13.9 cm).

tremendous crash', fortunately without anyone being injured. As the year progressed, however, things started to improve, the firm re-built the cone, re-lit furnaces that had been extinguished earlier for lack of orders, and began to re-engage the hands. Once more pressed-glass manufacturers were competing with each other for orders, and Edward Moore was determined not to allow Gateshead to win all the business. Towards the end of the year, the workmen went on full time again; they re-lit more furnaces, and a number of fresh hands were engaged, but still they could not complete the orders that were flooding in quickly enough.

Business was again booming by early 1882 and continued to do so for the rest of the century; during these years many new designs were produced and improvements made in the manufacture of coloured opaque glass. Edward Moore himself was instrumental in inventing new colours, and took out patents to protect them. Two of them, patents nos. 4821 and 4822, were submitted to the Patent Office in March 1887. The first specification, entitled 'Improvements in the Manufacture of Opaque Glass of a Certain New Colour', reads as follows:

> My invention relates to the production of a description of opaque glass of a soft shade of green colour, similar to what is termed 'Celadon' as a colour in porcelain manufacture. According to my invention I produce opaque glass of this colour by means of a mixture of

81 *Above* Blue Marbled Vitro-Porcelain candlestick, c. 1885. Unmarked, but appears in the catalogue of Edward Moore, c. 1885. Height 7½ in (19 cm).

82 *Above right* Blue Marbled Vitro-Porcelain 'swan' vase moulded with three swans linked by chains, beneath a zigzag border, c. 1880. Height 6¾ in

(17.1 cm). Vases like this have in the past been attributed to Sowerby's of Gateshead. There is no direct evidence for this, however, and the 'swan' vases appear in many colours which are not associated with Sowerby's, but which *are* colours patented by Edward Moore & Co. It is therefore probable that the vases were made by Edward Moore.

the oxide of uranium with the black oxide of copper added to the ordinary batch used in making opaque glass metal; or I obtain as desirable a shade of soft green by substituting peroxide of iron or Crocus Martis and black oxide of copper in suitable proportions instead of the above mentioned oxide of uranium and black oxide of copper by which latter means I obtain similar and satisfactory results at less expense than by using the oxide of uranium and the black oxide of copper.

When employing the oxide of uranium and the black oxide of copper in lieu of Crocus Martis and black oxide of copper I use 15ozs of oxide of uranium together with three ounces of the black oxide of copper to every one cwt of white opaque batch. I may employ with equally good results oxide of uranium or any compound containing an equal quantity of oxide of uranium; Crocus Martis or other form of peroxide of iron; black oxide of copper or any salt or compound of copper containing protoxide of copper.

The specification goes on to give a detailed description of the recipe, and states that the ingredients are combined and worked as in the manufacture of ordinary flint glass, ending with Edward Moore's declaration as to the claim he was making with his invention:

The addition to an opaque batch of the oxide of uranium or any compound containing an equal quantity of oxide of uranium in conjunction with the black oxide of copper or any salt or compound of copper containing protoxide of copper or Crocus Martis or other form of peroxide of iron and the black oxide of copper or any salt or compound of copper containing protoxide of copper combined in such proportions as to produce the desired shade of soft opaque green metal or glass which I term 'Eau de Nil'.[50]

The second specification submitted to the Patent Office was also for a new colour in opaque glass and was accepted on 3 May 1887. Patent no. 4822 was entitled 'The Manufacture of Opaque Glass of a New Colour', and gave the recipe for the colour, which was a type of caramel brown:

My invention relates to the production of opaque glass of a new colour, namely a soft shade of light brown or fawn colour and I obtain this colour by adding to an ordinary batch used in making opaque glass any of the following colouring substances: Flowers of Sulphur or calcined oats or other calcined cereal or vine stalks, or similar substances as used in the production of topaz colour in clear or translucent glass.

The following ingredients in the proportions stated are those I have found to answer when combining Flowers of Sulphur with the cryolite batch employed for the manufacture of opaque glass.

Sand ....7 cwts
Carbonate of lime or carbonate of Baryta ....1 cwt
Pure Alkali 58% ....3 cwts
Cryolite ....1 cwt 2 qtrs
Flowers of Sulphur at the rate of 16oz per cwt of batch ....12 lbs 8 ozs

These ingredients are combined and worked as in the manufacture of ordinary flint glass.

When employing the other ingredients named in lieu of Flowers of Sulphur I use calcined oats; or, other calcined cereal; or, vine stalks, at the rate of 8 ounces to every one cwt. of the aforesaid opaque batch.

I would here remark that I do not confine myself to the proportions above given of any of the named colouring materials nor to the precise materials and proportions employed in producing the opaque batch to which such colouring materials are added as such may be varied without departing from the peculiar character of my invention. Having now particularly described and ascertained the nature of my said invention and in what manner the same is to be performed I declare that what I claim is: the addition to an ordinary opaque batch of any of the materials ordinarily employed in colouring clear glass a topaz colour, such as Flowers of Sulphur, calcined oats or other calcined cereal, vine stalks or other similar materials so as to produce a soft shade of light brown or fawn colour.[51]

We can see, then, that the mixing of materials to make new colours was a fairly complex process, and one that had to be carefully controlled – although a clause was always inserted in the specifications to allow the manufacturers to alter the materials and proportions employed.

83 Three vases with thistle bowls moulded with palmettes beneath a zigzag border in marbled Vitro-Porcelain of unusual colours: the one in the centre is a slate blue colour and the other two are a mixture of caramel, blue-grey, black and white, *c.* 1880-1900. Height 7½ in (19 cm). Like the vase in Plate 82, these unmarked vases were probably originally manufactured by Edward Moore & Co; they were later produced by George Davidson & Co. who acquired the Edward Moore moulds in 1913. A catalogue produced by George Davidson & Co., of unknown date, shows similar moulded designs on other products, but the colours in which the vases appear point to an Edward Moore origin.

XXIX *Above* Sugar bowl and
cream jug in Opal glass with
moulded shell decoration.
Design registered by W. H.
Heppell 6 December 1881.
Height of bowl 4 in (10.1 cm),
height of jug 3¾ in (9.5 cm).

XXX *Right* Covered butter
dish in Opal glass with
moulded shell decoration.
Design registered by W. H.
Heppell 6 December 1881.
Height 4½ in (11.4 cm).

XXXI *Above* Figure of 'Punch' in an unusual green colour, *c.* 1875. John Derbyshire trade mark. Height 6¼ in (15.8 cm).

XXXII *Above right* Ornament in the form of Cleopatra's Needle in Opal glass, *c.* 1880. Maker unknown. Height 8½ in (21.6 cm). A similar model was made as a pomade jar and registered 13 October 1879 by G. V. de Luca, a firm of merchants' agents in London.

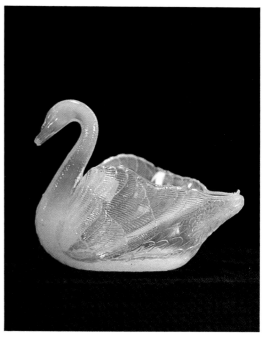

XXXIII *Right* Swan flower-holder in opalescent glass. Design registered by Burtles, Tate 8 January 1885, Rd.No. 20086. Height 2½ in (6.3 cm), length 3 in (7.6 cm).

This enabled them to improve on the colours at any time without re-submitting the original invention, and accounts for the slightly differing shades of the same colour one encounters on the finished article: experiments were taking place all the time.

As the decade progressed, as well as introducing new colours, Moore enlarged his range of goods whenever the opportunity arose by buying moulds from companies that were closing down. The well-known firm of Joseph Webb of the Coalbourn Hill Glass Works, Stourbridge, had been registering and producing pressed glass for some years with a reputation for good design and high quality. When Joseph, the founder, died the business was carried on by a partnership trading under the name of 'Jane Webb, Joseph Hammond and Henry Fitzroy Webb, the executors of the late Joseph Webb', and it continued to make pressed glass, registering many designs at the Design Registry Office, until 1888. When the firm ceased trading, the whole stock of moulds was bought by Edward Moore. A report in the *Pottery Gazette* on 1 November of that year shows that the combination of the Webbs' moulds and Moore's expertise was felt to be a promising one:

> Messrs Edward Moore & Co., pressed glass manufacturer, South Shields, have bought the whole stock of moulds held by the executors of the late Joseph Webb, Coalbourn Hill Glass Works, Stourbridge. Many of the designs formerly sold by Joseph Webb's firm were well known throughout the trade, and Messrs Moore & Co., producing these in good metal as they are doing, can scarcely fail to secure for them a good sale of these and their other patterns. A full line of samples can be seen at the showrooms of Mr John A. Leslie (agent), 67 St Mary Axe, London EC.[52]

In December the new patterns were included in the stock shown in an illustrated sheet of patterns in a supplement to the *Pottery Gazette*, and it was stated that 'these shapes in conjunction with a variety of new registered patterns are being incorporated in a new edition of their pattern book which is now in the press'.[53]

It will be inevitable, then, that the collector will encounter articles bearing the Joseph Webb factory registration on pieces that appear in the Edward Moore pattern sheets and available catalogues: we see here again an example of the interchangeability of moulds within the pressed-glass industry.

On the night of 4 July 1891 Edward Moore's glass works were completely destroyed by fire. Flames were first noticed by the watchman between 9 and 10 p.m., and soon the police, fire brigade and two steam tugs from the river were playing their hoses on the buildings. Their efforts were to no avail, however, and by 3.30 on Sunday morning the place was completely gutted, leaving only the five cones standing. The damage was roughly estimated at £45,000 and 400 hands were thrown idle. Despite this catastrophe the company was able to reconstruct the works, and production began again in May 1892.

From the time production started again until the end of the century, Edward Moore & Co. continued to bring out new designs in pressed-glass goods. They effected a notable improvement in their metal, bringing it up to the standard of what the trade then called 'Manchester glass', a reference to the fact that by the end of the nineteenth century the pressed-glass houses of Manchester had surpassed those of the north-east in the quality of glass they produced. The new metal had a hard, clear ring about it, and although still considered a cheap commodity, could hold its own amongst more expensive goods. One very good design, though a fine imitation of cut glass, was not a copy of any cut-glass pattern ever seen. It consisted of a series of flutes arranged in fan-shape, that is, open at the top and converging to a point at the bottom. These fan shapes, arranged alternately upside down, formed the ornamentation of the outside of, say, the bowl of a celery. In fact, it seems that the firm concentrated on the quality of the glass and of its decoration rather than trying to produce new wares: the *Pottery Gazette* noted that the company was 'paying more particular attention to the perfection of the metal and the originality of the decorations than to the production of new shapes'.[54] Edward Moore played his part in raising the standard of pressed glass produced in the north-east, for often by the end of the century glass from the Tyne and Wear was spoken of as 'North-Country stuff', and it was he who helped revive respect for it. Unfortunately, Edward Moore never used a trade mark, and the only way in which we can identify some of his products is by brief descriptions of his registered designs, by using the pattern sheets which he issued in the trade journal, and with the help of the few existing catalogues.

On 4 May 1900 Edward Moore died at his home in Wellington Street, South Shields, at the age of 64. His obituary paid tribute to his energetic business ability and his capabilities in his public career. He was a member of the town council, and had filled the office of mayor. The firm was continued by his son and widow during the Edwardian period, but in 1913 the company was wound up and ceased trading. The stock was sold off and the majority of the moulds were bought by Thomas Davidson of the Teams Glass Works, Gateshead.

CHAPTER THREE

LANCASHIRE
MANUFACTURERS

We now turn to the north-west of England for the other pressed-glass making centre that concerns the collector today. Lancashire had been renowned for its glass-making activities since the eighteenth century, when the industry was centred on Liverpool, Prescot, and Warrington, but it was not until the nineteenth century that Manchester became a centre for the trade. By the time the status of city had been conferred on Manchester by Queen Victoria in 1853, however, glass-making was well established, and by the end of the Victorian era Manchester was the most prestigious centre of the pressed-glass trade.

Unfortunately, the history of pressed glass in Lancashire was not documented nearly as well as that in the north-east, and contemporary records are very difficult to find: the trade journals of the time tended to ignore the area until brief reports appeared in the second half of the century, and even these are decidedly lacking in detail. Because of this lack of information, the history of the pressed-glass manufacturers in the Manchester area will have to be confined to those companies about which we do have some information and those of their products that are of particular interest to the collector.

Manchester was situated in a favourable position for glass-making, for the basic raw materials in the form of sand and chemicals were always at hand, coal to fire the furnaces was in abundance, and there was a network of canals and railways that enabled access not only to the rest of the country but to ports such as Liverpool and Hull as an outlet for foreign trade. One other major advantage, and one which was greatly to benefit the pressed-glass side of the trade, was the close proximity of the engineering and foundry workshops, where moulds and presses could be made to order, and it was this link between the glass-maker and the iron-worker that made Manchester the centre for the leading pressed-glass producers of the north-west. The pressed-glass trade was first set up in the Ancoats district, and later spread to the Hulme district, these two areas becoming the established glass-making centres.

JOHN DERBYSHIRE

Perhaps the best known of the pressed-glass houses in Manchester was that of John Derby-shire of the Regent Road Flint Glass Works, Salford. This was the only firm in Manchester

115

84 *Above* Four flint glass goblets from the different glass works of the Derbyshire family. From left to right: (1) design registered by James Derbyshire, British Union Flint Glass Works, 13 April 1869 (2) design registered by James Derbyshire & Brothers, Bridgewater Flint Glass Works 16 June 1866 (3) design registered by John Derbyshire, Regent Road Flint Glass Works, 8 August 1873, pattern number 256 (4) design registered by John Derbyshire, Regent Road Flint Glass Works, 8 August 1873, pattern number 258. Heights 6⅜ in (16.2 cm), 6 in (15.2 cm), 6¼ in (15.9 cm) and 6¾ in (17.1 cm) respectively.

86 *Below* Lion paperweight in black glass. Design registered by John Derbyshire, Regent Road Flint Glass Works, 3 July 1874. Trade marked. Height 5 in (12.7 cm), length 7¼ in (18.4 cm).

85 *Above* Flint glass celery vase with Greek key decoration and frosted glass. Design registered by James Derbyshire, British Union Flint Glass Works, 16 May 1865. Height 11 in (27.9 cm).

that used a trade mark – the initials JD superimposed over an anchor (see page 134) – and it is through this mark that the collector is able to identify with certainty the articles made by this firm. The Derbyshires were a glass-making family, and we first hear of them in Manchester with the name of James Derbyshire, a brother, who established a factory in 1858, at 248 City Road, Hulme, known as the British Union Flint Glass Works. By 1868 another factory had been established in Trentham Street, Hulme, which was called The Bridgewater Flint Glass Works, and was controlled by the brothers James, John and Thomas Derbyshire. It was during this period that we first find design registrations which can be attributed both to the Derbyshire brothers and the Hulme factories, although anything from either of the Hulme works is quite rare today and very much sought after.

It appears that the brothers continued to operate together, trading under the name of J. J. and T. Derbyshire, until 1873, when John left the company and set up a pressed-glass business of his own at Regent Road, Salford, which traded as John Derbyshire, Regent Road Flint Glass Works, Salford. This company had a life of only four years, for in 1876 the Salford works were renamed The Regent Flint Glass Co., and mention of John Derbyshire ceases. It was during these four years that the trade mark of JD superimposed on an anchor was used by John Derbyshire on his pressed-glass goods, often accompanied by the diamond registration mark, but not always. Meanwhile, James Derbyshire and Sons, as the parent company had become, continued operating the glass works at City Road, Hulme, and by the 1880s were also listed at the Regent Road Works, Salford. Whether any of the moulds made by John and bearing his trade mark were ever used by the family firm after 1876 is not known for certain, but all articles bearing the JD and anchor plus a diamond registration mark belong to the period 1873-6.

87 Neo-classical vase in matt black glass. Design registered by John Derbyshire, Regent Road Flint Glass Works, 23 April 1876. Trade marked. Height 5⅝ in (14.3 cm).

Like the other pressed-glass manufacturers, John Derbyshire produced a good range of utilitarian tableware, and on 8 August 1873 he registered his first designs, which included two goblets, both of which bear the pattern number beneath the trade mark. Similar goblets were produced at the Hulme factory by James Derbyshire in 1864, 1865, 1866 and 1869. For some reason not many of these goblets have survived, and are now extremely rare. They are all marked.

Of all the pressed glass produced by John Derbyshire at Salford, perhaps the most famous are his three-dimensional allegorical pieces, and, indeed, these are the most sought-after by collectors today. On 3 July

1874 he registered his most successful design, a paperweight in the form of a recumbent lion, modelled on the lions by Sir Edwin Landseer at the foot of Nelson's Column in Trafalgar Square in London. They appear in clear, frosted, and coloured glass. Another lion was produced with its front paws crossed, but was not registered and only bears the trade mark.

In 1876 a winged sphinx paperweight was produced: this took the form of the sphinx depicted in Greek mythology, represented with a body like that of a lion with wings, and with the breasts and upper parts of a woman. This differed from the Egyptian sphinx in that the latter had a human head (male or female) on the body of a lion (not winged) and was always in a recumbent posture, with the forepaws stretched forward, and a head-dress resembling an old-fashioned wig. The Greek sphinx, on the other hand, is represented in a variety of postures and was frequently used by the Greeks as an architectural ornament.

The Greek winged sphinx produced by John Derbyshire is in a recumbent posture and appears in frosted flint and black glass. The production of a sphinx by John Derbyshire was probably inspired by the current interest in Egyptology with talk of moving the obelisk known as Cleopatra's Needle from Egypt to London, and as another Manchester firm, Molineaux, Webb and Co., had already registered and produced an Egyptian sphinx in black glass in July 1875, it was appropriate that he should choose the Greek sphinx. When Cleopatra's Needle

88 The original design submitted to the Registrar of Designs by John Derbyshire for his winged sphinx paperweight. Registered 9 March 1876.

eventually reached London in 1878, it, too, was produced in pressed glass, but not, as far as is known, by John Derbyshire.

Other paperweights produced by John Derbyshire included a greyhound, which was registered in September 1874 – this was obviously inspired by nineteenth-century Staffordshire figure ornaments; a figure of Britannia in November 1874, and a pair of figures depicting Punch and Judy, which were not registered, but bear the trade mark of JD over an anchor. These figures are some of the most interesting articles in pressed glass to be produced in Manchester in the nineteenth century. No more designs were registered by John Derbyshire after May 1876, but by using a trade mark on those he did produce during his short term at Salford, he ensured himself a place in the history of pressed glass.

89 *Above* Figure of Britannia in frosted glass. Design registered by John Derbyshire, Regent Road Flint Glass Works, 26 November 1874. Trade marked. Height 7¾ in (19.7 cm).

90 *Above right* Figure of Judy in flint glass, *c.* 1875. John Derbyshire trade mark. Height 6¼ in (15.8 cm).

91 *Right* Greyhound paperweight in flint glass. Design registered by John Derbyshire 11 September 1874. Trade marked. Height 4¼ in (10.8 cm), length 7¼ in (18.4 cm).

Molineaux, Webb & Co.

One of the oldest, and the largest, glass works in Manchester was that of Molineaux, Webb & Co., Kirby Street, Ancoats, which was established in 1827. Not much is known about the early history of this company, but in *Pigot's Manchester Directory* for 1830 a firm called Maginnis, Molineux & Co., of Kirby Street, is listed for the first time, under the heading of glass manufacturers and merchants. From the *Directory* for 1832 we can see that Maginnis and Molineux had dissolved the partnership, for two new firms appear – Molineux, Webb, Ellis & Co., and Robinson, Perrin & Maginnis. In the 1832 alphabetical section we find David Webb, glasscutter; Jesse Webb, glass-maker; Thomas Webb, glass manufacturer; and William Webb, glass-blower. It will be noticed that at the time the name Molineaux was spelt differently. In the 1833 *Directory* a Thomas Molineux is listed as a glass manufacturer, with William Maginnis and Co., glass manufacturers.

The founder of the firm was Thomas Webb II, who in 1827 built some glass furnaces amidst green fields and trees at Ancoats, and who made his fortune manufacturing glass bowls to fit round the lights of railway lamps at the time of the railway boom. Webb also made lenses for ships' lights and, later, domestic and fancy glassware. Pressed glass was being made by Molineaux, Webb at least as early as 1848, the date of a letter sent to the Warrington firm of Robinson & Skinner by Thomas Webb II explaining the working conditions and wages at Molineaux, Webb at the time:

> The men do not work by time – they all work by piece. Making as much as they can in 6 hours – sometimes more, sometimes less – according to circumstances. Eleven moves constitute a week's work – for which we pay as follows: Pressers 21-23s. Melters 21-24s, gatherers 14-16s. Boys, not apprentices, 4s. A place consists of presser, melter, gatherer, and three boys – viz sticker-up, taker-in, and warmer-in. All work above 11 moves is overwork and paid for at the following rates: presser 1s 9d per move, melter 1s 9d per move, gatherer 1s per move and the 3 boys 4d each per move. Such are the general trends, we have one or two pressers and melters at 2s per move.[55]

The letter continues with an insight into how the men can earn more money 'with diligence', how satisfied and unsatisfied some are, and how making dishes seemed to be the worst job. A table is included in the letter indicating the numbers by which all work 'is reckoned' and also 'shews the amount of each article literally made for us in 6 hours'. This extant letter gives us our earliest knowledge of the working of a pressed-glass house in nineteenth-century England, and as such is invaluable. Unfortunately, no pressed glass can be identified from the Molineaux, Webb factory from this period, and it is not until the 1860s, when they began to register designs, that we can make positive identification.

Most of the output of the firm comprised general utilitarian pressed-glass tableware, and one of its most distinctive designs was the Greek key pattern with the outer surface partly roughened or obscured. This first appeared, and was registered, in 1864, and can be seen mainly on comports and dishes, celery vases, plates, cream jugs and sugar basins. As has been

92 *Above* Flint glass biscuit barrel, cover and stand with Greek key and frosted decoration. Base registered by Molineaux, Webb 22 December 1864; barrel registered 24 June 1867; lid registered 26 August 1867. Height 8¼ in (21 cm), diameter of base 8¼ in (21 cm). The lids and bases were often used for other domestic items such as butter dishes and preserve jars, hence the different dates of registration for each piece.

93 *Above* Flint glass comport with Greek key and frosted decoration. Design registered by Molineaux, Webb 27 September 1864. Height 6 in (15.2 cm), diameter of dish 7¾ in (19.7 cm).

94 *Below* Egyptian sphinx paperweight in matt black glass. Design registered by Molineaux, Webb 26 July 1875. Height 5½ in (14 cm), length 8 in (20.3 cm).

mentioned, the firm produced a very popular Egyptian sphinx in matt black glass imitating Wedgwood's black basalt; this appears to have been its only three-dimensional ornament. It was registered on 26 July 1875 and described as a paperweight. During the next decade many designs were produced, one popular design being the 1883 'Duchess' pattern, which recalled the 'cut-glass' fashion in pressed glass of earlier years. The following year saw further designs imitating cut glass, and the company began to issue pattern sheets to the *Pottery Gazette*. A brief report appeared in this journal in April 1884:

> We have received from Messrs Molineaux, Webb & Co., flint glass manufacturers, Kirby-street, Ancoats, Manchester, samples of a new pressed service which they are just bringing out, in imitation of a cut pattern. The set will comprise five sizes of oval dishes, five sizes of round dishes, four sizes comports, butters, basins, creams, celery etc. We certainly have not seen pressed goods more nearly resembling cut than the samples before us. The metal is brilliant, and the appearance is altogether good. Illustrated sheets of these goods will be distributed with our next issue. Messrs Molineaux, Webb & Co., have a deservedly high reputation for saleable goods.[56]

95 Flint glass sugar bowl in imitation cut glass. Design registered by Molineaux, Webb 28 January 1890, Rd. No. 143153. Height 4 in (10.1 cm), diameter 5 in (12.7 cm).

The firm continued to pioneer new designs in tableware throughout the remainder of the century, often augmenting its range of goods with ornamental articles of a novel design, such as flower holders for table decoration in opalescent glass, which seem to have been perennially popular with most pressed-glass houses in nineteenth-century England, whatever the fashion in tableware prevailing at the time. Molineaux, Webb survived well into the twentieth century, and in 1927, when the firm ceased trading, it was noted that 'the factory, both inside and out, is as it was in 1827', a fitting tribute to the builders of Manchester's first glass works.[57]

BURTLES, TATE & CO.

The next most important glass house producing pressed glass in Manchester of interest to the collector is that of Burtles, Tate & Co., Poland Street Glass Works, Oldham Road. Founded in 1858, and specialising in flint, coloured and ornamental fancy glass, the firm is perhaps best known to the collector for its pressed-glass ornaments in colours that closely imitate those produced by George Davidson of Gateshead in Pearline. In the early 1880s the company was operating two glass houses, one in Poland Street, and the other at Bolton, known as the Victoria Glass Works, where table glass was the main output. In 1887, a new glass works was erected in German Street, Manchester, near to the Poland Street works, and the company was able to close the Bolton factory and concentrate its glass-making activities within the two glass works in Manchester. It was from these works that some of the most interesting designs emanated in the late 1880s and early 1890s. It will be noted that most of the ornamental designs of interest to the collector were registered after 1884, the year the new series of registered numbers began, and Burtles, Tate marked the registered numbers (Rd. Nos.) on their wares within an oblong box. One of the first ornamental designs registered was a flower holder in the shape of a swan, No. 20086, in 1885, and then in 1886 an elephant flower holder, No. 64234. Novelties became a feature of this firm's productions, and in 1891 an interesting report appeared in the *Pottery Gazette* about one of them:

> Messrs Burtles, Tate & Co., Manchester, have a very good show of glass novelties of all descriptions, very tastefully displayed by their agent, Mr B. J. Stone, at the London rooms of the firm, 17 Ely Place, E.C. Any one seeing this firm's samples now, and remembering them some years ago, would hardly recognise them as the production of the same manufac-

96 Pair of swan posy holders in black glass. Design registered by Burtles, Tate 8 January 1885, Rd. No. 20086. Height 2½ in (6.3 cm), length 3 in (7.6 cm). Most of the black swan designs were made for the Australian market since these birds are indigenous to that country.

PERCIVAL, VICKERS & Co.

(LIMITED),

BRITISH AND FOREIGN

FLINT GLASS WORKS,

MANCHESTER.

MANUFACTURERS of EVERY DESCRIPTION and COLOUR of TABLE GLASS,

CUT, ENGRAVED, ETCHED, PLAIN, AND PRESSED.

RETORTS, &c., for CHEMICAL MANUFACTURERS,

DECK AND PORT LIGHTS FOR SHIPS' USE.

London Show Rooms—QUEEN ANNE'S CHAMBERS, HOLBORN VIADUCT.   Agent—Mr. W. SIVEWRIGHT.

SAMPLES AND PRICES ON APPLICATION.

BURTLES, TATE, & Co.,

FLINT GLASS MANUFACTURERS,

POLAND STREET,

MANCHESTER.

MANUFACTURERS OF

FLINT AND COLOURED PRESSED, BLOWN, OR CUT GLASS

OF EVERY DESCRIPTION,

AND ALL KINDS OF CONFECTIONERS' GLASS,

FOR HOME AND EXPORT TRADE.

London Show Rooms:—23, THAVIES INN, E.C.

SAMPLES AND PRICES ON APPLICATION.

turers. Messrs Burtles, Tate & Co., are not only quite up to date with the particular goods in demand, but they do not hesitate to bring out a succession of novelties . . .

The most pleasing novelty we saw in our inspection of these samples last week was the 'Topas Opalescent' ware. This is a striking imitation of the old Venetian Topas of the fourteenth century. The best effects are the result of a very clever manipulation of the metal after the article has been shaped. When the vase, or jug, or any other article has been made, the Topas effect is produced by a dexterous subjection of one part of it (in the case of a flower vase, the top part) to the heat of the 'glory hole', the quality of the work turned out depending upon the skill of the operator. As this Topas opalescent can be produced from any of the colours generally used, we anticipate a great sale for it . . .[58]

As can be seen from the above description, Burtles, Tate's new novelty was very similar to that produced by George Davidson & Co. in Gateshead in 1889, under the direction of Thomas Davidson, where it was patented using the name 'Pearline'. And, indeed, the Topas ware resembled this type of glass in colour and shading, the only difference being that the Topas glass appeared in a wider variety of colours than did the Pearline glass, for Thomas Davidson patented his glass in two colours only, Blue and Primrose. Nevertheless, both types of glass are very attractive in appearance, and both are very collectable today, whether made in Manchester or Gateshead.

One very popular colour in the Topas ware was Uranium, which was greenish-yellow in appearance. A variation on this type of glass, meanwhile, called 'Sunrise', appeared in 1891, and although the technique used to produce it was applied mostly on Burtles, Tate's blown glass, it was also experimented with on some pressed glass and can sometimes be seen on their swan flower holders. An account of this glass was given by the *Pottery Gazette* in 1892:

Messrs Burtles, Tate & Co. have already been very successful in some striking effects produced by a dexterous manipulation of the metal after the article has been shaped. There are several varieties of these now to be seen at their rooms, the latest of which has just been introduced. This is appropriately called the 'Sunrise' and bids fair to become as popular as their 'Uranium'. The 'Sunrise' effect is produced by a clever shading of the opalescent glass, this deepens gradually from yellow or amber to pink, with ruby edges. The 'Sunrise' is really a development of, and we think a great improvement upon, their Topas opalescent ware.[59]

The output from the two glass works of Burtles, Tate in the later 1890s was prolific, and in both ornamental and utilitarian pressed glass the firm excelled. The *Pottery Gazette* commented that 'there are few makers who can compete with them in this particular line. With "cheap lines" this firm are very far ahead of the foreign glass maker, the quality of the metal being of sterling value.'[60] The firm continued into the present century, and was acquired by Butterworth Bros. of Manchester in 1924.

97 *Opposite* Advertisement from the *Pottery Gazette* of 1 December 1880 for two Manchester pressed-glass manufacturers, Percival, Vickers and Burtles, Tate.

MINOR MANUFACTURERS

One of the first registrations for pressed glass in Manchester was a design for a dish in 1847 by Percival & Yates of The British & Foreign Flint Glass Works, Jersey Street, Manchester. Established in 1844, the firm was first known as Percival & Yates, Glass Manufacturers, and it was not until it was well established that a Mr Vickers joined the company, the firm then trading as Percival, Yates and Vickers. Some time in the early 1870s Yates appears to have left the company, for the name changes once again to become Percival, Vickers & Co. Ltd., Manufacturers of Flint and Coloured Glass, Cut, Moulded, and Engraved. There is very little information available about this glass factory, apart from a few designs registered and the occasional pattern sheet issued in the *Pottery Gazette*. Percival, Vickers produced many attractive designs in pressed glass and seem to have concentrated on general tableware. In 1881 they produced a novel design to commemorate the death of Benjamin Disraeli, Earl of Beaconsfield, which they later transferred on to their blown glass where it was printed:

> Messrs Percival, Vickers & Co. Ltd, with two of their furnaces working, report things quiet, although working as full as usual, some part of the manufactures going into stock; I may notice this firm have just got out a very good plate of the late Earl Beaconsfield, K. G., which they are transferring by the printing process on to gas globes, water sets, etc.[61]

The firm continued to make pressed glass into the twentieth century, enjoying a large home trade, with showrooms in London at Queen Anne's Chambers, Holborn Viaduct, and eventually ceased trading in 1914.

Two other glass houses in Manchester produced pressed glass in the second half of the nineteenth century, but not much is known about their history. They were modest in size, and registered only a few designs. The first was Thomas Kidd & Co., Holt Town Glass Works, Gibbon Street, Bradford Road, Ancoats. The firm was a producer of flint and coloured pressed glass and, like Greener & Co. of Sunderland, was noted for its novelties in 'Penny Glassware'; each article cost one penny and the goods produced ranged from such things as salt cellars, dishes, ash trays, vases, and plates to swans, dogs and bird glasses. For the Queen's Diamond Jubilee in 1897 Thomas Kidd & Co. produced a five-inch commemorative plate with a medallion portrait in the centre and the inscription 'Queen Victoria: England's Greatest Queen: Fairest And Noblest The World Has Ever Seen'. They also produced a three-dimensional bust of the Queen, which often appears in black glass, and can also be found in translucent brown, blue and clear. The firm was registered as a limited company on 12 November 1891 and continued into the early years of the twentieth century.

The other pressed-glass manufacturer worthy of note in Manchester was Andrew Ker & Co., Prussia Street Flint Glass Works. This was another modest glass house which only registered three designs of interest to the collector today, the first two under the name of Ker, Webb & Co: the first, a flower vase, was registered on 13 June 1872, the second, a piano footrest, on 27 May 1873, and the third, a glass dish, on 19 December 1876. The works appear to have closed down in the late 1880s.

98 *Above* Standing dish (or comport) with frosted glass decoration and heavily moulded stem. Design registered by Percival, Vickers 1 March 1878. Height 7¼ in (18.4 cm), diameter 6¾ in (17.1 cm).

99 *Above* Opaque black glass bust of Queen Victoria produced by Thomas Kidd for the Diamond Jubilee in 1897. Height 3½ in (8.9 cm).

100 *Below* An example of Thomas Kidd's Penny Glassware. A small plate made for the Silver Wedding of the Prince and Princess of Wales in 1888. Diameter 5 in (14 cm).

EPILOGUE

As the twentieth century dawned, the pressed-glass industry was on the wane. There were several reasons for this. Probably the main cause of decline was foreign competition, and to this was allied the perennial problem of restrictive work practices.

Ever since the invention of the process of pressing glass in the early years of the century there had been frequent labour disputes in the glass industry. The basic problem was that, as with other inventions which made possible faster production and lessened the need for skilled labour, the workers feared that their employers would cut jobs and pay. Rates of pay, speed of working, length of the working week and so on were constantly in dispute and there was a complete lock-out in 1858-9. Conversely, since the men were paid by the piece rather than the time worked, innovations which might temporarily slow their rate of production while they learned new techniques were viewed with suspicion, and thus progress was sometimes retarded – this was the case, as we have seen, with the introduction of spring snaps in Lancashire in the 1860s.

Several reports in the *Pottery Gazette* refer to the restrictive practices adopted by the unions, and show that these enabled European and American competitors to undercut English manufacturers. For instance, a report in December 1884 describes the difference between the English and European systems:

> On the Continent, if a man is a poor workman he gets smaller wages, this being a question between himself and his employer according to his ability. In England, supposing a man comes to work – say a wine workman – who is an unsteady, idle workman, who does not earn a week's work in eight turns, he starts at the same rate of wages, under the same conditions and numbers, etc., as his neighbour (who is perhaps an industrious, steady, clever, workman), who in the same time makes two weeks' wages, and of course there is no comparison between the two. Yet the number of articles required in the eight turns cannot be increased because the poor workman could not then earn his wages. How different on the Continent! There the good workman would have his wages raised, while the poor workman would either have to work for a smaller wage or leave. Again, a man who is not a com-

petent workman and who does not produce a full quantity of work per week, takes up room which might be utilized by a clever workman; and still if this man is sent to the manufacturer by the Glass Makers' Union he must be employed. The Continental manufacturer may have as many apprentices as he likes, and if a young man is clever he is advanced: not as here, where we cannot put on an apprentice if there is a journeyman out of employment, until we have tried him, although we know that he will not suit. Of course this increases the number of *competent men*, and thus tends to raise both the standard and the competition of the workmen. In fact 'the weakest goes to the wall'. In England we are allowed only a limited number of apprentices; and these are only allowed to be bound if there are no journeymen out of work. I am sure that the Glass Makers' Union have lots of men on their books drawing money under the head of 'unemployed', who would not be employed for any length of time in any glass works, and they are 'unemployed' not from shortness of work (in many cases) but because glass manufacturers will not light and work a furnace, and place eight or nine such chairs on it, who altogether produce, perhaps, as much work as three or four competent and clever men do, occupying, perhaps, half of another furnace.[62]

The writer of this article also commented on the fact that by this time, the quality of the glass of the north-eastern firms had fallen below that of the Lancashire manufacturers.

I have endeavoured in these few lines to point out some of the causes, etc., which enable the foreign manufacturer to undersell his English neighbour so completely; and although their glass is not as good as the best English glass or the pressed glass of the Manchester and Warrington and Birmingham districts, still it is quite equal to many of the productions of Newcastle and the northern districts.

By 1890, the *Pottery Gazette* was bemoaning the depressed state of the English pressed-glass trade, and blaming it on excessive competition, both home and foreign:

For a long time past there has been an unsettled and uneasy feeling throughout the pressed-glass trade. All connected with it – manufacturers, wholesale dealers and retailers alike – have been complaining. Competition, both home and foreign, has demoralised prices to such an extent that in many cases the bare cost of production has not been realised. Many suggestions for altering this unsatisfactory condition of things have from time to time been made, but none have had any prospect of adoption.[63]

Part of the problem for the English pressed-glass makers at this time seems to have been design. The following extract seems to suggest that neither the continental manufacturers nor the American firms were strong in design, but that the Americans were good at other aspects of production. Since the continental manufacturers, as we have seen, did not suffer from the English disease of restrictive working practices, falling standards in England's main strength, design, boded ill for the trade:

The most curious part of this trade is, that the only country which can even now succeed in making it (pressed glass) besides ourselves is the United States; Belgium, Holland, France and Germany are as clumsy at it as they were years ago, and the States excel in everything but design; and in this latter art England is fast losing ground, forgetting that design and quality are factors not to be set aside in the commercial free-trade fight for supremacy: cheapness is not everything in pressed glass . . .

It would be a mistake to say that pressing of glass has improved in England the last few years; the fight for cheapness has let in the better class from the United States, and our design seems to have left us, which the foresight and commercial ability of Sowerby & Neville brought to bear in their twenty years' partnership.[64]

A further retarding factor in the English pressed-glass trade was the depression of 1877-85, which meant that, just as the industry had developed sufficiently to produce large quantities of glass in a huge variety of designs, its main customers, the working classes, could least afford to buy it. Thus many glass works fluctuated between virtual closure and full working, and some of the impetus of development was lost.

In the 1900s, moreover, fashions began to change and pressed glass gradually declined in popularity. Finally, during World War I, thousands of the metal moulds were melted down to be made into armaments. Many of the most famous pressed-glass houses continued to trade, but turned to producing industrial goods, such as pavement lights and glass covers for ships' lights.

Nevertheless, what were once cheap wares produced for the masses have since come to be increasingly valued. The best pieces of nineteenth-century pressed glass now fetch sums approaching four figures, and pressed glass is a busy collectors' field. The huge variety of attractive and unusual wares in collections and elsewhere today shows the originality and skill of the Victorian glass-makers, and allows us to continue to appreciate this fascinating branch of the glass-maker's craft.

DESIGN REGISTRATIONS

REGISTRATION MARKS

Glass articles made by the press-moulding technique and manufactured between 1842 and 1883 sometimes bear a diamond-shaped registration mark. This indicates that the design was registered at the Patent Office Design Registry and was protected by the Act of Parliament governing the registration at the time. The mark can be used to determine the exact date of registration, and with the help of the official Register held at the Public Record Office (the relevant parts of which are reproduced in this Appendix) the name of the firm or person registering the design can be ascertained. There were two cycles of diamond-shaped marks, the first running from 1842 to 1867 and the second from 1868 to 1883. The information can be gained by first reading off the various figures and letters appearing in the corners of the diamond and then relating them to the table below in the manner outlined.

In the first cycle, the year of registration is represented by a letter of the alphabet at the top of the diamond, the month is shown by a letter on the left and the day of the month by a figure on the right; the bottom figure represents the parcel or bundle number. In the second cycle the year of registration moves to the right of the diamond, the month to the bottom, the day of the month to the top, and the parcel or bundle number appears on the left. On all the diamonds will be seen a ring at the top enclosing Roman numerals. This indicates the class of goods the article was registered under; for glass the Roman numerals III will appear.

By following this simple procedure the collector should have no difficulty in determining the date of registration on articles that bear the diamond-shaped mark. However, it should not be taken for granted that all examples bearing this mark were manufactured in this country, as several foreign manufacturers and agents registered designs that were to be sold in England, and they, too, sought protection from piracy of their designs. Sometimes a retailer's name appears in the register instead of that of the glass manufacturer, and this makes attribution of a particular item to a glass manufacturer more difficult, unless the manufacturer happened to use a trade mark, as for example Sowerby & Co. did when they made a 'Queen Ann' candlestick for J. Mortlock & Co. of Oxford Street and Orchard Street, London.

In 1883 the Patents, Designs and Trade Marks Act merged all the various categories of designs, both useful and ornamental, into one continuous series to begin on 1 January 1884.

These appear on the glass as a serial number prefixed with the abbreviation 'Rd. No.' starting with No. 1 on 1 January 1884. It must be remembered, however, that with all systems of registration the official mark will show only the date that the design was first introduced, and this is not necessarily the date of manufacture.

(a) 1842 to 1867

Years		Months
1842 – X	1855 – E	January – C
1843 – H	1856 – L	February – G
1844 – C	1857 – K	March – W
1845 – A	1858 – B	April – H
1846 – I	1859 – M	May – E
1847 – F	1860 – Z	June – M
1848 – U	1861 – R	July – I
1849 – S	1862 – O	August – R
1850 – V	1863 – G	September – D
1851 – P	1864 – N	October – B
1852 – D	1865 – W	November – K
1853 – Y	1866 – Q	December – A
1854 – J	1867 – T	

(R may be found as the month mark for 1-19 September 1857, and K for December 1860.)

(b) 1868 to 1883

Years		Months
1868 – X	1876 – V	January – C
1869 – H	1877 – P	February – G
1870 – C	1878 – D	March – W
1871 – A	1879 – Y	April – H
1872 – I	1880 – J	May – E
1873 – F	1881 – E	June – M
1874 – U	1882 – L	July – I
1875 – S	1883 – K	August – R
		September – D
		October – B
		November – K
		December – A

(For 1-6 March 1878, G was used for the month and W for the year.)

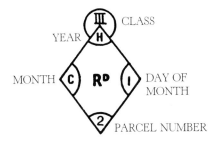

1 January 1843

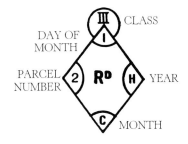

1 January 1869

Trade Marks

Collectors of pressed glass today are fortunate in being able to identify a great many of their pieces through the manufacturers' use of a trade mark on their products, although not every manufacturer used this form of protection and identification. The Trade Marks Registration Act of 1875 first made provision for the registration of trade marks, and the first official registration date was January 1876. Only five pressed-glass manufacturers in the nineteenth century used a trade mark on their goods – four in the north-east and one in Manchester.

Of these only two appear to have bothered to register their mark: John Sowerby of the Ellison Glass Works, Gateshead, with his famous peacock's head crest, and Henry Greener of the Wear Flint Glass Works, Sunderland, with a heraldic crest mark in the form of a demi-lion rampant, facing left and holding in his right paw a five-pointed star. Both these trade marks were registered in the first year of official registration, 1876, and were stated not to have been used before 13 August 1875, the date on which the Act became law. The other two trade marks used by north-east manufacturers were the second 'Greener' mark adopted when the firm was taken over by James A. Jobling in 1885, and that of George Davidson. Jobling's mark was a family heraldic crest of a demi-lion holding a battleaxe in both paws. Davidson also adopted a heraldic crest – that of a demi-lion rampant issuing from a mural crown and facing left. One other trade mark used on pressed glass which is of great interest to the collector is that of the Manchester firm of John Derbyshire of the Regent Road Flint Glass Works, Salford. This takes the form of an anchor superimposed on the initials JD, and had a life of only four years (1873-6 inclusive).

These trade marks, along with the diamond registration mark, help us to identify some of the pressed glass manufactured in nineteenth-century England with some degree of certainty. It has been said, however, that some of the marks were copied at the time, especially the products of the firm of Sowerby & Co. It is doubtful that this practice was rife in England, but certainly Sowerby's were concerned about it, for their advertisements at the time warned their customers: 'All designs registered. – Sowerby & Co. will esteem it a favour by being informed of any infringement of their designs or Trade Mark.' A report in the *Pottery Gazette* in 1880, although not naming Sowerby, was obviously referring to this firm's dilemma:

> An important house in the pressed glass trade has its registered designs copied under the very shadow of its own works, and they are informed there is no remedy. The moulds are made of iron and the registration is for glass. These moulds are shipped to Holland, where goods are made from them of an inferior quality, to the great injury of the house in question. Of course the goods cannot be imported as long as the registration lasts; but they sell them throughout the continent.[65]

There appears to be no record of any proceedings in law against anyone guilty of this infringement, so it must be assumed the practice was short-lived and died a natural death. With the passage of time, it is probable that few of these spurious pieces still exist, for compared with the vast output of the Sowerby factory at the time, the amount of copying would have been negligible, and the ratio compared with the genuine article infinitesimal.

Occasionally the collector will encounter the word 'Deposé' on pieces of pressed glass made by Sowerby's of Gateshead, accompanied by the peacock trade mark and sometimes the diamond registration mark. Because of the concern engendered by copying, especially from abroad, and because Sowerby's was exporting to the continent, John Sowerby included this word, French for 'Registered', on his registered designs that were for export. He began this practice in 1877 and continued it for the remainder of the century. These pieces were made in Gateshead, registered in London, and sold abroad, therefore few articles will be found in this country bearing the Deposé mark; those pieces that have found their way back to England are quite rare.

In 1896 Sowerby's built a glass works near Antwerp in Belgium for the manufacture of pressed glass, but the venture was short-lived, for a year later the factory was blown down in a hurricane. Rebuilding took place immediately, but the factory never achieved success and Sowerby's abandoned the project in the early twentieth century. At one time it was thought that articles appearing with the Deposé mark on them were manufactured at this factory, but this is not so, as articles appear with this mark long before the Belgian venture took place.

The following are the five trade marks found on English pressed glass:

Sowerby, Gateshead
Used 1875-c. 1930

George Davidson,
Gateshead
Used c. 1880-90

Henry Greener,
Sunderland
Used 1875-85

Greener & Co.,
Sunderland
Used c. 1885-1900

John Derbyshire, Salford
Used 1873-6

LIST OF DESIGN REGISTRATIONS

The Ornamental Designs Act of 1842 established various categories for registering designs: Class III was for glass. The records of the Patent Office and Industrial Property Department of the Board of Trade, which are housed at the Public Record Office, Kew, include Registers and volumes of Representations of these Class III designs. The Registers give the registered number, the exact date of registration, type of design, and the maker's name and address but not necessarily the name of the designer, whilst the volumes of Representations, containing a representation of a design, give a drawing or photograph of the article. Registered designs between 1842 and 1884 should carry a diamond mark (see pages 131-2).

The following list is in two parts. The first part is a complete list of all registered designs in Class III (glass) from 1 September 1842 to 16 January 1884, the dates the register began and ended for those articles carrying a diamond registration mark. The list comprises four columns and gives the date of registration, the parcel number, the number of the design, and the name of the person or company registering the design, together with the name of the place in which the person or company was based. The full address of the proprietor has been omitted, since the town or place of residence is sufficient for identification purposes. By consulting the table and diagram on page 132, the collector can find the exact date of registration for those pieces bearing the diamond registration mark, and with the help of this list establish the person registering the design who, in most cases for pressed glass, was the manufacturer. The design number in column three corresponds with the drawing or photograph submitted with the registration at the time. These can be found in the four volumes of Representations held at Kew. Since this number establishes in which volume the design can be found, the collector, armed with it and with the registered date, should have no difficulty in finding the design illustration. Where a design is registered individually in the list that follows, it will in most cases also be possible to check the type of article from a written description in the Registers. When a design is registered in a batch, however, eg Design Nos 378063-5, no written description appears and the collector should go straight to the volumes of Representations. It should be noted that the list in this book, being in full, gives registered designs in Class III other than pressed glass. It is necessary to give the whole list because in some instances it is not possible to determine whether or not an article registered is made of pressed glass unless one actually has the article.

In 1883, as has been explained, the Patents, Designs and Trade Marks Act amalgamated all the categories into which designs had previously been divided, and registered the articles in a single numerical series beginning with the first registration in January 1884. Glass was included in Class 4 along with many other categories such as ceramics, pottery, metals, etc. The second part of the list, beginning in February 1884, gives all registrations submitted by glass manufacturers and most glass merchants up to 1900; the collector needs simply to look at the Rd. No. on the piece of glass he is trying to identify, find the number in the sequence in the list and read off the manufacturer and the date. It will be noted that some manufacturers gave their London showroom address rather than the place of manufacture, but in most cases the manufacturer's glass works appear.

DATE	PARCEL NO.	DESIGN NO.	MANUFACTURER OR REGISTRAR
1842			
Sept. 1	9	1461	Henry Cope Junr, London
Sept. 6	1	1480	Rice Wm. Harris, Birmingham
Sept. 14	1	1684	Frederick Gye Junr, London
Sept. 28	4	1774	Sir John Scott Lillie, Knt, London
Oct. 27	6	2132	Reeves & Sons, London
Oct. 28	5	2138	Alfred Ward, London
Nov. 19	3	2319	Chance Bros & Co., Birmingham
Nov. 19	3	2320	Chance Bros & Co., Birmingham
Nov. 19	3	2321	Chance Bros & Co., Birmingham
Nov. 28	2	2508	Philip James Luntley, London
1843			
Jan. 25	7	4338	Apsley Pellatt, London
March 15	1	5857	Rice Wm Harris, Birmingham
April 24	5	6689	Apsley Pellatt, London
June 17	7	7559	Apsley Pellatt, London
June 17	7	7560	Apsley Pellatt, London
Sept. 8	8	9809	Palmer & Co, London
Oct. 7	5	10385	Thomas Taylor, London
1844			
Jan. 18	8	14658	Apsley Pellatt, London
Feb. 27	8	16636	John Christy & Alfred Joy, London
July 29	9	20328	Alfred Joy, London
July 30	3	20335	Apsley Pellatt, London
1845			
April 1	4	27045	Robert Walter Winfield, Birmingham
April 14	7	27232	Crosse & Blackwell, London
May 10	2	27481	Uriah Lane, Brighton
May 14	4	27509	Uriah Lane, Brighton
May 14	4	27510	Uriah Lane, Brighton
May 14	4	27511	Uriah Lane, Brighton
May 14	4	27512	Uriah Lane, Brighton
May 14	4	27513	Uriah Lane, Brighton

DATE	PARCEL NO.	DESIGN NO.	MANUFACTURER OR REGISTRAR
May 15	2	27515	Uriah Lane, Brighton
May 23	3	27641	Charles Heaton & Co., London
June 7	7	28035	Phillipson & Co., London
July 9	3	28723	Joseph Wingrave, London
July 17	4 or 5	28865	Wilson & Southern, Sheffield
Aug. 12	3	29718	Joseph Wingrave, London
Aug. 19	1	29847	Apsley Pellatt, London
Aug. 26	3	29930	Charles Heaton & Co., London
Sept. 23	6	30428	Isaac Clifton, London
Nov. 6	5	31057	Charles & May, London
Dec. 5	5	31721	The Aire & Calder Bottle Co., London
Dec. 9	2	31877	The Aire & Calder Bottle Co., London
Dec. 24	1	32479	William Binnion, Birmingham
Dec. 24	2	32480	William Wray Western Pigott, London
Dec. 31	3	32643	William Binnion, Birmingham
1846			
Jan. 12	3	32954	Robert Walter Winfield, Birmingham
Feb. 13	4	33765	Crosse & Blackwell, London
Feb. 19	2	33917	Robert Walter Winfield, Birmingham
March 20	4	34443	Anthony Thatcher, Pontefract, Yorkshire
March 31	1	34522	Anthony Thatcher, Pontefract, Yorkshire
April 9	1	34577	R. Torbock & Co., London
April 15	5	34601	William Binnion, Birmingham
May 9	4	34929	William Binnion, Birmingham
May 14	3	34943	Anthony Thatcher, Pontefract, Yorkshire
June 12	4	35283	The Aire & Calder Bottle Co., London
June 22	9	35385	The Aire & Calder Bottle Co., London
June 26	3	35778	Jonas Defries, London
July 7	1	35925	The Aire & Calder Bottle Co., London
July 7	1	35926	The Aire & Calder Bottle Co., London
Aug. 1	1	36441	Rice Harris, Birmingham
Aug. 1	1	36442	Rice Harris, Birmingham
Aug. 1	1	36443	Rice Harris, Birmingham
Aug. 1	1	36444	Rice Harris, Birmingham
Aug. 1	1	36445	Rice Harris, Birmingham
Aug. 1	1	36446	Rice Harris, Birmingham

Date	Parcel No.	Design No.	Manufacturer or Registrar
Aug. 20	1	36925	Anthony Thatcher, Pontefract, Yorkshire
Aug. 25	3	36987	William Binnion, Birmingham
Aug. 27	3	36992	Anthony Thatcher, Pontefract, Yorkshire
Sept. 5	4	37202	Anthony Thatcher, Pontefract, Yorkshire
Sept. 8	1	37224	Anthony Thatcher, Pontefract, Yorkshire
Oct. 7	4	37676	Griffiths & Son, London
Oct 14	2	37706	Samuel Chambers, Birmingham
Nov. 26	4	38329	George Upton & Co., London
Dec. 7	2	38643	Molineux & Co., Manchester
1847			
Jan. 2	5	39810	Hammond Turner & Sons, Birmingham
Jan. 7	2	39960	John Weekes Kincaird, London
March 17	10	42074	The Aire & Calder Bottle Co., London
March 25	3	42296	Percival & Yates, Manchester
April 12	3	42604	Vincent Price, London
April 16	2	42634	W.H.B. & J. Richardson, Stourbridge
April 16	2	42635	W.H.B. & J. Richardson, Stourbridge
May 10	6	43137	The Aire & Calder Bottle Co., London
May 10	6	43138	The Aire & Calder Bottle Co., London
May 19	3	43245	Arthur Young & Co., London
May 31	4	43426	The Aire & Calder Bottle Co., London
June 3	3	43462	Felix Summerly, London
June 17	1	43655	Percival & Yates, Manchester
June 22	1	43729	John Cliff Quince, London
June 30	6	43850	Percival & Yates, Manchester
July 5	4	43915	John Dockree, London
July 6	2	43924	W.H.B. & J. Richardson, Stourbridge
July 6	2	43925	W.H.B. & J. Richardson, Stourbridge
July 6	2	43926	W.H.B. & J. Richardson, Stourbridge
July 6	2	43927	W.H.B. & J. Richardson, Stourbridge
July 17	3	44041	Robert Best, Birmingham
July 29	5	44616	The Aire & Calder Bottle Co., London
Oct. 1	5	46131	F. & C. Osler, Birmingham
Oct. 12	3	46292	The Aire & Calder Bottle Co., London
Oct. 14	6	46306	Charles Lloyd, Birmingham
Oct. 20	5	46484	Charles Rowley, Birmingham

Date	Parcel No.	Design No.	Manufacturer or Registrar
Oct. 23	3	46519	F. & C. Osler, Birmingham
Oct. 25	2	46523	John Fell Christy & Co., London
Oct. 28	1	46662	Alexis Soyer, London
Nov. 2	1	46748	F. & C. Osler, Birmingham
Nov. 5	2	46788	Percival & Yates, Manchester
Nov. 5	2	46789	Percival & Yates, Manchester
Nov. 27	2	47344	Percival & Yates, Manchester
Dec. 9	5	47532	Crosse & Blackwell, London
Dec. 11	4	47601	Crosse & Blackwell, London
Dec. 28	2	48516	Crosse & Blackwell, London
1848			
Jan. 6	5	48718	Joseph Barlow, London
Jan. 11	3	48858	R.W. Winfield, Birmingham
Jan. 17	5	49021	John Davis, nr. Stourbridge
Jan. 26	2	49205	The Yorkshire Bottle Co., London
Feb. 7	5	49700	Cornelius Bagnall & John Westwood, London
Feb. 11	2	49779	Percival & Yates, Manchester
Feb. 22	7	50271	John Combs & Son, London
Feb. 26	3	50369	The Yorkshire Bottle Co., London
Feb. 26	6	50378	The Aire & Calder Bottle Co., London
Feb. 28	2	50413	Crosse & Blackwell, London
Feb. 29	6	50463	Cornelius Bagnall & John Westwood, London
March 2	4	50520	The Aire & Calder Bottle Co., London
March 18	4	50942	Jonas Defries, London
March 18	4	50943	Jonas Defries, London
March 18	4	50944	Jonas Defries, London
March 20	5	50988	Henry Pershouse, Birmingham
March 27	10	51199	William Binnion, Birmingham
March 30	2	51213	Joseph Wingrave & Co., London
May 10	5	51882	Jonas Defries, London
May 25	1	52120	Alexis Soyer, London
May 30	1	52158	W.H.B. & J. Richardson, Stourbridge
May 30	1	52159	W.H.B. & J. Richardson, Stourbridge
May 30	1	52160	W.H.B. & J. Richardson, Stourbridge
June 1	6	52179	W.H.B. & J. Richardson, Stourbridge
June 13	4	52328	W.H.B. & J. Richardson, Stourbridge

DATE	PARCEL NO.	DESIGN NO.	MANUFACTURER OR REGISTRAR
June 13	4	52329	W.H.B. & J. Richardson, Stourbridge
July 3	2	52554	Anthony Thatcher, Pontefract, Yorkshire
July 21	4	53121	A. Bissett, London
Aug. 2	6	53633	John West & John Henry Weston, London
Aug. 17	2	53881	John West & John Henry Weston, London
Aug. 30	3	54128	John West & John Henry Weston, London
Aug. 30	3	54129	John West & John Henry Weston, London
Aug. 30	3	54130	John West & John Henry Weston, London
Aug. 30	3	54131	John West & John Henry Weston, London
Sept. 7	3	54273	George & Robert Macdonus, London & Dublin
Sept. 7	4	54274	Joseph Guise, London
Sept. 23	5	54552	Elton & Everton, London
Oct. 2	1	54664	Joseph Green, Birmingham
Oct. 28	2	55052	Westwood & Moore, Brierley Hill, Staffordshire
1849			
Jan. 4	6	57024	Westwood & Moore, Brierley Hill, Staffordshire
Jan. 12	5	57319	Joseph Wingrave & Co., London
Feb. 28	5	58596	Westwood & Moore, Brierley Hill, Staffordshire
March 12	1	58852	David Wilkinson, Manchester
April 2	7	59335	Crosse & Blackwell, London
April 18	1	59584	Thomas Gammon, Birmingham
April 24	3	59686	W.H.B. & J. Richardson, Stourbridge
May 8	2	59872	R.W. Winfield, Birmingham
May 22	2	60072	Thomas Gammon, Birmingham
June 8	8	60692	John Davis, Staffordshire
July 3	1	61115	F. & C. Osler, Birmingham & London
July 5	6	61144	R.W. Winfield, Birmingham
July 18	4	61373	David Wilkinson, Manchester
Oct. 1	3	62740	John Cliff Quince, London
Oct. 12	6	62918	Thomas Gammon, Birmingham
Oct. 13	2	62923	W.H.B. & J. Richardson, Stourbridge
Oct. 16	4	62989	Westwood & Moore, Brierley Hill, Staffordshire
Oct. 17	6	63006	Henry Trinder, London
Nov. 5	5	63401	Alfred Bird, Birmingham
Nov. 19	6	64172	Badger Brothers & Co., Dudley, Worcestershire
Nov. 20	3	64184	The Aire & Calder Bottle Co., London

DATE	PARCEL NO.	DESIGN NO.	MANUFACTURER OR REGISTRAR
Nov. 22	3	64320	F. & C. Osler, Birmingham & London
Nov. 23	5	64359	Crosse & Blackwell, London
1850			
Jan. 31	4	66954	William Rowe, London
Jan. 31	4	66955	William Rowe, London
Feb. 6	9	67167	Henry Trinder, London
Feb. 15	8	67468	Sherwood & Co., St Helens, Lancashire
Feb. 15	8	67467	Sherwood & Co., St Helens, Lancashire
Feb. 27	2	67781	Penry Rees, London
March 4	3	67831	William Kidd, London
March 4	3	67832	William Kidd, London
March 11	11	68066	A. Thatcher, Yorkshire Bottle Co., London
March 12	6	68073	John R. Isaac, Liverpool
April 16	2	68834	Felix John McManus, London
April 19	8	69046	Wm Hancock, R. Brown & R. Davis, London
May 23	4	69516	George Sherwood & Co., St Helens, Lancashire
May 23	4	69517	George Sherwood & Co., St Helens, Lancashire
May 30	2	69601	John Kilner, Dewsbury
May 31	4	69607	John Cliff Quince, London
June 29	3	70042	Joseph Sterry & Sons, London
July 11	3	70296	F. & C. Osler, Birmingham & London
July 17	4	70377	Badger Bros, Dudley, Worcestershire
July 19	5	70488	Thomas Yates, Liverpool
July 23	5	70609	George Mosley, London
July 24	7	70622	George J. Green, Birmingham
Aug. 7	5	71064	Henry Pershouse, Birmingham
Aug. 16	5	71179	John Kilner, London
Aug. 17	3	71202	John Kilner, London
Sept. 18	3	71983	John Kilner, London
Oct. 9	3	72397	W.H.B. & J. Richardson, Stourbridge
Oct. 15	4	72500	Crosse & Blackwell, London
Oct. 25	6	73130	J.H. Brown, London
Nov. 5	3	73334	Thomas Gammon, Birmingham
Nov. 9	2	73428	Thomas Bragg, Birmingham
Nov. 29	4	73917	Jonas Defries, London
Dec. 14	2	74530	John Cliff Quince, London

DATE	PARCEL NO.	DESIGN NO.	MANUFACTURER OR REGISTRAR
1851			
Jan. 11	3	75674	W.H.B. & J. Richardson, Stourbridge & London
Jan. 11	3	75675	W.H.B. & J. Richardson, Stourbridge & London
Jan. 13	15	75738	Eugene Rimmel, London
Jan. 20	5	75885	John Cliff Quince, London
Jan. 22	8	75988	Eliezer Edwards, Birmingham
Feb. 14	9	76783	George Lloyd & Thomas Summerfield, Birmingham
March 29	6	77954	Hallmarke, Aldebert & Hallmarke, London
April 1	6	78039	Benjamin Black, London
April 2	3	78049	Lloyd & Summerfield, Birmingham
April 2	3	78050	Lloyd & Summerfield, Birmingham
April 17	7	78476	Philip Benjamin, London
April 17	8	78477	Lloyd & Summerfield, Birmingham
June 10	4	79180	Henry David Green Truscott, London
July 4	3	79537	Frederic Pellatt, London
July 21	6	79749	George Joseph Green, Birmingham
Sept. 12	2	80554	Davis Greathead & Green, Stourbridge
Oct. 11	3	80929	Joseph Webb, Stourbridge
Oct. 21	2	81056	Hancocks, Rixon & Dunt, London
Oct. 24	3	81078	Davis, Greathead & Green, Stourbridge
Oct. 24	6	81081	F. & C. Osler, Birmingham & London
Oct. 31	4	81217	Berens Blumberg & Co., London
Nov. 18	7	81613	W.H.B. & J. Richardson, Stourbridge
Dec. 26	2	82568	Robert Lancaster, Bolton, Lancashire
1852			
Jan. 10	3	82737	Thomas Gammon, Birmingham
Feb. 9	1	83700	Crosse & Blackwell, London
Feb. 14	5	83811	George Twigg, Birmingham
Feb. 16	4	83825	Westwood & Moore, Brierley Hill, Staffordshire
March 3	4	84128	Hancock, Rixon & Dunt, London
March 3	8	84129	Hancock, Rixon & Dunt, London
March 4	4	84136	Archibald Ross & Robert Henderson, Sunderland
March 4	5	84137	Jonas Defries, London
March 4	5	84138	Jonas Defries, London

Date	Parcel No.	Design No.	Manufacturer or Registrar
March 5	4	84155	George Twigg, Birmingham
March 10	4	84217	Archibald Hilson Ross, Sunderland
March 12	4	84228	Hancock, Rixon & Dunt, London
March 12	4	84229	Hancock, Rixon & Dunt, London
March 17	4	84264	Archibald Hilson Ross & Robert Henderson, Sunderland
March 18	5	84300	Joseph Webb, Stourbridge
March 19	4	84308	William Young, London
March 23	1	84386	Joseph Webb, Stourbridge
April 6	1	84598	John Walsh Walsh, Birmingham
April 14	4	84673	John Marten, London
April 14	4	84674	John Marten, London
April 20	1	84816	Twigg & Silvester, Birmingham
May 1	2	84947	Crosse & Blackwell, London
May 11	5	85064	A. Marion & Co., London
June 29	3	85540	Jonas Defries, London
July 21	3	85790	J. Bevan & Co., London
July 23	5	85806-11	William Churcher, London
Aug. 30	4	86391	Alfred Hely, London
Nov. 3	5	87525	William Fontaine, London
Nov. 13	3	87658	Dieley & Son, Stourbridge
Nov. 16	5	87723	Howard Brothers, London
Dec. 9	2	88218	King & Co., London
1853			
Jan. 28	8	89210	Davis, Greathead & Green, Stourbridge
Feb. 5	5	89520	Dieley & Son, Stourbridge
Feb. 14	6	89681	John Cliff Quince, London
April 12	7	90767	John Walsh Walsh, Birmingham
May 17	3	91193	Wood & Perkes, Barnsley, Yorkshire
May 17	6	91227	Stott Walker, London
May 30	2	91284	Stott Walker, London
May 30	2	91285	Stott Walker, London
June 9	2	91341	Hodge & Roberts, London
June 10	4	91381	Robert Best, Birmingham
June 23	2	91476	Joseph Webb, Stourbridge
July 9	1	91634	John Walsh Walsh, Birmingham

Date	Parcel No.	Design No.	Manufacturer or Registrar
July 22	1	91764	Blackwood & Co., London
Aug. 19	5	92120	Joseph Tylor & Son, London
Oct. 3	4	92734-55	Chance Bros., Birmingham
Oct. 15	4	92927	William Reichenbach, London
Nov. 5	4	93185	Jonas Defries & Sons, London
Nov. 11	5	93328	John Rothwell, Manchester
Dec. 14	6	93615	Price's Patent Candle Co., London
Dec. 17	1	93626	Joseph Webb, Stourbridge
1854			
Jan. 9	5	94308	Stott Walker, London
Jan. 21	4	94728	Davis, Greathead & Green, Stourbridge
Feb. 6	2	94906	William Reichenbach, London
Feb. 14	3	95056	Benjamin Richardson, Stourbridge
Feb. 17	1	95065	William Reichenbach, London
Feb. 22	6	95155	William Blanure Tate, London
March 3	2	95237	Thomas Jackson, London
May 6	5	95745	Blackwood & Co., London
May 24	3	95928	John J. Willway, Bristol
June 3	3	96004	Benjamin Richardson, Stourbridge
June 15	2	96056	Joseph Webb, Stourbridge
July 27	2	96491-3	George Novra, London
Aug. 2	3	96543	Jonas Defries & Sons, London
Aug. 3	1	96544	Joseph Webb, Stourbridge
Aug. 22	1	96657	George Novra, London
Aug. 26	2	96703	Benjamin Richardson, Stourbridge
Aug. 30	1	96720-1	George Novra, London
Sept. 21	5	96898	Jonas Defries & Sons, London
Oct. 7	2	97145	William Reichenbach, London
Oct. 7	2	97146	William Reichenbach, London
Oct. 9	5	97161	F. Kensitt & Co., Middlesex
Oct. 14	1	97190	Thomas Turner, Redditch
Oct. 14	2	97191	Davis, Greathead & Green, Stourbridge
Oct. 17	5	97249	Jonas Defries & Sons, London
Oct. 23	6	97346	Benjamin Richardson, Stourbridge
Nov. 16	2	98170	Benjamin Richardson, Stourbridge
Nov. 18	4	98201	Joseph Webb, Stourbridge

Date	Parcel No.	Design No.	Manufacturer or Registrar
Nov. 23	1	98238	William Reichenbach, London
1855			
Jan. 29	7	99187	Price's Patent Candle Co., London
Feb. 10	7	99344	Crosse & Blackwell, London
Feb. 22	5	99466	Price's Patent Candle Co., London
March 3	6	99572	Charles Wellbourne Slee, London
March 10	3	99632	Davis, Greathead & Green, Stourbridge
April 10	4	99823	John McLachlan, London
April 18	4	99882	John Walsh Walsh, Birmingham
April 18	5	99883	Joseph Lane, Manchester
June 9	5	100296	F. & C. Osler, London and Birmingham
June 14	2	100452	Hodge & Roberts, London
June 23	3	100549	Hodge & Roberts, London
Aug. 1	2	100997	James Syon Nibbs, Bakewell, Derbyshire
Aug. 1	3	100998	Davis, Greathead & Green, Stourbridge
Aug. 28	1	101235	John Pinkerton, London
Oct. 22	4	102292	John Smith, London
Nov. 9	3	102519	Alfred Tooth, London
Nov. 10	4	102537	William Reichenbach, London
Nov. 12	3	102545	Samuel Harraden, London
Nov. 17	2	102701	Henry Neve, London
Nov. 21	3	102728	Aubin Chappiris, London
1856			
Feb. 9	3	103724	Benjamin Richardson, Stourbridge
Feb. 11	4	103731	Crosse & Blackwell, London
Feb. 13	4	103739	Jonas Defries & Sons, London
March 25	6	104212	Benjamin Richardson, Stourbridge
April 5	3	104307	William Reichenbach, London
April 17	3	104379	Eliezer Edwards, Birmingham
May 1	4	104614	John Kilner, London
May 14	1	104728	William Young, London
June 23	2	105196	Peter Robinson & Edward Bolton, Warrington, Lancashire
Sept. 8	3	106216	Benjamin Richardson, Stourbridge
Sept. 20	3	106366	Benjamin Richardson, Stourbridge

Date	Parcel No.	Design No.	Manufacturer or Registrar
Oct. 1	6	106452	William Reid, London
Oct. 7	7	106554	Solomon Maw, London
Oct. 8	4	106559	Louis Groux & Charles Francis Hayward, London
Oct. 8	4	106562	Louis Groux & Charles Francis Hayward, London
Oct. 9	2	106571	George Ensell & Co., Birmingham
Nov. 5	2	106915	John Pinkerton, London
Nov. 15	2	107070	George Bell & Co., London
Nov. 18	1	107566	William England, Sheffield
Dec. 18	4	108055	Andrew Brundish, Birmingham
1857			
Jan. 5	2	108485	Owen Parry, London
Jan. 5	2	108486	Owen Parry, London
Jan. 14	5	108575	James Joseph Bastien, London
Jan. 30	4	108815	James Lewis, London
Feb. 10	8	108985	B. Hurwitz, London
March 21	3	109434	Joseph Webb, Stourbridge
April 30	4	109830	Eliezer Edwards, Birmingham
May 14	3	109909	Jonas Defries & Sons, London
May 16	7	109943	Crosse & Blackwell, London
June 9	2	110109	Benjamin Richardson, Stourbridge
July 2	1	110293	Wootten & Powell, Birmingham
Aug. 20	2	110942	James Couper & Sons, Glasgow
Aug. 20	2	110943	James Couper & Sons, Glasgow
Aug. 24	1	111017	F. & C. Osler, Birmingham & London
Sept. 12	2	111228	Frederick Simpson, Red Hill, Surrey
Nov. 6	3	111878	Benjamin Richardson, Stourbridge
Nov. 7	4	111901	George Brown, York
Nov. 11	2	111917	Hodge & Reed, London
Dec. 17	3	112427	James Couper & Sons, Glasgow
Dec. 19	4	112467	Ambrose Hall, Limerick
Dec. 21	1	112469-70	R.W. Winfield & Son, Birmingham
1858			
Feb. 24	7	113105-7	Isaac Hawker Bedford, Birmingham
March 9	3	113179	Nibbs & Hinks, Birmingham

Date	Parcel No.	Design No.	Manufacturer or Registrar
March 18	4	113236	John Henry Weston & James Frederick Curel, London
March 20	7	113260	William Reichenbach, London
April 13	5	113410	George Edward Ashton, London
April 15	1	113422	James Goodchild, London
May 10	4	113685	John Jex Long, Glasgow
May 11	5	113728	John Cannington & Co., Liverpool
June 2	2	113907	Powell & Ricketts, Bristol
June 23	5	114047	F. & C. Osler, Birmingham & London
June 24	3	114071	William Blamire Tate, London
June 29	2	114082	Benjamin Richardson, Stourbridge
July 29	3	114531	Matthew Whieldon, Burslem, Staffordshire
Aug. 28	2	114989	Joseph Webb, Stourbridge
Sept. 16	5	115551-3	Henry Emery, London
Oct. 27	2	116444	David Jacobs, London
Dec. 10	5	117356	Edward Ashton, London
Dec. 21	6	117501	Angus & Greener, Sunderland
1859			
Jan. 1	2	117763	Tower & Arrol, Glasgow
Jan. 4	5	117809	Joseph Hutchin, Liverpool
Feb. 11	5	118467	Joseph Sedger, London
Feb. 21	5	118630	Mrs Eliza Hunt, London
March 14	5	118804	Robert Cogan, London
May 20	6	119975	Davis, Greathead & Green, Stourbridge
May 21	4	119980	Finch, Hill & Paraire, London
June 14	7	120352	James Copcutt, London
July 8	2	120613	Thomas Dawkins, London
Sept. 22	5	122349	William Leggatt Gilbart, Birmingham
Sept 23	4	122368-70	Tucker & Son, London
Oct. 26	6	123473	J. & F. Lloyd & Co., London
Nov. 25	1	124288	Clarke & Timmins, Birmingham
1860			
Jan. 19	5	125806	Weston Curel & Symons, London
Feb. 4	7	126202	Samuel Limobeer, London
Feb. 28	3	126847	Peter Peel, Birmingham

Date	Parcel No.	Design No.	Manufacturer or Registrar
April 14	4	128002	Francis Mordan, London
April 17	8	128066	James Hinks, Birmingham
Sept. 5	1	132703	Wootton & Powell, Birmingham
Sept. 25	3	133418	Francis Spark, London
Nov. 10	7	135384	Benton & Stone, Birmingham
Nov. 23	6	136029	James Lewis, London
1861			
Jan. 3	2	137154	James Syson Nibbs, Birmingham
Jan. 26	2	137646	James Hinks, Birmingham
Feb. 12	4	138254	George Mathieson, Glasgow
March 6	10	138724	David Kenny & Robert Brown, Glasgow
March 14	4	138947	James Hinks, Birmingham
March 20	10	139075	Jonas Defries & Sons, London
March 20	10	139076	Jonas Defries & Sons, London
March 28	4	139266	Weston, Curel & Co., London
March 30	1	139286-90	J. & J.D. Cook, Glasgow
April 8	6	139493	R.W. Winfield & Son, Birmingham
April 24	2	140188	Frederic Lewis, Dublin
May 23	1	140932	Edward Morris, Reading
June 5	7	141261	Dobson & Pearce, London
June 5	7	141262	Dobson & Pearce, London
June 27	1	141573	Edward Moore & Co., South Shields
June 29	4	141642	Edward Moore & Co., South Shields
Aug. 5	3	142371	Pearce & Co., London
Aug. 21	3	142814	Frederic Lewis, Dublin
Aug. 21	3	142815	Frederic Lewis, Dublin
Dec. 12	5	147545	Edwin Martin Thornton, London
Dec. 19	4	147792	David. H. Jacobs, London
1862			
Jan. 13	7	148562	Robert Hennell & Sons, London
Feb. 12	5	149306	Henry Chatwin, Birmingham
Feb. 22	7	149521	Isaac Barnes, Birmingham
Feb. 22	7	149522	Isaac Barnes, Birmingham
Feb. 24	6	149561	James Syson Nibbs, Birmingham
March 3	9	149776	Crosse & Blackwell, London

DESIGN REGISTRATIONS

Date	Parcel No.	Design No.	Manufacturer or Registrar
April 7	10	150512	Crosse & Blackwell, London
April 7	10	150513	Crosse & Blackwell, London
April 8	6	150526	William Johnston, Glasgow
April 11	6	150809	Mercer Hampson Simpson Jnr., Birmingham
April 28	6	151261-5	Dobson & Pearce, London
May 7	1	151468	Robinson Donald & Co., Glasgow
May 9	10	151570-2	R.W. Winfield & Son, Birmingham
May 20	5	151915	Dobson & Pearce, London
May 20	6	151916	Thomas March, Lord Chamberlain's Office, London
June 12	6	152426	A.W. Digby & Co., London
June 25	2	152722	Alfred Dunn of Naylor & Co., London
Aug. 16	6	153822	Messenger & Sons, Birmingham
Sept. 9	6	154589	Robert Woods, London
Oct. 1	3	155257	Eliezer Edwards, Birmingham
Oct. 16	5	156470-2	Alfred Dunn of Naylor & Co., London
Oct. 23	5	156712	Johnston, Fraser & Co., Glasgow
Oct. 23	9	156718	George Piercy Tye, Birmingham
Dec. 10	4	158230	James Hinks & Son, Birmingham
Dec. 15	6	158400	Jonas Defries & Sons, London
Dec. 15	6	158401	Jonas Defries & Sons, London
Dec. 15	7	158402	S. Mordan & Co., London
1863			
March 26	5	160895	S. Mordan & Co., London
April 8	7	161282	Napoleon Price, London
May 12	3	162269	Dobson & Pearce, London
June 9	2	163192	Isaac Barnes, Birmingham
June 16	5	163551	Dobson & Pearce, London
July 1	4	163900	Isaac Barnes, Birmingham
July 8	8	164119	Bewley & Draper, Dublin
July 9	8	164138	E. Edwards, Birmingham
Oct. 16	5	167365	Alfred Dunn, Naylor & Co., London
Nov. 4	8	168189	Nicholas Jacquel, Paris
Nov. 5	5	168202	Hodd & Linley, London
Nov. 25	6	169480	Hodd & Linley, London
Dec. 8	6	169986	Septimus Presse, London

DATE	PARCEL NO.	DESIGN NO.	MANUFACTURER OR REGISTRAR
Dec. 24	6	170523	Jonas Defries & Sons, London
Dec. 24	6	170524	Jonas Defries & Sons, London
Dec. 26	1	170526	Jonas Defries & Sons, London
1864			
Jan. 11	11	170914	The Tutbury Glass Co., Tutbury, Staffordshire and London
Feb. 6	6	171561	Alfred Dunn, Naylor & Co., London
Feb. 6	6	171562	Alfred Dunn, Naylor & Co., London
March 8	1	172348-52	Dobson & Pearce, London
March 18	11	172681	James Lewis, London
May 11	6	174479	Frederic Lewis, Dublin
May 25	4	174857	Emily Temple, London
June 8	5	175314	Swan & Co., London
June 14	4	175421	James Derbyshire & Bro., Hulme, Manchester
June 15	3	175494	Samuel & Charles Bishop, St Helens, Lancashire
June 17	9	175749	Dobson & Pearce, London
June 17	9	175750	Dobson & Pearce, London
June 21	8	175803	Dobson & Pearce, London
July 2	5	175961	Johnston, Fraser & Co., Glasgow
July 6	3	175994	J.T. Stroud & Co., Birmingham
July 9	4	176163	Johnston, Fraser & Co., Glasgow
July 13	5	176508	John Burgess & Son, London
Aug. 17	6	177744	George Robinson, Stourbridge
Aug. 27	4	178045	Molineux & Webb, Manchester
Aug. 27	4	178046	Molineux & Webb, Manchester
Oct. 11	3	179038	Boulton & Mills, Stourbridge
Oct. 24	7	180385	J. Defries & Sons, London
Nov. 2	1	180696	Andrew Guille, Glasgow
Nov. 2	4	180699	James Derbyshire & Bro., Hulme, Manchester
Nov. 8	2	181208	Richard Dent, London
Nov. 10	12	181314	James Lewis, London
Dec. 10	7	182248	James Derbyshire & Bro., Hulme, Manchester
Dec. 22	6	182483	Molineux, Webb & Co., Manchester
1865			
Jan. 18	1	183352	Percival, Yates & Vickers, Manchester

DATE	PARCEL NO.	DESIGN NO.	MANUFACTURER OR REGISTRAR
Jan. 18	1	183353	Percival, Yates & Vickers, Manchester
Feb. 14	8	183953	Alfred Edmund Edwardes, Twickenham, Middlesex
March 17	11	184910	Pellatt & Co., London
March 17	11	184917	Pellatt & Co., London
March 21	6	185030	Percival, Yates & Vickers, Manchester
March 31	2	185472	John Conolly Binns, Dublin
April 7	8	185841	Elkington & Co., London
April 24	5	183295	S. & C. Bishop & Co., St Helens, Lancashire
May 1	7	186461	Alderson, Higginbottom & Co., Warrington, Lancashire
May 1	8	185462	Molineux, Webb & Co., Manchester
May 1	8	186463	Molineux, Webb & Co., Manchester
May 3	1	186478	Hodgetts, Richardson & Pargeter, Stourbridge
May 12	6	186808	Molineux, Webb & Co., Manchester
May 16	4	186847	James Derbyshire & Bro., Hulme, Manchester
May 29	3	187182	Molineux, Webb & Co., Manchester
May 29	3	187183	Molineux, Webb & Co., Manchester
May 30	4	187204	James Hinks & Son, Birmingham
June 14	3	187536	Robinson & Bolton, Warrington
June 23	3	187749	Dobson & Pearce, London
June 25	6	188496	James Walker, London
Aug. 15	4	189066	James Derbyshire & Bro., Hulme, Manchester
Aug. 18	4	189121	Percival, Yates & Vickers, Manchester
Aug. 18	4	189122	Percival, Yates & Vickers, Manchester
Aug. 25	6	189321	James Derbyshire & Bro., Hulme, Manchester
Sept. 5	1	189511-3	George Burt, Birmingham
Sept. 7	3	189534	Mohr & Smith, Birmingham
Sept. 11	1	189615	Robinson & Bolton, Warrington, Lancashire
Sept. 11	1	189616	Robinson & Bolton, Warrington, Lancashire
Sept. 12	2	189705	James Derbyshire & Bro., Hulme, Manchester
Sept. 21	10	189948	David Jacobs, London
Sept. 29	5	190325	John Henry Weston, London
Oct. 4	4	190755-8	Molineaux, Webb & Co., Manchester
Oct. 23	4	191244	Richard Gent, London
Oct. 31	8	191555	Molineaux, Webb & Co., Manchester
Nov. 4	4	191995	Franz Steigerwald & Co., London

DATE	PARCEL NO.	DESIGN NO.	MANUFACTURER OR REGISTRAR
Nov. 6	3	192008	Richard Gent, London
Nov. 23	8	192790	Hall & Dutson, Birmingham
Nov. 23	8	192791	Hall & Dutson, Birmingham
Nov. 23	9	192792	David Henry Jacobs, London
Nov. 29	10	192966	Thomas Norman, London
Dec. 6	4	193264	Crosse & Blackwell, London
Dec. 14	5	193419	James Derbyshire & Bro., Hulme, Manchester
Dec. 14	6	193420	James Couper & Sons, Glasgow
1866			
Jan. 18	6	194616-8	Molineaux, Webb & Co., Manchester
Jan. 20	2	194685	Molineaux, Webb & Co., Manchester
Jan. 30	7	194825	Molineaux, Webb & Co., Manchester
Jan. 31	8	194844	William Brooke, Leeds, Yorkshire
Feb. 1	9	194871	W.B. Tate, London
Feb. 2	6	194948	D. Hulett & Co., London
Feb. 15	2	195262	Molineaux, Webb & Co., Manchester
Feb. 17	1	195272	Robinson & Bolton, Warrington, Lancs
March 1	5	195623	Kenny & Brown, Glasgow
March 1	10	195639	Dobson & Pearce, London
March 16	6	195956	S. & C. Bishop & Co., St Helens, Lancashire
March 27	1	196244	James Green, London
April 6	9	196366-8	James Hayward MacKay, London
April 7	6	196419	Alfred Arculus, Birmingham
April 7	6	196420	Alfred Arculus, Birmingham
April 21	5	196684	Richard Gent, London
May 2	2	197022	Richard Gent, London
May 4	6	197096	Thomas Charles March, St James's Palace, London
May 8	2	197154	Eliezer Edwards, Birmingham
May 10	4	197298	McDermott, Connolly & Co., Gateshead-on-Tyne
May 22	17	197656	Thomas Charles March, St James's Palace, London
May 22	17	197657	Thomas Charles March, St James's Palace, London
May 24	1	197703	Angus & Greener, Sunderland

Date	Parcel No.	Design No.	Manufacturer or Registrar
May 24	1	197704	Angus & Greener, Sunderland
June 16	4	198277	James Derbyshire & Bro., Hulme, Manchester
June 16	5	198278	Woodall, Keen & Woodall, Birmingham
Aug. 15	8	199959	Joseph Perkins Teagle & Edwin Martin, London
Aug. 25	6	200233	Angus & Greener, Sunderland
Sept. 22	5	201596	Eugene Rimmell, London
Sept. 26	5	201705	George Fisher, London
Oct. 12	1	202372	Eugene Rimmell, London
Nov. 10	6	203523	S. & C. Bishop & Co., St Helens, Lancashire
Nov. 28	5	204182	Michael & Lewis Beck, London
Dec. 27	3	205210	Hodgetts, Richardson & Pargeter, Wordsley, nr. Stourbridge
Dec. 29	1	205228	Pellatt & Co., London
1867			
Jan. 5	6	205330	Pellatt & Co., London
Jan. 14	8	205511	James Green, London
Jan. 26	4	205812	Angus & Greener, Sunderland
Feb. 1	1	205852	Pellatt & Co., London
Feb. 1	1	205853	Pellatt & Co., London
Feb. 8	7	205997	John Dobson, London
Feb. 23	9	206280	H.P. Downing, Birmingham
Feb. 25	5	206304	James Derbyshire & Bro., Hulme, Manchester
March 14	9	206745	Sidney Brown, London
March 16	3	206845	Thomas Charles March, St James's Palace, London
April 4	10	207202	Sidney Brown, London
April 11	5	207427	Mohr & Smith, Birmingham
April 16	7	207561	James Lewis, London
May 21	2	208419	James Hinks & Son, Birmingham
May 21	2	208420	James Hinks & Son, Birmingham
May 21	3	208421	Richard Gent, London
May 22	10	208455	S. & C. Bishop & Co., St Helens, Lancashire
May 28	5	208519	James Hinks & Son, Birmingham
June 7	7	208779	Samuel Chandler & Son, London
June 24	3	209086	Molineaux, Webb & Co., Manchester
June 26	8	209161	Angus & Greener, Sunderland

DATE	PARCEL NO.	DESIGN NO.	MANUFACTURER OR REGISTRAR
June 29	4	209222	John Whitehouse & Sons, Birmingham
July 2	4	209332	J.M. Johnson & Sons, London
July 16	2	209574	Percival, Vickers & Co. Ltd., Manchester
July 16	2	209575	Percival, Vickers & Co. Ltd., Manchester
Aug. 10	3	210199	Molineaux, Webb & Co., Manchester
Aug. 16	5	210325	William Blamire Tate, London
Aug. 26	5	210484	Molineaux, Webb & Co., Manchester
Aug. 30	3	210619	Napoleon Montanari, London & Paris
Sept. 10	4	210941	Molineaux, Webb & Co., Manchester
Sept. 10	4	210942	Molineaux, Webb & Co., Manchester
Oct. 18	4	212432	Robinson & Bolton, Warrington, Lancashire
Oct. 19	4	212674-7	Thomas Webb & Sons, Stourbridge
Nov. 14	5	213851	Richardson & Smith, Stourbridge
Nov. 25	6	214321	Frederick Cadby, Birmingham
Nov. 26	9	214357	Angus & Greener, Sunderland
Nov. 26	9	214358	Angus & Greener, Sunderland
Dec. 2	4	214597	Edward Webb, Stourbridge
Dec. 21	6	215150	Edward Jackson Hollidge, London
1868			
Jan. 13	1	215734	Molineaux, Webb & Co., Manchester
Jan. 17	11	215917	Francis Mordan, London
Jan. 31	9	216348	Molineaux, Webb & Co., Manchester
Jan. 31	13	216361	S. & C. Bishop & Co., St Helens, Lancashire
Jan. 31	13	216362	S. & C. Bishop & Co., St Helens, Lancashire
Feb. 8	4	216632	Molineaux, Webb & Co., Manchester
Feb. 21	4	216996-7	J. Defries & Sons, London
Feb. 27	6	217101	Gustav Bohm, Offenbach, Germany & London
Feb. 28	4	217107-9	The Tutbury Glass Co., Staffordshire
March 5	11	217207	Edward Moore & Co., South Shields
March 6	7	217227	Percival, Vickers & Co. Ltd., Manchester
March 27	6	217676	Phillips & Pearce, London
March 30	7	217715	P. Rappolt & Co., London
April 1	7	217728	Angus & Greener, Sunderland
April 29	7	218486	Ker, Webb & Co., Manchester
May 4	6	218561	Angus & Greener, Sunderland
May 21	4	218866	Berman & Wild, London

Date	Parcel No.	Design No.	Manufacturer or Registrar
May 29	8	218984	Frederick Cadby, Birmingham
May 29	11	218988	James Derbyshire & Bro., Hulme, Manchester
June 6	2	219163-5	Berman & Wild, London
June 11	6	219303	S. & C. Bishop & Co., St Helens, Lancashire
July 11	4	219769	Molineaux, Webb & Co., Manchester
July 29	1	220059	Henry Durandu, Liverpool
Aug. 1	1	220230	Edward Tombs, London
Aug. 6	8	220317	Richard Gent, London
Aug. 20	6	220898-900	Molineaux, Webb & Co., Manchester
Sept. 4	7	221205	Frederick Travis, Liverpool
Sept. 5	7	221220	S. & C. Bishop & Co., St Helens, Lancashire
Sept 10	8	221497	Ker, Webb & Co., Manchester
Sept. 10	9	221498	Boulton & Mills, Stourbridge
Sept. 12	2	221520	E. Edwards, Birmingham
Sept. 15	5	221563	Isidore Leveaux & Co., London
Sept. 17	5	221689	Angus & Greener, Sunderland
Sept. 19	8	221795	Percival, Vickers & Co. Ltd., Manchester
Oct. 13	5	222546	H.W. & L. Dee, London
Oct. 21	7	223307	J. Defries & Sons, London
Oct. 23	4	223322	Percival, Vickers & Co. Ltd., Manchester
Nov. 6	11	224027	James Lewis, London
Dec. 2	7	225010	S. Maw & Son, London
Dec. 4	16	225286	McMaster, Hodgson & Co., Dublin
Dec. 14	6	225440	Percival, Vickers & Co. Ltd., Manchester
Dec. 21	4	225673	Percival, Vickers & Co. Ltd., Manchester
Dec. 30	4	225973	Elijah Atkins, Birmingham
1869			
Jan. 1	9	226052	S. & C. Bishop & Co., St Helens, Lancashire
Jan. 20	5	226509	Elijah Atkins, Birmingham
Jan. 20	5	226510	Elijah Atkins, Birmingham
Jan. 28	8	226743	Thomas Padmore & Sons, Birmingham
Feb. 1	12	226916	Molineaux, Webb & Co., Manchester
Feb. 1	12	226917	Molineaux, Webb & Co., Manchester
Feb. 11	1	227266	Charles Joseph King, London
Feb. 22	12	227410	James Derbyshire & Bro., Hulme, Manchester
Feb. 24	4	227429	Elijah Atkins, Birmingham

Date	Parcel No.	Design No.	Manufacturer or Registrar
Feb. 24	4	227430	Elijah Atkins, Birmingham
March 24	7	228147-8	S. & C. Bishop & Co., St Helens, Lancashire
March 27	1	228202	Molineaux, Webb & Co., Manchester
March 31	2	228286	H.W. & L. Dee, London
March 31	2	228287	H.W. & L. Dee, London
April 5	3	228427	John Sharp, London
April 13	7	228612	James Derbyshire & Bro., Hulme, Manchester
April 20	9	228782	Angus & Greener, Sunderland
April 26	5	228889	Percival, Vickers & Co., Manchester
May 20	7	229522	C.A. & E. Speyer & Co., London
June 8	6	229958	W.P. & G. Phillips & Pearce, London
July 1	6	230596	Ker, Webb & Co., Manchester
July 2	6	230631	Loewenthal & Hesse, Manchester
July 5	3	230716	Edward Bolton, Warrington, Lancashire
July 6	9	230802	William Thomas Tongue, Wolverhampton
July 31	8	231430	Henry Greener, Sunderland
Aug. 12	8	231927	Henry Greener, Sunderland
Aug. 26	5	232473	Sidney Brown, London
Sept. 9	6	232893	Ensell & Baker, Birmingham
Sept. 13	8	233022-4	Henry Bauerrichter & Co., London
Sept. 15	5	233092	Sidney Brown, London
Sept. 27	6	233716	Henry Bauerrichter & Co., London
Oct. 16	3	234517	Percival, Vickers & Co. Ltd., Manchester
Oct. 19	8	234789	Eugene Rimmel, London
Oct. 28	1	235182	F. Fletcher, London
Nov. 2	1	235568	Richard Gent, London
Nov. 3	11	235690	A. Kenyon, Manchester
Nov. 4	9	235710	James Lewis, London
Nov. 4	9	235711	James Lewis, London
Nov. 6	3	235821	Percival, Vickers & Co. Ltd., Manchester
Nov. 10	6	236001	Richard Gent, London
Nov. 10	7	236002	Ker, Webb & Co., Manchester
Nov. 16	13	236235	Sidney Brown, London
Dec. 7	7	236921	Henry Greener, Sunderland
Dec. 14	3	237141	James Couper & Sons, Glasgow
Dec. 15	4	237158	Lloyd & Summerfield, Birmingham
Dec. 18	1	237228	Johnston, Fraser & Co., Glasgow

Date	Parcel No.	Design No.	Manufacturer or Registrar
Dec. 23	8	237550	Percival, Vickers & Co. Ltd., Manchester
1870			
Jan. 3	3	237741	Molineaux, Webb & Co., Manchester
Jan. 7	4	237893	E.H. Downes, Manchester
Jan. 12	8	238052	Hodgetts, Richardson & Pargeter, Stourbridge
Jan. 14	11	238105	Henry Greener, Sunderland
Jan. 15	10	238145	Edward Bolton, Warrington, Lancashire
Jan. 15	14	238151	J.J. Hicks, London
Jan. 28	6	238431	Edward Bolton, Warrington, Lancashire
Feb. 3	12	238593-4	Boulton & Mills, Stourbridge
Feb. 7	11	238637	William Thomas Standish, London
Feb. 8	9	238658	Leon Pyke, London
Feb. 16	7	238916	James Hateley, Birmingham
Feb. 21	7	239056	Louis Petre & Son, London
Feb. 22	4	239084	Molineaux, Webb & Co., Manchester
Feb. 24	9	239136	Burtles, Tate & Co., Manchester
Feb. 28	8	239241	Hodgetts, Richardson & Pargeter, Stourbridge
Feb. 28	8	239242	Hodgetts, Richardson & Pargeter, Stourbridge
March 22	3	239748	Joseph Ratcliff & Sons, Birmingham
March 26	8	240010	Percival, Vickers & Co. Ltd., Manchester
April 2	4	240217	Molineaux, Webb & Co., Manchester
April 29	7	241052	William Henry Gritton, London
May 5	11	241259	Alfred Arculus, Birmingham
May 19	11	241590	Peter Bicker Caarten, London
May 26	6	241961	Molineaux, Webb & Co., Manchester
May 26	8	241963-4	Gustav Boehm, London
May 27	10	242010	Gustav Boehm, London
June 10	4	242418	Frederick Cadby, Birmingham
June 21	3	242570	J.J. & T. Derbyshire, Hulme, Manchester
June 23	2	242642	James Hickisson, London
July 6	2	242968-70	Molineaux, Webb & Co., Manchester
July 18	4	243267	James Bond, London
Aug. 1	1	243554	Percival, Vickers & Co. Ltd., Manchester
Aug. 29	7	244354	Loewenthal & Hesse, Manchester
Sept 1	6	244491	W. Gammon & Co., Birmingham
Sept. 13	8	244871	Allen & Baker, Birmingham

Date	Parcel No.	Design No.	Manufacturer or Registrar
Sept. 22	7	245051	Edward Hand Jefferys, Sheffield
Sept. 22	7	245052	Edward Hand Jefferys, Sheffield
Oct. 6	1	245563	Frederick Kingston Gurney & John Henry Gurney, London
Oct. 12	5	245730	J. Barnett, London
Oct. 22	6	246153	Hodgetts, Richardson & Pargeter, Stourbridge
Oct. 27	8	246394	Richard Gent, London
Nov. 1	5	246500	Chance & Malin, Birmingham
Nov. 4	7	246924	H.W. & L. Dee, London
Nov. 10	11	247081	Henry Greener, Sunderland
Nov. 14	10	247322	James Lewis, London
Nov. 18	2	247463	Molineaux, Webb & Co., Manchester
Nov. 18	2	247464	Molineaux, Webb & Co., Manchester
Nov. 22	4	247945	Henry Thacker & Co., London
Nov. 23	6	247983	Walter Thornhill, London
Dec. 9	9	248459	S. & C. Bishop & Co., St Helens, Lancashire
Dec. 23	1	249039	Felix Sultana, London
Dec. 24	10	249099	S. & C. Bishop & Co., St Helens, Lancashire
1871			
Jan. 17	7	249600	Molineaux, Webb & Co., Manchester
Jan. 24	3	249808-10	Molineaux, Webb & Co., Manchester
Jan. 25	8	249882	Boulton & Mills, Stourbridge
Jan. 26	4	249890-3	Gregoir Antoin Hunanian, London
Jan. 28	11	249969	Boulton & Mills, Stourbridge
Feb. 16	5	250430	Blackwood & Co., London
Feb. 24	8	250600	Blackwood & Co., London
March 1	4	250678	Boulton & Mills, Stourbridge
March 2	8	250723	Henry Greener, Sunderland
March 8	5	250835	Boulton & Mills, Stourbridge
March 15	9	251012	J.J. & T. Derbyshire, Hulme, Manchester
March 16	8	251034	John Binns & Phillip Pargeter, London
March 22	3	251131-3	Stuart & Mills, Stourbridge
April 29	9	252159	Edward Bolton, Warrington, Lancashire
May 25	12	252823	John Henry Wood, London
June 7	5	253067	Percival, Vickers & Co. Ltd., Manchester
June 21	6	253471	N. Dingwall, London

DATE	PARCEL NO.	DESIGN NO.	MANUFACTURER OR REGISTRAR
July 17	1	254050	Boulton & Mills, Stourbridge
July 18	3	254058	Phillips & Pearce, London
Aug. 3	7	254641	Henry White Wickins, London
Aug. 17	4	254864	Philip Pargeter, Stourbridge
Aug. 22	4	254993	William Henry Hewitt, Birmingham
Sept. 2	2	255351	Chance & Malins, Birmingham
Sept. 6	7	255383	Ker, Webb & Co., Manchester
Sept. 8	8	255459	Dietz & Co., London
Sept 30	10	256264	Percival, Vickers & Co. Ltd., Manchester
Oct. 3	4	256336	Burtles, Tate & Co., Manchester
Oct. 13	9	256680	Isaac Barnes, Birmingham
Nov. 6	9	257538	Loewenthal & Hesse, London
Nov. 24	10	257989	H. Boch Binks, London
Dec. 7	5	258445	Percival, Vickers & Co. Ltd., Manchester
1872			
Jan. 5	6	259270	James Lewis, London
Jan. 10	8	259391	James Buckley, Birmingham
Jan. 27	12	260050	M. Kuhn, Paris
Jan. 29	11	260064	Akerman, Worrall & Phillips, London
Feb. 2	1	260183-6	Sowerby & Co., Gateshead-on-Tyne
Feb. 12	1	260397	Woodall, Keen & Woodall, Birmingham
Feb. 12	6	260404-5	Sowerby & Co., Gateshead-on-Tyne
Feb. 15	8	260472	Gustav Boehm, London
Feb. 22	6	260648-50	Hodgetts, Richardson & Son, Stourbridge
Feb. 29	8	260802	Sowerby & Co., Gateshead-on-Tyne
March 2	12	260854	The Crown Perfumery Co., London
March 14	2	261125-7	Hodgetts, Richardson & Son, Stourbridge
March 15	18	261182	Akerman, Worrall & Phillips, London
March 19	6	261264	H.W. Wickins, London
March 25	5	261445	J.J. & T. Derbyshire, Hulme, Manchester
March 28	7	261532	W.T. Copeland & Sons, London
April 16	8	261950	John Frederic Cooke, London
April 19	3	262010	Norton & White, Birmingham
April 23	5	262193	Burtles, Tate & Co., Manchester
May 2	7	262405	Percival, Vickers & Co. Ltd., Manchester
May 11	9	262680	J.J. & T. Derbyshire, Hulme, Manchester

Date	Parcel No.	Design No.	Manufacturer or Registrar
May 30	7	263032	Percival, Vickers & Co. Ltd., Manchester
June 11	4	263314	Percival, Vickers & Co. Ltd., Manchester
June 13	3	263362	Ker, Webb & Co., Manchester
June 18	2	263495	James Alfred Fussell, Birmingham
June 21	6	263540	Jane Webb & Joseph Hammond, trading as the executors of the late Joseph Webb, Stourbridge
June 22	1	263543	E.A. Rippingille, London
July 5	7	263929	F.S. Cleaver & Sons, London
July 18	6	264288	Robert Sallmann, London
Aug. 28	2	265528	John Hanbury, Birmingham
Oct. 2	8	266734	S. Mordan & Co., London
Nov. 6	11	267727	J.J. & T. Derbyshire, Hulme, Manchester
Nov. 7	7	267742	Sowerby & Co., Gateshead-on-Tyne
Nov. 7	7	267743	Sowerby & Co., Gateshead-on-Tyne
Nov. 19	5	267990	Boissière & Ch. Augueulle, France
Nov. 21	12	268074-6	William Singleton, Sheffield
Dec. 2	7	268325	Akerman, Worrall & Phillips, London
Dec. 10	7	268734	Henry Greener, Sunderland
Dec. 11	4	268739	J.J. & T. Derbyshire, Hulme, Manchester
Dec. 13	7	268786	Mappin & Webb, Sheffield
Dec. 14	8	268810	J.J. & T. Derbyshire, Hulme, Manchester
Dec. 19	3	268883-4	Jane Webb & Joseph Hammond, trading as the executors of the late Joseph Webb, Stourbridge
Dec. 23	3	269194	Percival, Vickers & Co. Ltd., Manchester
1873			
Jan. 3	4	269476	Ker, Webb & Co., Manchester
Jan. 10	3	269593	Charles Joseph King, London
Jan. 15	4	269694	Percival, Vickers & Co. Ltd., Manchester
Feb. 1	10	270083	William Burrows, Derby
Feb. 12	1	270351	Daniel Pearce, Hammersmith
Feb. 17	8	270525	Henry Herbert, London
March 5	7	271027	Akerman & Worrall, London
March 7	6	271070-2	D. Beck & Co., Birmingham
March 12	1	271146	W. & F. Mortlock, London
April 5	2	271867	Isaac Barnes, Birmingham
April 10	15	272048	Akerman & Worrall, London

DATE	PARCEL NO.	DESIGN NO.	MANUFACTURER OR REGISTRAR
April 16	4	272132	Jane Webb & Joseph Hammond, trading as the executors of the late Joseph Webb, Stourbridge
April 29	1	272381-2	Percival Jones, Dublin
April 29	7	272424	Daniel Pearce, London
May 3	9	272649	F.H. Atkins & Co., London
May 7	2	272685-8	Percival, Vickers & Co. Ltd., Manchester
May 16	4	272981	Philip Pargeter, Stourbridge
May 26	12	273170	Edward Bolton, Warrington
May 27	5	273177	Boulton & Mills, Stourbridge
May 27	6	273178	Ker, Webb & Co., Manchester
June 14	5	273730	Lloyd & Summerfield, Birmingham
June 20	13	273866	Sowerby & Co., Gateshead-on-Tyne
July 31	5	274743	Sowerby & Co., Gateshead-on-Tyne
Aug. 6	10	274906-10	H. Barrett, London
Aug. 8	7	274961-3	John Derbyshire, Salford, Manchester
Aug. 8	9	274965	Howes & Burley, Birmingham
Sept. 2	9	275756	John Derbyshire, Salford, Manchester
Sept. 6	2	275856	Hodgetts, Richardson & Son, Stourbridge
Sept. 25	12	276524-5	James Bromwich, London
Oct. 13	4	277150	J. Defries & Sons, London
Oct. 14	5	277158	Thomas Riddell, London
Oct. 21	8	277328	George Busby, Birmingham
Oct. 28	5	277629-30	Thomas Riddell, London
Oct. 31	12	277834-5	Daniel Pearce, London
Nov. 3	13	277869	Akerman & Worrall, London
Nov. 13	8	278266	Percival, Vickers & Co. Ltd., Manchester
Nov. 14	5	278292	E.H. Downs, Manchester
Nov. 20	9	278481	Benjamin Hastwell, London
Nov. 29	6	278712	Edward Berman & Co., London
Dec. 10	11	279179	Jane Webb & Joseph Hammond, trading as the executors of the late Joseph Webb, Stourbridge
Dec. 15	7	279245	La Baronne Gabrielle de Foelckersahm, London
Dec. 20	5	279324	Edward Berman & Co., London
1874			
Jan. 6	6	279532	John Derbyshire, Salford, Manchester
Jan. 6	9	279535	Lewes Henry Beck, London

Date	Parcel No.	Design No.	Manufacturer or Registrar
Jan. 15	6	279876	Sowerby & Co., Gateshead-on-Tyne
Jan. 20	5	279940	Douglas Coates Crawford, Chertsey, Surrey
Feb. 3	5	280197	John Derbyshire, Salford, Manchester
Feb. 14	10	280493-5	Molineaux, Webb & Co., Manchester
Feb. 18	3	280566	Henry Manton Jnr, Birmingham
Feb. 23	2	280660	Thomas Seago & Benjamin John Johnson, Birmingham
March 13	1	281092	Maw Son & Thompson, London
March 13	10	281119	Isaac Barnes, Birmingham
March 28	8	281435-6	Pellatt & Wood, London
April 9	3	281670-5	Samuel Evans, Birmingham
April 11	6	281767	Franz Eisert, London
April 13	3	281771	A. Aronsberg & W.H. Gritton, London
April 17	3	281842	Ker, Webb & Co., Manchester
April 22	8	281933	Sowerby & Co., Gateshead-on-Tyne
May 12	6	282260	John Derbyshire, Salford, Manchester
May 15	10	282371	Ellis Pearson, Maldon, Surrey
May 20	10	282496	Philip Pargeter, Stourbridge & Percival Jones, Dublin
May 26	10	282585	Daniel Judson & Sons, London
May 29	2	282648	John Hanbury, Birmingham
June 1	8	282663-4	Sowerby & Co., Gateshead-on-Tyne
June 10	4	282882	Toy & Jones, Birmingham
June 15	1	282961	Jane Webb & Joseph Hammond, trading as the executors of the late Joseph Webb, Stourbridge
June 24	4	283214	George Treble & Son, London
July 3	4	283406	John Derbyshire, Salford, Manchester
July 13	3	283567	Toy & Jones, Birmingham
July 29	8	284031	Percival, Vickers & Co. Ltd., Manchester
Aug. 10	8	284291	Percival Jones, Dublin
Aug. 17	5	284431	Sowerby & Co., Gateshead-on-Tyne
Aug. 25	4	284581	John Short Downing, Birmingham
Aug. 26	5	284672	William Henry Heppell & Co., Newcastle-on-Tyne
Aug. 27	9	284695	Henry Greener, Sunderland
Sept. 4	8	284903	Dietz & Co., London
Sept. 10	6	285016	Sowerby & Co., Gateshead-on-Tyne

Date	Parcel No.	Design No.	Manufacturer or Registrar
Sept. 11	5	285175	John Derbyshire, Salford, Manchester
Sept. 11	9	285179	Frank Lyon, London
Sept. 24	6	285632	Walter C. Stone, Exeter
Oct. 2	8	285831-4	R. & J. Beck, London
Oct. 3	9	285851	R. & J. Beck, London
Oct. 12	3	286172	Thomas & Harding, London
Oct. 23	12	286498	John Dawson Kiddell, London
Oct. 26	5	286525	Hodgetts, Richardson & Son, Stourbridge
Oct. 28	7	286561	Edward Bolton, Warrington, Lancashire
Nov. 26	3	287474	Charles Joseph Adie, Birmingham
Nov. 26	5	287495	John Derbyshire, Salford, Manchester
Dec. 2	15	287613	W. G. Parkin & Co., Sheffield
Dec. 21	1	288011	A. Dittrich, London
Dec. 21	4	288015	Jane Webb & Joseph Hammond, trading as the executors of the late Joseph Webb, Stourbridge
1875			
Jan. 1	2	288210	Sowerby & Co., Gateshead-on-Tyne
Jan. 7	8	288295	Thomas Lane & Son, Birmingham
Jan. 16	7	288498-500	Seago, Johnson & Co., Birmingham
Jan. 28	11	288858	Robinson & Son & Skinner, Warrington, Lancashire
Jan. 29	2	288863	John Short Downing, Birmingham
Jan. 29	9	288889	J.J. Hicks, London
Feb. 4	9	289067-8	C. J. Padgett, London
Feb. 6	10	289098-9	Thomas & Harding, London
Feb. 8	11	289165	Judson & Son, London
Feb. 12	9	289283	Molineaux, Webb & Co., Manchester
Feb. 15	6	289314	James Lewis, London
Feb. 22	6	289493	Kinmond & Co., Leamington
Feb. 26	4	289645-7	Molineaux, Webb & Co., Manchester
March 1	8	289713	Henry Defries, London
March 8	1	289799	John Short Downing, Birmingham
March 9	2	289821	Seago, Johnson & Co., Birmingham
March 13	5	289894	Thomas Lane & Son, Birmingham
March 24	5	289145	Frank Lyon, London
March 30	4	290191-2	John Short Downing, Birmingham

Date	Parcel No.	Design No.	Manufacturer or Registrar
April 3	10	290263-4	G. V. de Luca, London
April 19	5	290778	Sowerby & Co., Gateshead-on-Tyne
April 23	14	290890	Hodgetts, Richardson & Son, Stourbridge
April 26	14	290913	Beater Bros. & Co., London
May 14	9	291347	Daniel Pearce, London
May 24	5	291499-501	D. Beck & Co., Birmingham
May 27	4	291532	Daniel Pearce, London
June 5	9	291873-4	Sowerby & Co., Gateshead-on-Tyne
June 12	9	292040-1	Hodgetts, Richardson & Son, Stourbridge
June 16	6	292113	Thomas Gray & Co., Gateshead-on-Tyne
June 21	7	292201	Ortner & Houle, London
July 13	7	292783	Woodall & Son, Birmingham
July 19	2	292980	Benjamin Newham & Co., Sheffield
July 26	3	293100	Molineaux, Webb & Co., Manchester
Aug. 5	8	293356	John Derbyshire & Co., Salford, Manchester
Aug. 23	5	293890	James Scott, Birmingham
Aug. 24	6	293942	Hyde & Co., London
Sept. 8	4	294315-8	William Richards & Son, Birmingham
Sept. 10	6	294376-9	Sowerby & Co., Gateshead-on-Tyne
Sept. 14	16	294522	Joseph Polak, Birmingham
Sept. 15	1	294523	Charles Harris & Frederick Jones, Birmingham
Sept. 18	4	294575	Hodgetts, Richardson & Son, Stourbridge
Sept. 23	6	294653-4	Edward Bolton, Warrington, Lancashire
Oct. 16	10	295133	Molineaux, Webb & Co., Manchester
Oct. 23	3	295362	William Henry Heppell, Newcastle-on-Tyne
Oct. 28	4	295444	Sowerby & Co., Gateshead-on-Tyne
Nov. 13	4	295919	William Henry Heppell & Co., Newcastle-on-Tyne
Nov. 15	7	295973	W.J. Bishop, London
Nov. 25	7	296342	John Perkins, Nottingham
Dec. 3	15	296556	Edward Cetti & John Louis Guanziroli, London
Dec. 6	5	296641	Thomas Webb & Sons, Stourbridge
Dec. 6	7	296643	John Derbyshire & Co., Salford, Manchester
Dec. 17	16	297041-2	Sowerby & Co., Gateshead-on-Tyne
Dec. 22	5	297157	Thomas Webb & Sons, Manchester

Date	Parcel No.	Design No.	Manufacturer or Registrar
1876			
Jan. 9	5	297633	Seago & Co., Birmingham
Jan. 14	6	297634	Thomas Webb & Sons, Stourbridge & London
Feb. 2	1	298055-7	G. V. de Luca, London
Feb. 11	1	298309	James Lewis, London
Feb. 19	1	298446	Whittingham & Percival, Manchester
Feb. 25	8	298609	William Ford trading as John Ford, Edinburgh
Feb. 26	9	298626-7	Thomas Webb & Sons, Stourbridge & London
March 6	3	298870-6	Sowerby & Co., Gateshead-on-Tyne
March 9	4	299022-3	John Derbyshire & Co., Salford, Manchester
March 9	7	299050-4	Sowerby & Co., Gateshead-on-Tyne
March 11	10	299158	Hodgetts, Richardson & Son, Stourbridge
March 18	7	299251-2	F. & C. Osler, Birmingham & London
March 22	3	299305	Oswald Thiel, Birmingham
March 27	13	299424-6	Sowerby & Co., Gateshead-on-Tyne
March 28	1	299427	Hodgetts, Richardson & Son, Stourbridge
March 28	7	299473	Sowerby & Co., Gateshead-on-Tyne
April 4	7	299697	Joseph Benson, Sheffield
April 11	10	299826	Daniel Pearce, London
April 28	2	300300	John Derbyshire & Co., Salford, Manchester
May 3	10	300371	Boulton & Mills, Stourbridge
May 8	6	300419-20	Sowerby & Co., Gateshead-on-Tyne
May 9	10	300456	F.H. Atkins & Co., London
May 11	6	300487	Henry Manton Jnr, Birmingham
May 13	3	300619	Charles Harris, Birmingham
May 17	9	300655	John Derbyshire & Co., Salford, Manchester
May 20	2	300672	Sykes, Macvay & Co., Castleford, Yorkshire
May 24	5	300748	Sowerby & Co., Gateshead-on-Tyne
May 29	19	300940	Sowerby & Co., Gateshead-on-Tyne
June 6	2	301058-67	Whittingham & Percival, Manchester
June 14	2	301236-8	Whittingham & Percival, Manchester
June 15	8	301266	John Short Downing, Birmingham
June 17	3	301298	Boulton & Mills, Stourbridge
June 20	1	301312	Sowerby & Co., Gateshead-on-Tyne
June 21	1	301326-7	Sowerby & Co., Gateshead-on-Tyne
June 21	5	301331	Henry Pether, London
June 30	7	301579	Percival, Vickers & Co. Ltd., Manchester

DATE	PARCEL NO.	DESIGN NO.	MANUFACTURER OR REGISTRAR
July 14	8	301951	Wittman & Roth, London
July 19	6	301999	E. Cetti & Co., London
July 24	13	302114-5	Sowerby & Co., Gateshead-on-Tyne
July 29	6	302199	Henry Greener, Sunderland
July 29	8	302201	Gustave Marquot, France
Aug. 16	7	302625	Barrow & Co., Birmingham
Aug. 18	10	302804-5	Sowerby & Co., Gateshead-on-Tyne
Aug. 26	4	302912	Joseph Kidd, Manchester
Sept. 1	3	303199	Albert Bradbrook, London
Sept. 7	9	303379	Sykes Macvay & Co., Castleford, Yorkshire
Sept. 25	1	303830	Barrow & Co., Birmingham
Oct. 2	3	303996	Seago & Co., Birmingham
Oct. 11	5	304306	Louis Henry Beck, London
Oct. 16	8	304363-6	Sowerby & Co., Gateshead-on-Tyne
Oct. 17	6	304378-80	Benjamin Newham & Co., Sheffield
Nov. 15	4	305209	Sowerby & Co., Gateshead-on-Tyne
Nov. 17	7	305227	Isaac Barnes, Birmingham
Nov. 28	10	305541	James Derbyshire & Sons, Hulme, Manchester
Nov. 30	8	305579	Aston & Marlow, Birmingham
Dec. 5	9	305705	William Ramsey, London
Dec. 8	3	305778	James Aston, Birmingham
Dec. 11	4	305832	Frederick Vanstan, London
Dec. 18	2	306083	Sykes, Macvay & Co., Castleford, Yorkshire
Dec. 19	16	306149	Andrew Ker, Manchester
Dec. 20	8	306185	Lloyd & Summerfield, Birmingham
1877			
Jan. 16	8	306884	George Davidson & Co., Gateshead-on-Tyne
Jan. 16	11	306887	Sowerby & Co., Gateshead-on-Tyne
Jan. 22	7	307126	Thomas Rule, Harrogate
Jan. 31	11	307426	Henry Brett & Co., London
Feb. 1	7	307433	Warren, Stokes & Co., Dublin
Feb. 12	9	307674	Slack & Brownlow, Manchester
Feb. 13	8	307686-96	Sowerby & Co., Gateshead-on-Tyne
Feb. 17	1	307869	James Aston, Birmingham
Feb. 21	10	307910	J. T. Crawford, London
Feb. 26	8	308957-8	Sowerby & Co., Gateshead-on-Tyne

Date	Parcel No.	Design No.	Manufacturer or Registrar
Feb. 28	15	308104	George Davidson & Co., Gateshead-on-Tyne
March 1	5	308122-3	Sowerby & Co., Gateshead-on-Tyne
March 7	11	308257-8	F. & C. Osler, Birmingham
March 8	13	308328	T. Maw Son & Thompson, London
March 13	10	308414	Sowerby & Co., Gateshead-on-Tyne
March 15	1	308495	Sowerby & Co., Gateshead-on-Tyne
March 19	5	308644	Sowerby & Co., Gateshead-on-Tyne
March 21	4	308667	The Regent Flint Glass Co., Manchester
March 22	12	308713-5	Sowerby & Co., Gateshead-on-Tyne
March 23	7	308776	Sowerby & Co., Gateshead-on-Tyne
March 29	4	308876	Sowerby & Co., Gateshead-on-Tyne
April 18	3	309484-5	Seago & Co., Birmingham
April 19	5	309542	John Davis & Co., Stourbridge
April 19	6	309543	Boulton & Mills, Stourbridge
April 23	7	309621	Crosse & Blackwell, London
April 26	6	309695	Max Sugar, London
April 28	12	309765	Max Sugar, London
May 4	4	309902	The Regent Flint Glass Co., Manchester
May 22	4	310358	Ellis Allan & Co., Glasgow
May 24	6	310446	W. Lester, London
May 24	10	310450-1	G.V. de Luca, London
May 31	9	310595-7	Sowerby & Co., Gateshead-on-Tyne
June 4	14	310657	Bolton, Son & Wood, Warrington, Lancashire
June 21	10	311138	James Lewis, London
July 20	6	312061	Emil August Thomson, Manchester
July 20	12	312070-1	Sheldon & Passey, Birmingham
July 21	3	312121	Eugene Valade, Paris
Aug. 2	6	312457	William Lester, London
Aug. 9	1	312701	Jehoida A. Rhodes, Sheffield
Sept. 4	3	313707	James Henry Stone, Birmingham
Sept. 17	2	314156-7	Wittmann & Roch, London
Sept. 18	7	314265-85	Sowerby & Co., Gateshead-on-Tyne
Sept. 24	1	314482	Samuel Heath, Birmingham
Oct. 4	12	314938	Samuel H. Martin, London
Oct. 13	12	315269	G.V. de Luca, London
Oct. 17	2	315429	Molineaux, Webb & Co., Manchester
Oct. 29	6	315664-74	Sowerby & Co., Gateshead-on-Tyne

DATE	PARCEL NO.	DESIGN NO.	MANUFACTURER OR REGISTRAR
Oct. 30	6	315683	The Spirit Ageing Co., Glasgow
Nov. 15	5	316299	Jehoida A. Rhodes, Sheffield
Nov. 20	4	316490-2	Sowerby & Co., Gateshead-on-Tyne
Nov. 24	10	316623	R. Hedges, London
Dec. 3	2	316776	Molineaux, Webb & Co., Manchester
Dec. 6	3	316862	Molineaux, Webb & Co., Manchester
Dec. 17	12	317233-4	Sowerby & Co., Gateshead-on-Tyne
Dec. 19	1	317277-80	Sowerby & Co., Gateshead-on-Tyne
1878			
Jan. 5	1	317583-4	Archibald Hodge & Co., Glasgow
Jan. 18	2	317822	Frederick William Brownlow, Hulme, Manchester
Feb. 2	14	318371	Eugène Bon-Rougier, France
Feb. 9	14	318467	Widmore Hyatt, Dudley
Feb. 9	5	318468	James Henry Stone, Birmingham
Feb. 20	3	318789-95	Sowerby & Co., Gateshead-on-Tyne
March 1	8	319090	Percival, Vickers & Co. Ltd, Manchester
March 14	10	319413	W. & J. Milne, Edinburgh
March 16	9	319533	E. Remy Martin & Co., France
March 19	6	319555	Samuel Roodhouse, Leeds
March 20	7	319585-9	Sowerby & Co., Gateshead-on-Tyne
March 21	6	319599	H.W. & L. Dee, London
March 22	8	319619-20	Sowerby & Co., Gateshead-on-Tyne
April 9	10	320276	J. Defries & Sons, London
April 12	1	320330	William Frederick Williams, London
May 11	8	321308	Samuel Jones Tranmore, County of Chester
May 13	3	321340	Jane Tyzack, Sheffield
May 14	9	321368-79	Sowerby & Co., Gateshead-on-Tyne
May 27	22	322009	Sardin, Roux Bazin & Co., London & France
May 30	16	322080	Hookers Cream Milk Co. Ltd., London
June 8	11	322393	Henry Greener, Sunderland
June 25	10	322819-25	Sowerby & Co., Gateshead-on-Tyne
June 28	10	322947	H.W. & L. Dee, London
July 8	9	323400	Sowerby & Co., Gateshead-on-Tyne
July 16	5	323711	W.H. Gritton, London
July 27	15	324317	F. & C. Osler, Birmingham

DATE	PARCEL NO.	DESIGN NO.	MANUFACTURER OR REGISTRAR
July 29	4	324321-2	Sowerby & Co., Gateshead-on-Tyne
Aug. 2	12	324501	I. Barnes & Co., Birmingham
Aug. 12	6	324929-32	Sowerby & Co., Gateshead-on-Tyne
Aug. 16	11	325096-101	Sowerby & Co., Gateshead-on-Tyne
Aug. 28	4	325439	Joseph Wilson Hollyer, Birmingham
Aug. 30	16	325534	Sowerby & Co., Gateshead-on-Tyne
Aug. 31	8	325547	Henry Greener, Sunderland
Sept. 5	14	325782	F. & C. Osler, Birmingham
Sept. 7	2	325876	Robert Gourlay, Glasgow
Sept. 23	6	326775-6	George Davidson & Co., Gateshead-on-Tyne
Oct. 15	4	327641	James Webb, Joseph Hammond & Henry Fitzroy Webb trading as the executors of the late Joseph Webb, Stourbridge
Oct. 19	3	327771	J. Gill & E. Rawlinson, Manchester
Oct. 26	12	328347	William Boyd & Co., Glasgow
Oct. 26	14	328349	Oscar Braumuller, London
Nov. 4	10	328740-51	Sowerby & Co., Gateshead-on-Tyne
Nov. 7	17	328919	Sowerby & Co., Gateshead-on-Tyne
Nov. 12	6	329010	Francis Thomas Bond. M.D., Gloucester
Nov. 20	11	329376	Sowerby & Co., Gateshead-on-Tyne
Nov. 21	12	329408	Henry Rawlings, London
Nov 28	12	329744	I. Barnes & Co., Birmingham
Dec. 10	13	330210	Westwood & Moore, Brierley Hill
Dec. 13	9	330326	George Cooke, Manchester
Dec. 13	16	330348-52	Sowerby & Co., Gateshead-on-Tyne
Dec. 18	10	330470	Henry Greener, Sunderland
Dec. 23	2	330604	Sowerby & Co., Gateshead-on-Tyne
1879			
Jan. 2	3	330816	Edward Green & Edward Unsworth Green, London & France
Jan. 8	10	330964	Sowerby & Co., Gateshead-on-Tyne
Jan. 13	3	331138	William Boyd & Co., Glasgow
Jan. 17	11	331370	Daniel Pearce, London
Jan. 21	1	331421	James Barwell, Son & Fisher, Birmingham
Jan. 21	8	331450	William Ramsey, London
Feb. 8	8	332051-4	Sowerby & Co., Gateshead-on-Tyne

DATE	PARCEL NO.	DESIGN NO.	MANUFACTURER OR REGISTRAR
Feb. 8	9	332055	William McKinlay Percy, Glasgow
Feb. 12	17	332195	Sowerby & Co., Gateshead-on-Tyne
March 8	8	333128-9	Hodgetts, Richardson & Son, Stourbridge
March 10	9	333167-73	Sowerby & Co., Gateshead-on-Tyne
March 17	11	333424-9	Sowerby & Co., Gateshead-on-Tyne
March 20	9	333557	Ernest Unger, London
March 20	10	333558-60	F. & C. Osler, Birmingham
March 27	4	333762-3	H.J. Humphreys & Co., Glasgow
April 1	13	333955	Mountain Horsley & Collett, London
April 28	7	334634-43	Sowerby & Co., Gateshead-on-Tyne
May 6	9	334930	James Wilson, London
May 10	12	335118	Groves & Co., London
May 14	3	335175	H.W. & L. Dee, London
June 4	1	335845	The Rochester Tumbler Co., Pittsburgh, Pennsylvania, USA
June 6	10	335969-72	Sowerby & Co., Gateshead-on-Tyne
June 14	2	336135	Jane Webb, Joseph Hammond & Henry Fitzroy Webb trading as the executors of the late Joseph Webb, Stourbridge
June 25	16	336445	Dalby & Pearson, Birmingham
June 30	14	336594-5	Sowerby & Co., Gateshead-on-Tyne
July 3	6	336725	John Shaw & Sons, Sheffield
July 4	5	336759-61	Pellison, Père & Co., France
July 10	7	337071	Thomas Webb & Sons, Stourbridge
July 10	8	337072	William Thomas Sugg, London
July 17	1	337178	Dalby & Pearson, Birmingham
July 21	2	337344	Jane Webb, Joseph Hammond & Henry Fitzroy Webb trading as the executors of the late Joseph Webb, Stourbridge
July 22	6	337409-15	Sowerby & Co., Gateshead-on-Tyne
July 22	7	337416	Henry Greener, Sunderland
July 24	16	337492	Wheeler & Shanks, Dublin
July 29	7	337572	Jane Webb, Joseph Hammond & Henry Fitzroy Webb trading as the executors of the late Joseph Webb, Stourbridge
July 29	13	337623-7	Sowerby & Co., Gateshead-on-Tyne
Aug. 1	13	337775	S. Mordan & Co., London

DATE	PARCEL NO.	DESIGN NO.	MANUFACTURER OR REGISTRAR
Aug. 8	12	338015	Henry Greener, Sunderland
Aug. 11	7	338093	Matthew Turnbull, Sunderland
Aug. 14	13	338286-7	W.H. Heppell & Co., Newcastle-on-Tyne
Aug. 14	15	338294-8	Sowerby & Co., Gateshead-on-Tyne
Aug. 26	14	338734	Frederick Tiemens, Dresden, Saxony
Sept. 4	7	339194-200	Sowerby & Co., Gateshead-on-Tyne
Sept. 12	9	339494	John Jackson Wheeler, London
Sept. 12	13	339498-502	Sowerby & Co., Gateshead-on-Tyne
Sept. 18	13	340002-6	Sowerby & Co., Gateshead-on-Tyne
Sept. 19	19	340104	Henry Greener, Sunderland
Sept. 23	2	340206	Molineaux, Webb & Co., Manchester
Sept. 23	13	340254	Sowerby & Co., Gateshead-on-Tyne
Sept. 24	15	340369	George W.W. Edwards, Wolverhampton
Nov. 17	9	342941	H. W. & L. Dee, London
Dec. 2	21	343724-31	Sowerby & Co., Gateshead-on-Tyne
Dec. 15	9	344257	G.V. de Luca, London
1880			
Jan. 5	2	344911	Molineaux, Webb & Co., Manchester
Jan. 7	2	344960	Molineaux, Webb & Co., Manchester
Jan. 9	11	345042-4	Sowerby & Co., Gateshead-on-Tyne
Jan. 12	3	345071	W. Lester Smith, Birmingham
Jan. 14	2	345166-8	Molineaux, Webb & Co., Manchester
Jan. 20	14	345451	Abraham Fitton, Manchester
Feb. 4	13	346020-1	The Rochester Tumbler Co., Pittsburgh, Pennsylvania, USA
Feb. 13	3	346369	The Rochester Tumbler Co., Pittsburgh, Pennsylvania, USA
Feb. 16	13	346506	Mina Beresch, London
Feb. 17	9	346543	W.H. Heppell & Co., Newcastle-on-Tyne
March 11	9	347465	W.J. Bush & Co., London
March 20	20	347818	John Shaw & Sons, Sheffield
March 23	12	347895	G. V. de Luca, London
March 31	13	348165	G.W. Winfield & Co., Birmingham
April 1	9	348189-91	M.I. Verhouteren Jnr, London
May 5	12	349527	C.B. Stamp, London
May 10	16	349740	Henry Solomon Wellcome, London

DATE	PARCEL NO.	DESIGN NO.	MANUFACTURER OR REGISTRAR
May 11	13	349789	William Pratt, Birmingham
May 14	5	349879	Henry Tonkinson, Sunderland
May 21	3	350028	William Twigg & Co., Birmingham
May 22	1	350065	Daniel Pearce, London
May 24	8	350083-93	Sowerby & Co., Gateshead-on-Tyne
May 28	11	350211	Sykes Macvay & Co., Castleford, Yorkshire
May 28	15	350218	J. H. Aveling, M.D., London
May 31	15	350246	S. Williamson & Sons, London
June 8	6	350486	Ferdinand Mullens trading as Francis Maria Farina, Cologne
June 17	3	351024	Percival, Vickers & Co. Ltd., Manchester
June 17	19	351062	Burtles, Tate & Co., Manchester
June 19	16	351191	W.H. Heppell & Co., Newcastle-on-Tyne
June 23	5	351354	Edmund William Boulding, Liverpool
June 23	17	351455	Roland Bourne, Birmingham
July 1	8	351728	Alfred Arculus, Birmingham
July 5	11	351866	Westwood & Moore, Brierley Hill, Staffordshire
July 5	12	351867	T.W. Watson, London
July 13	11	352133-7	Sowerby & Co., Gateshead-on-Tyne
July 20	4	352408	F. William Mackinlay Percy, Glasgow
July 21	14	352519	Johnstone, Sadler & Norris, London
July 26	10	352840-5	Sowerby & Co., Gateshead-on-Tyne
July 27	9	352870	Percival, Vickers & Co. Ltd., Manchester
Aug. 14	14	353716	R. M. Brundige, New York, USA
Aug. 23	4	354091	Barwell Son & Fisher, Birmingham
Sept. 7	1	354935	W.H. Heppell & Co., Newcastle-on-Tyne
Sept. 14	1	355154-8	Sowerby & Co., Gateshead-on-Tyne
Sept. 24	9	355627-9	Sowerby & Co., Gateshead-on-Tyne
Sept. 29	16	355979	Young's Paraffin Light & Mineral Oil Co. Ltd., Birmingham
Oct. 5	1	356111	Thomas Pargeter Richardson, Wordsley, Staffordshire
Oct. 12	5	356515	Caroline Amelia Elizabeth Swallow, Manchester
Oct. 18	14	356807	John Walsh Walsh, Birmingham
Nov. 2	1	357608	John Walsh Walsh, Birmingham
Nov. 5	5	357730	Percival, Vickers & Co. Ltd., Manchester
Nov. 9	1	357951	James Bird, Bilston, Staffordshire

Date	Parcel No.	Design No.	Manufacturer or Registrar
Nov. 9	2	357952	Ungar & Co., London
Nov. 22	2	358659	Pembrook & Dingley, Birmingham
Nov. 23	16	358798	J. Defries & Sons, London
Nov. 29	14	359014	J. Defries & Sons, London
Dec. 1	17	359134	Young's Paraffin Light & Mineral Oil Co. Ltd, Birmingham
Dec. 3	15	359237-9	J. Defries & Sons, London
Dec. 8	14	359361	Henry Greener, Sunderland
Dec. 10	7	359464	Watkin Bros., Leicester
Dec. 18	15	359806	W.H. Heppell & Co., Newcastle-on-Tyne
Dec. 21	4	359877	Obed. Charles Hawkes, Birmingham
Dec. 22	13	359928	Burroughs, Wellcome & Co.
1881			
Jan. 5	2	360315-6	Obed. Charles Hawkes, Birmingham
Jan. 7	15	360486-7	J. Defries & Sons, London
Jan. 12	16	360656	Edward Berman & Co., London
Jan. 31	9	361355	B. Temple, Hackney
Feb. 8	4	361535-6	John Shaw & Sons, Sheffield
Feb. 16	14	361810	J. Defries & Sons, London
Feb. 28	10	362243	George William Hughes, Birmingham
March 1	8	362318	Max Sugar, London
March 1	12	362328	Henry Greener, Sunderland
March 4	4	362453	Hodgetts, Richardson & Son, Stourbridge
March 11	2	362734-44	Sowerby & Co., Gateshead-on-Tyne
March 19	11	363048-9	Sowerby & Co., Gateshead-on-Tyne
March 23	9	363194-203	Young's Paraffin Light & Mineral Oil Co. Ltd., Birmingham
March 30	8	363454-8	William Thomas Sugg, London
April 4	6	363648	William Pratt, Birmingham
April 9	9	363798	John Gough, Birmingham
April 20	9	364167	Sowerby & Co., Gateshead-on-Tyne
April 21	13	364187	Henry Greener, Sunderland
April 30	17	364574	Samuel Elijah Culver, London
May 19	9	365165	Sowerby & Co., Gateshead-on-Tyne
May 31	6	365634	Thomas Wimpenny, Leeds
June 14	9	366032	Henry Greener, Sunderland

DATE	PARCEL NO.	DESIGN NO.	MANUFACTURER OR REGISTRAR
June 22	16	366273	R.H.C. Wilson, London
June 24	10	366408	Henry Greener, Sunderland
July 16	9	367237	Crichton & Curry, London
Aug. 19	15	368638	J. Defries & Sons, London
Sept. 2	23	369483	Robert Gardner Bird & Co., London
Sept. 19	9	370198-9	Alfred Augustus Hely, London
Sept. 21	16	370370-9	Sowerby & Co., Gateshead-on-Tyne
Sept. 23	20	370469	J. Defries & Sons, London
Sept. 26	1	370524	W.H. Heppell & Co., Newcastle-on-Tyne
Sept. 28	3	370618-9	Molineaux, Webb & Co. Ltd., Manchester
Oct. 12	5	371262	Molineaux, Webb & Co. Ltd., Manchester
Oct. 14	2	371343	William Bartlett & Sons, Redditch
Oct. 22	15	372018	Percival, Vickers & Co. Ltd., Manchester
Nov. 7	3	372860	W.H. Heppell & Co., Newcastle-on-Tyne
Nov. 8	10	372967	Max Sugar, London
Nov. 15	15	373268-9	A. Dollmann, London
Nov. 26	6	373918	William Sugg & Co. Ltd., London
Dec. 6	8	374432	J. Defries & Sons, London
Dec. 6	13	374437	W.H. Heppell & Co., Newcastle-on-Tyne
Dec. 7	17	374475	Henry Greener, Sunderland
Dec. 8	8	374497	Harwood Sons & Harrison, Birmingham
Dec. 12	13	374629-31	Messrs. Hawkes, Birmingham
Dec. 14	6	374682-6	Sowerby & Co., Gateshead-on-Tyne
Dec. 15	9	374773	J. Defries & Sons, London
Dec. 15	10	374774-8	Sowerby & Co., Gateshead-on-Tyne
Dec. 23	1	375013-4	Hawkesford & Booth, Birmingham
Dec. 28	7	375151-5	B. Verity & Sons, London
1882			
Jan. 2	1	375281	Molineaux, Webb & Co., Manchester
Jan. 24	7	375360	George Whybrow, London
Jan. 26	8	376428	Hodgetts, Richardson & Son, Stourbridge
Feb. 9	20	376905	Sowerby's Ellison Glass Works Ltd., Gateshead-on-Tyne
Feb. 16	19	377222	R.W. Winfield & Co., Birmingham
March 4	10	378022-3	Henry Greener, Sunderland
March 7	15	378063-5	Samuel Gratrix Jnr & Brother, Manchester

Date	Parcel No.	Design No.	Manufacturer or Registrar
March 17	4	378495	Percival, Vickers & Co. Ltd., Manchester
March 17	8	378506	Phillip M. Beck, London
March 28	19	378997-8	J. Defries & Sons, London
April 8	10	379366	John William Webb & Robert Richard Sinclair, London
April 12	7	379463	Henry Gething Richardson, Stourbridge
April 24	2	379826	John Short Downing, Birmingham
April 28	1	380077	James Dixon & Sons, Sheffield
April 28	13	380132-4	Sowerby's Ellison Glass Works Ltd., Gateshead-on-Tyne
May 23	9	381369	Edward Edwards, Stourbridge
May 25	1	381436	Percival, Vickers & Co. Ltd., Manchester
May 25	12	381481	Henry Greener, Sunderland
May 30	11	381677-9	William Sugg & Co. Ltd., London
July 1	10	382831	Sidney Brown, London
July 1	12	382838	J. Defries & Sons, London
July 5	18	383007	J. Defries & Sons, London
July 19	6	383640	Henry Greener, Sunderland
July 31	1	384159	Walton & Co., London
Aug. 9	14	384453-5	Sowerby's Ellison Glass Works Ltd., Gateshead-on-Tyne
Aug. 18	16	384998	Hedges & Butler, London
Aug. 29	13	385624-5	Sowerby's Ellison Glass Works Ltd., Gateshead-on-Tyne
Aug. 31	16	385736	E.R. Durkee & Co., New York, USA
Sept. 7	2	386038	William James, Birmingham
Sept. 22	3	386878	Dalby & Pearson, Birmingham
Sept. 25	8	387036	Henry Howe, London
Sept. 26	9	387075-7	J. Defries & Sons, London
Oct. 3	4	387378	Charles Ward & Sons, London
Oct. 25	16	388896	Sowerby's Ellison Glass Works Ltd., Gateshead-on-Tyne
Oct. 31	11	389157-8	John Walsh Walsh, Birmingham
Nov. 1	3	389169	Drykin & Sons, Birmingham
Nov. 15	11	390018	Henry Churchman, Horsham, Sussex
Nov. 17	3	390103-4	Thomas Webb & Sons, Stourbridge
Nov. 24	17	390584-6	W.H. Heppell & Co., Newcastle-on-Tyne

Date	Parcel No.	Design No.	Manufacturer or Registrar
Nov. 27	1	390615	Percival Vickers & Co. Ltd., Manchester
Nov. 27	2	390616	Dalby & Pearson, Birmingham
Nov. 29	11	390709-10	Joseph Shaw, Walsall, Birmingham
Dec. 1	13	390833-5	W. James, Birmingham
Dec. 9	18	391302	H. Vander Weyde, London
Dec. 19	15	391669	Walton & Co., Newton-le-Willows, Lancashire
Dec. 28	12	392018-9	Walter Thornhill, London
1883			
Jan. 6	5	392521-3	William James, Birmingham
Jan. 25	20	393243-4	John Walsh Walsh, Birmingham
Feb. 3	11	393638-43	Sowerby's Ellison Glass Works Ltd., Gateshead-on-Tyne
Feb. 12	9	394098	Henry Greener, Sunderland
Feb. 14	11	394205	Percival, Vickers & Co. Ltd., Manchester
Feb. 16	10	394320	Jonas & Jules Lang, London
Feb. 24	15	394680	Henry Morrell, London
March 12	1	395417-8	Young's Paraffin Light & Mineral Oil Co. Ltd., Birmingham
March 19	6	395786	Henry G. Richardson, Stourbridge
March 27	5	396091	Boulton & Mills, Stourbridge
March 31	9	396305	Henry Greener, Sunderland
April 6	1	396530	Muckley & Co., Stourbridge
April 12	22	396835	Rudolph Edward Frank, London
April 17	3	397022	Percival, Vickers & Co. Ltd., Manchester
April 27	5	397473	Josiah Lane, Birmingham
May 1	16	397604	Henry Greener, Sunderland
May 8	4	397827	John Castle, Birmingham
May 8	5	397828	Henry Gething Richardson, Stourbridge
May 16	2	398241	Edmund Fowle, Bickley, Kent
May 23	6	398435	Hopgood & Co., Isle of Wight
May 28	18	398610	Allen & Hanburys, London
June 1	11	398825	Henry Adolph Wetzell, London
June 6	10	398981	G. V. de Luca, London
June 7	20	399063	J. Defries & Sons, London
June 7	22	399065	Wittmann & Roth, London
June 9	7	399144	S. Mordan & Co., London

Date	Parcel No.	Design No.	Manufacturer or Registrar
June 12	14	399313	Burtles, Tate & Co., Manchester
June 15	3	399455	J. Forrest & Son, Glasgow
June 29	14	400089-90	Hermann Schulder, Solingen, Germany
Aug. 2	4	401665	Hames Batchelor & Co., London
Aug. 11	9	402039	Allen & Hanburys, London
Aug. 17	11	402378	William Ramsey Junior & Co., Glasgow
Aug. 24	2	402690	Percival, Vickers & Co. Ltd., Manchester
Aug. 31	5	403109	Pembrook & Dingley, Birmingham
Sept. 13	18	403804	Thomas Webb & Sons, Stourbridge
Sept. 15	1	403905	Richard Dendy Sadler, London
Sept. 24	13	404322	W.B. Simmons & Co., London
Oct. 2	19	404649	W. Reynolds & Sons, London
Oct. 6	10	404899	James Lewis & Arthur Lewis, London
Oct. 12	15	405338	William Barker & Son, London
Oct. 13	14	405367	George Robert Cheshire, London
Oct. 15	8	405382-3	Richard Dendy Sadler & Wm. Bagley, London
Nov. 2	12	406456	Percival, Vickers & Co. Ltd., Manchester
Nov. 9	16	406731	John J. Wheeler, London
Nov. 13	15	406880-1	Richard Dendy Sadler & Wm. Bagley, London
Nov. 14	11	406942-3	Thomas Webb & Sons, Stourbridge
Nov. 14	12	406944	Henry Greener, Sunderland
Nov. 17	11	407253-4	James & Grieve, Edinburgh
Nov. 28	2	407766	Khoosh Bitters Co. Ltd., Liverpool
Dec. 12	11	408221	Cuthbert Britton Slee & Herbert Hutton Slee trading as Batty & Co., London
1884			
Jan. 16	1	408895	John Phillips, London

Date	Rd. No.	Manufacturer or Registrar
1884		
Feb. 7	1415	Percival, Vickers & Co. Ltd, Manchester
Feb. 9	1627	Barnes & Company, Birmingham
Feb. 9	1628	Barnes & Company, Birmingham
Feb. 14	1909	John Walsh Walsh, Birmingham
Feb. 29	2659	H.G. Richardson & Sons, Stourbridge

Date	Rd. No.	Manufacturer or Registrar
March 14	3613	Burtles, Tate & Co., Manchester
March 14	3614	Burtles, Tate & Co., Manchester
March 15	3658	Reuben Jackson, Sheffield
March 17	3760	Charles Riley & Co., London
March 27	4242	Alfred & James Davies, Stourbridge
April 2	4489	John Walsh Walsh, Birmingham
April 2	4589	Edward Webb, Stourbridge
April 7	4833	Sowerby's Ellison Glass Works Ltd, Gateshead-on-Tyne
April 18	5418	Henry Johnson, London
April 29	5849	Sowerby's Ellison Glass Works Ltd, Gateshead-on-Tyne
May 8	6481	Sowerby's Ellison Glass Works Ltd, Gateshead-on-Tyne
May 10	6658	Percival, Vickers & Co. Ltd, Manchester
June 5	7978	Sowerby's Ellison Glass Works Ltd, Gateshead-on-Tyne
June 5	7979	Sowerby's Ellison Glass Works Ltd, Gateshead-on-Tyne
June 7	8013	John Walsh Walsh, Birmingham
July 15	9805	Alfred & James Davies, Stourbridge
July 15	9806	Alfred & James Davies, Stourbridge
July 15	9807	Alfred & James Davies, Stourbridge
July 15	9808	Alfred & James Davies, Stourbridge
July 25	10277	Thomas Webb and Sons, Stourbridge
Aug. 2	10595	Max Sugar, London
Aug. 11	10966	Sowerby's Ellison Glass Works Ltd, Gateshead-on-Tyne
Aug. 11	10967	Sowerby's Ellison Glass Works Ltd, Gateshead-on-Tyne
Aug. 12	11109	Thomas Webb and Sons, Stourbridge
Aug. 15	11344	Max Sugar & Co., London
Sept. 10	12723	Silber & Fleming, London
Sept. 11	12758	Thomas Webb and Sons, Stourbridge
Sept. 11	12759	Thomas Webb and Sons, Stourbridge
Sept. 12	12839	Thomas Webb and Sons, Stourbridge
Sept. 12	12840	Thomas Webb and Sons, Stourbridge
Sept. 19	13563	Sowerby's Ellison Glass Works Ltd, Gateshead-on-Tyne
Sept. 24	13792	Sowerby's Ellison Glass Works Ltd, Gateshead-on-Tyne
Oct. 3	14390	Henry Greener, Sunderland
Oct. 16	15256	H.G. Richardson, Stourbridge
Oct. 18	15332	Percival, Vickers & Co. Ltd, Manchester
Oct. 18	15353	Stevens & Williams, Stourbridge
Oct. 23	15711	Thomas Webb and Sons, Stourbridge

DATE	RD. NO.	MANUFACTURER OR REGISTRAR
Nov. 7	16475	Boulton and Mills, Stourbridge
Nov. 13	16828	Thomas Webb and Sons, Stourbridge
Nov. 13	16829	Thomas Webb and Sons, Stourbridge
Nov. 17	17102	George Cole, London
Nov. 17	17103	George Cole, London
Nov. 27	17721	George Cole, London
Dec. 10	18749	Percival, Vickers & Co. Ltd, Manchester
Dec. 16	18990	H.B. Johnson, London
Dec. 18	19238	Edmond Rocher, Clichy (Seine), France
Dec. 30	19704	George Cole, London
Dec. 23	19740	Mills, Walker & Co., Stourbridge
Dec. 23	19742	Mills, Walker & Co., Stourbridge
Dec. 27	19743	Cannington, Shaw & Co., St Helens, Lancashire
1885		
Jan. 6	19937	Sowerby's Ellison Glass Works Ltd, Gateshead-on-Tyne
Jan. 8	20079	George Cole, London
Jan. 8	20085	Burtles, Tate & Co., Manchester
Jan. 8	20086	Burtles, Tate & Co., Manchester
Jan. 14	20355	Percival, Vickers & Co. Ltd, Manchester
Jan. 21	20775	Sowerby's Ellison Glass Works Ltd, Gateshead-on-Tyne
Jan. 21	20860	Jane Webb & Henry Fitzroy Webb, Stourbridge
Jan. 21	20861	Jane Webb & Henry Fitzroy Webb, Stourbridge
Jan. 21	20862	Jane Webb & Henry Fitzroy Webb, Stourbridge
Jan. 22	20930	Edward Edwards, Stourbridge
Jan. 23	20936	Percival, Vickers & Co. Ltd, Manchester
Jan. 24	20972	Burtles, Tate & Co., Manchester
Jan. 28	21108	Burtles, Tate & Co., Manchester
Jan. 28	21109	Burtles, Tate & Co., Manchester
Jan. 28	21110	Burtles, Tate & Co., Manchester
Jan. 31	21284	Sowerby's Ellison Glass Works Ltd, Gateshead-on-Tyne
Feb. 2	21325	Burtles, Tate & Co., Manchester
Feb. 2	21326	Burtles, Tate & Co., Manchester
Feb. 2	21327	Burtles, Tate & Co., Manchester
Feb. 2	21328	Burtles, Tate & Co., Manchester
Feb. 2	21329	Burtles, Tate & Co., Manchester
Feb. 5	21616	Boulton & Mills, Stourbridge

Date	Rd. No.	Manufacturer or Registrar
Feb. 6	21620	James Hateley, Birmingham
Feb. 17	22179	Boulton & Mills, Stourbridge
March 5	23040	Molineaux, Webb & Co., Manchester
March 5	23041	Molineaux, Webb & Co., Manchester
March 5	23184	Yeatman & Co., London
March 10	23333	Molineaux, Webb & Co., Manchester
March 10	23334	Molineaux, Webb & Co., Manchester
March 10	23335	Molineaux, Webb & Co., Manchester
March 10	23336	Molineaux, Webb & Co., Manchester
March 10	23337	Molineaux, Webb & Co., Manchester
March 10	23338	Molineaux, Webb & Co., Manchester
March 11	23378	Molineaux, Webb & Co., Manchester
March 20	24100	Burtles, Tate & Co., Manchester
April 13	24953	Sowerby's Ellison Glass Works Ltd, Gateshead-on-Tyne
April 20	25435	Thomas Webb and Sons, Stourbridge
April 27	25863	Thomas Webb and Sons, Stourbridge
April 27	25864	Thomas Webb and Sons, Stourbridge
April 27	25865	Thomas Webb and Sons, Stourbridge
May 4	26173	Max Sugar & Co., London
May 7	26480	Burtles, Tate & Co., Manchester
May 28	27552	Percival, Vickers & Co. Ltd, Manchester
May 28	27553	Percival, Vickers & Co. Ltd, Manchester
June 1	27639	A. Barnes-coni, London
June 25	28921	A. Barnes-coni, London
June 29	29106	Burtles, Tate & Co., Manchester
July 1	29145	Percival, Vickers & Co. Ltd, Manchester
July 14	29780	Molineaux, Webb & Co., Manchester
July 14	29781	Molineaux, Webb & Co., Manchester
July 22	30244	Sowerby's Ellison Glass Works Ltd, Gateshead-on-Tyne
July 24	30345	Henry Johnson, London
Aug. 1	30704	Henry Johnson, London
Aug. 21	31844	Molineaux, Webb & Co., Manchester
Aug. 27	32253	Sowerby's Ellison Glass Works Ltd, Gateshead-on-Tyne
Sept. 3	32685	Henry Fitzroy Webb, Stourbridge
Sept. 19	33714	John Walsh Walsh, Birmingham
Sept. 19	33715	John Walsh Walsh, Birmingham
Sept. 26	34196	Burtles, Tate & Co., Manchester

Date	Rd. No.	Manufacturer or Registrar
Oct. 10	35293	Percival, Vickers & Co. Ltd, Manchester
Oct. 15	35660	Thomas Seage, Sheffield
Oct. 16	35709	·Alfred Arculus, Birmingham
Oct. 22	36184	John Walsh Walsh, Birmingham
Oct. 24	36408	George Cole, London
Oct. 31	36853	John Thornton, Warrington, Lancashire
Nov. 4	37109	George Cole, London
Nov. 4	37110	Sowerby's Ellison Glass Works Ltd, Gateshead-on-Tyne
Nov. 4	37111	Sowerby's Ellison Glass Works Ltd, Gateshead-on-Tyne
Nov. 23	38582	Henry Greener & Co., Sunderland
Dec. 1	38983	Stevens & Williams, Brierley Hill, Staffordshire
Dec. 3	39062	Sowerby's Ellison Glass Works Ltd, Gateshead-on-Tyne
Dec. 3	39063	Sowerby's Ellison Glass Works Ltd, Gateshead-on-Tyne
Dec. 3	39064	Sowerby's Ellison Glass Works Ltd, Gateshead-on-Tyne
Dec. 10	39328	Robinson Son & Skinner, Warrington, Lancashire
Dec. 11	39414	Edward Bolton, Warrington, Lancashire
Dec. 11	39415	Edward Bolton, Warrington, Lancashire
Dec. 16	39648	Joseph Benson, Sheffield
Dec. 18	39807	Burtles, Tate & Co., Manchester
Dec. 21	39898	George Cole, London
1886		
Jan. 1	40484	Percival, Vickers & Co. Ltd, Manchester
Jan. 29	42716	John Walsh Walsh, Birmingham
Feb. 10	42947	Sowerby's Ellison Glass Works Ltd, Gateshead-on-Tyne
Feb. 22	43650	James Testro & John Rickard, London
Feb. 25	43869	James Testro & John Rickard, London
March 8	44445	Burtles, Tate & Co., Manchester
March 9	44546	Blumberg & Co. Ltd, London
March 11	44659	Sowerby's Ellison Glass Works Ltd, Gateshead-on-Tyne
March 25	45759	Sowerby's Ellison Glass Works Ltd, Gateshead-on-Tyne
March 25	45768	H.G. Richardson, Stourbridge
March 26	45942	Percival, Vickers & Co. Ltd, Manchester
March 24	46252	Edward Webb, Stourbridge
March 30	46253	Jonas & Jules Lang, London
April 1	46498	H.G. Richardson, Stourbridge
April 16	47381-6	Alfred Arculus, Birmingham

Date	Rd. No.	Manufacturer or Registrar
April 21	47513	Sowerby's Ellison Glass Works Ltd, Gateshead-on-Tyne
April 21	47514	Sowerby's Ellison Glass Works Ltd, Gateshead-on-Tyne
April 20	47900	Mills, Walker & Co., Stourbridge
April 28	48212	Mills, Walker & Co., Stourbridge
May 4	48228	Sowerby's Ellison Glass Works Ltd, Gateshead-on-Tyne
May 5	48352	Henry Greener & Co., Sunderland
May 11	48909	Sowerby's Ellison Glass Works Ltd, Gateshead-on-Tyne
May 11	48910	Sowerby's Ellison Glass Works Ltd, Gateshead-on-Tyne
June 1	50071	Sowerby's Ellison Glass Works Ltd, Gateshead-on-Tyne
June 2	50165	Alfred Arculus, Birmingham
May 18	50168	Edward Webb, Stourbridge
June 10	50725	Boulton & Mills, Stourbridge
June 10	50726	Boulton & Mills, Stourbridge
June 12	50859	Alfred Arculus, Birmingham
June 15	51047	Thomas Webb and Sons, Stourbridge
June 22	51365	G.V. de Luca, London
July 13	52434	Sowerby's Ellison Glass Works Ltd, Gateshead-on-Tyne
July 26	53107	Sowerby's Ellison Glass Works Ltd, Gateshead-on-Tyne
Aug. 3	53466	Percival Jones, Dublin
Aug. 3	53468	Percival, Vickers & Co. Ltd, Manchester
July 30	53483	H.G. Richardson, Stourbridge
Aug. 6	53643	Sowerby's Ellison Glass Works Ltd, Gateshead-on-Tyne
Aug. 3	53731-3	Stuart & Sons, Stourbridge
Aug. 7	53734	Stuart & Sons, Stourbridge
Aug. 13	54040	A. & R. Cochran, Glasgow
Aug. 18	54314	Sowerby's Ellison Glass Works Ltd, Gateshead-on-Tyne
Aug. 18	54315	Sowerby's Ellison Glass Works Ltd, Gateshead-on-Tyne
Aug. 18	54316	Sowerby's Ellison Glass Works Ltd, Gateshead-on-Tyne
Aug. 14	54494	Thomas Webb & Sons, Stourbridge
Aug. 19	54702	Hauptman Albert & Co., Edinburgh
Aug. 27	55113	Stone, Fawdry & Stone, Birmingham
Aug. 26	55235	John Shaw & Sons, Sheffield
Aug. 30	55272	G. V. de Luca, London
Aug. 27	55275	Josiah Lane, Birmingham
Sept. 6	55693	Stevens & Williams, Brierley Hill, Stourbridge
Sept. 7	55773	Edward Webb, Stourbridge
Sept. 11	56047	Percival, Vickers & Co. Ltd, Manchester

Date	Rd. No.	Manufacturer or Registrar
Sept. 23	56961	Sowerby's Ellison Glass Works Ltd, Gateshead-on-Tyne
Sept. 23	56962	Sowerby's Ellison Glass Works Ltd, Gateshead-on-Tyne
Sept. 23	56963	Sowerby's Ellison Glass Works Ltd, Gateshead-on-Tyne
Oct. 7	58275	Edward Moore, South Shields
Oct. 8	58374	Thomas Webb & Sons, Stourbridge
Oct. 8	58375	Thomas Webb & Sons, Stourbridge
Oct. 19	59136	Boulton & Mills, Stourbridge
Oct. 29	60108	Percival, Vickers & Co. Ltd, Manchester
Nov. 1	60351	Edward Webb, Stourbridge
Nov. 8	60872	Edward Webb, Stourbridge
Nov. 15	61357	Stevens & Williams, Stourbridge
Nov. 23	62029	Thomas Webb and Sons, Stourbridge
Dec. 10	63267	F. & C. Osler, Birmingham
Dec. 14	63474	Stevens & Williams, Stourbridge
Dec. 15	63543	Edward Moore, South Shields
Dec. 22	64086	Sowerby's Ellison Glass Works Ltd, Gateshead-on-Tyne
Dec. 23	64106	Sowerby's Ellison Glass Works Ltd, Gateshead-on-Tyne
Dec. 28	64234	Burtles, Tate & Co., Manchester
1887		
Jan. 11	65229	Stevens & Williams, Stourbridge
Jan. 14	65339	Edward Moore & Co., South Shields
Jan. 17	65455	Burtles, Tate & Co., Manchester
Jan. 15	65543	John Walsh Walsh, Birmingham
Feb. 5	67263	Stevens & Williams, Stourbridge
Feb. 7	67425	Edward Moore, South Shields
Feb. 9	67648	Thomas Webb & Sons, Stourbridge
Feb. 7	67650	Ephraim Cutler, Birmingham
Feb. 18	68249	Edward Moore, South Shields
Feb. 21	68327	H.G. Richardson, Stourbridge
Feb. 24	68632	Ephraim Cutler, Birmingham
Feb. 28	68806	Stevens & Williams, Stourbridge
March 1	68846	Sowerby's Ellison Glass Works Ltd, Gateshead-on-Tyne
March 23	70422	Molineaux, Webb & Co., Manchester
March 12	70971	Joseph Price & Co., Gateshead-on-Tyne
April 6	71528	Molineaux, Webb & Co., Manchester
April 6	71546	John Shaw & Sons, Sheffield

Date	Rd. No.	Manufacturer or Registrar
April 9	71736	Henry Greener, Sunderland
April 12	71753	Edward Moore, South Shields
April 13	71816	Edward Moore, South Shields
April 14	71869	Percival, Vickers & Co. Ltd, Manchester
April 28	72790	Philip M. Black, London
April 28	72815	Edward Moore, South Shields
April 29	72884	Edward Moore, South Shields
April 29	72885	Edward Moore, South Shields
May 17	73836	Scotney & Earnshaw, London
May 26	74556	John Walsh Walsh, Birmingham
June 8	75015	Edward Moore, South Shields
June 8	75016	Edward Moore, South Shields
June 9	75091	Edward Moore, South Shields
June 9	75092	Edward Moore, South Shields
June 29	75942	Percival, Vickers & Co. Ltd, Manchester
July 11	76682	Alfred & James Davies, Stourbridge
July 12	76762-5	Alfred & James Davies, Stourbridge
July 13	76878	Edward Moore, South Shields
July 13	76879	Edward Moore, South Shields
July 13	76880	Edward Moore, South Shields
July 14	76935	Edward Moore, South Shields
July 25	77341	Edward Moore, South Shields
Aug. 2	77881	Sowerby's Ellison Glass Works Ltd, Gateshead-on-Tyne
Aug. 3	77967	Sowerby's Ellison Glass Works Ltd, Gateshead-on-Tyne
Aug. 2	78084	Sowerby's Ellison Glass Works Ltd, Gateshead-on-Tyne
Aug. 11	78551	Sowerby's Ellison Glass Works Ltd, Gateshead-on-Tyne
Aug. 13	78704	Sowerby's Ellison Glass Works Ltd, Gateshead-on-Tyne
Aug. 13	78754	Woodall & Son, Birmingham
Sept. 1	80012	Edward Moore, South Shields
Sept. 1	80013	Edward Moore, South Shields
Sept. 5	80167	Thomas Webb & Sons, Stourbridge
Sept. 10	80530	Sowerby's Ellison Glass Works Ltd, Gateshead-on-Tyne
Sept. 12	80632	Percival, Vickers & Co. Ltd, Manchester
Sept. 15	81051	Stevens & Williams, Stourbridge
Sept. 15	81160	Henry Greener & Co., Sunderland
Sept. 24	81959	Edward Moore, South Shields
Sept. 30	82606	Edward Moore, South Shields

DATE	RD. NO.	MANUFACTURER OR REGISTRAR
Oct. 12	83773	Edward Moore, South Shields
Oct. 7	83777	Sowerby's Ellison Glass Works Ltd, Gateshead-on-Tyne
Oct. 15	84001	Sowerby's Ellison Glass Works Ltd, Gateshead-on-Tyne
Oct. 18	84218	Sowerby's Ellison Glass Works Ltd, Gateshead-on-Tyne
Oct. 21	84747	Sowerby's Ellison Glass Works Ltd, Gateshead-on-Tyne
Nov. 1	85870	Sowerby's Ellison Glass Works Ltd, Gateshead-on-Tyne
Nov. 5	86246	Thomas Webb & Sons, Stourbridge
Nov. 15	87058	Sowerby's Ellison Glass Works Ltd, Gateshead-on-Tyne
Nov. 24	87776	Sowerby's Ellison Glass Works Ltd, Gateshead-on-Tyne
Nov. 24	87777	Sowerby's Ellison Glass Works Ltd, Gateshead-on-Tyne
Nov. 26	88120	Henry Greener & Co., Sunderland
Nov. 29	88124	Edward Moore, South Shields
Nov. 29	88125	Edward Moore, South Shields
Dec. 5	88730	Edward Moore, South Shields
1888		
Jan. 13	91359	Henry J. Manton, Birmingham
Jan. 14	91431	Sowerby's Ellison Glass Works Ltd, Gateshead-on-Tyne
Jan. 14	91432	Sowerby's Ellison Glass Works Ltd, Gateshead-on-Tyne
Jan. 11	91449	Henry Greener & Co., Sunderland
Jan. 23	92045	Edward Moore, South Shields
Feb. 18	93905	Percival, Vickers & Co. Ltd, Manchester
Feb. 17	94025	Stevens & Williams, Stourbridge
Feb. 18	94100	Mills, Walker & Co., Stourbridge
Feb. 18	94101	Mills, Walker & Co., Stourbridge
Feb. 25	94543	Henry Greener & Co., Sunderland
March 1	94820	Edward Moore, South Shields
March 7	95300	Sowerby's Ellison Glass Works Ltd, Gateshead-on-Tyne
March 12	95625	Edward Moore, South Shields
March 14	95775	Edward Moore, South Shields
March 16	95894	Sowerby's Ellison Glass Works Ltd, Gateshead-on-Tyne
March 16	95935	Henry Greener & Co., Sunderland
March 24	96547	Sowerby's Ellison Glass Works Ltd, Gateshead-on-Tyne
March 27	96775	Henry Greener & Co., Sunderland
March 27	96776	Henry Greener & Co., Sunderland
March 31	96945	George Davidson & Co., Gateshead-on-Tyne
April 18	98215	Sowerby's Ellison Glass Works Ltd, Gateshead-on-Tyne

Date	Rd. No.	Manufacturer or Registrar
April 18	98216	Sowerby's Ellison Glass Works Ltd, Gateshead-on-Tyne
April 13	98242	Frederick L. Jeyes, London
April 21	98551	Henry Greener & Co., Sunderland
April 23	98578	Burtles, Tate & Co., Manchester
April 25	98744	A. & P. Cochran, Glasgow
May 9	99715	Sowerby's Ellison Glass Works Ltd, Gateshead-on-Tyne
May 10	99911	H.G. Richardson, Stourbridge
May 12	100004	John Walsh Walsh, Birmingham
May 14	100207-8	J. Stembridge & Co., London
May 18	100404	G. V. de Luca, London
May 19	100456	Thomas Webb & Sons Ltd, Stourbridge
June 28	102902	Boulton & Mills, Stourbridge
July 11	103434	Henry Greener & Co., Sunderland
July 18	103949	John Walsh Walsh, Birmingham
July 17	103975	Henry Greener & Co., Sunderland
July 31	104759	Duncan Webb, Molineaux, Webb & Co., Manchester
Aug. 2	104890	Boulton & Mills, Stourbridge
Aug. 11	105464	Edward Bolton & Sons, Warrington, Lancashire
Aug. 14	105830	Thomas Webb & Sons Ltd, Stourbridge
Aug. 30	106892	Sowerby's Ellison Glass Works Ltd, Gateshead-on-Tyne
Aug. 31	106938	Sowerby's Ellison Glass Works Ltd, Gateshead-on-Tyne
Sept. 5	107316	Edward Moore, South Shields
Sept. 6	107409	Duncan Webb, Molineaux, Webb & Co., Manchester
Sept. 12	107808	John Walsh Walsh, Birmingham
Sept. 12	107809	John Walsh Walsh, Birmingham
Sept. 14	108018	Henry Greener & Co., Sunderland
Sept. 14	108019	Henry Greener & Co., Sunderland
Sept. 15	108129	Mills Walker & Co., Stourbridge
Sept. 29	109461	Henry Greener & Co., Sunderland
Sept. 29	109462	Henry Greener & Co., Sunderland
Oct. 1	109531	Burtles, Tate & Co., Manchester
Oct. 2	109612	Edward Moore, South Shields
Oct. 5	109926	G. V. de Luca, London
Oct. 11	110458-9	Robert Emmett Finley, Birmingham
Oct. 17	111269	Sowerby's Ellison Glass Works Ltd, Gateshead-on-Tyne
Oct. 17	111270	Sowerby's Ellison Glass Works Ltd, Gateshead-on-Tyne
Oct. 17	111282	Duncan Webb, Molineaux, Webb & Co, Manchester

Date	Rd. No.	Manufacturer or Registrar
Oct. 17	111290	Duncan Webb, Molineaux, Webb & Co, Manchester
Oct. 19	111661	Matthew Turnbull, Sunderland
Nov. 1	112468	John Thomas Creasy & James Dingwall, London
Nov. 1	112730-1	Robert Emmett Finley, Birmingham
Nov. 13	113560	Sowerby's Ellison Glass Works Ltd, Gateshead-on-Tyne
Nov. 15	113896	Henry Greener & Co., Sunderland
Nov. 14	114006	Boulton & Mills, Stourbridge
Nov. 17	114044	Sowerby's Ellison Glass Works Ltd, Gateshead-on-Tyne
Nov. 23	114474	Sowerby's Ellison Glass Works Ltd, Gateshead-on-Tyne
Nov. 28	115077	Percival, Vickers & Co. Ltd, Manchester
Dec. 14	115743	Henry Greener & Co., Sunderland
Dec. 12	115748	Stone, Fawdry & Stone, Birmingham
Dec. 17	115910	John Shaw & Sons, Sheffield
1889		
Jan. 9	117086	John Walsh Walsh, Birmingham
Jan. 9	117222	John Walsh Walsh, Birmingham
Jan. 14	117556	Burtles, Tate & Co., Manchester
Jan. 14	117557	Burtles, Tate & Co., Manchester
Jan. 17	117569	Sowerby's Ellison Glass Works Ltd, Gateshead-on-Tyne
Jan. 21	117815	Matthew Turnbull, Sunderland
Jan. 26	118285	A. & R. Cochran, Glasgow
Jan. 26	118358	Chance Bros. & Co. Ltd, Birmingham
Jan. 26	118359	Chance Bros. & Co. Ltd, Birmingham
Feb. 2	118864	Boulton & Mills, Stourbridge
Feb. 9	119318	Matthew Turnbull, Sunderland
Jan. 16	119542	William Davis, Birmingham
Feb. 23	120229	Sowerby's Ellison Glass Works Ltd, Gateshead-on-Tyne
Feb. 26	120437	Edward Moore, South Shields
Feb. 27	120451	H.G. Richardson, Stourbridge
March 4	120808	Burtles, Tate & Co., Manchester
March 19	121729-31	James Couper & Sons, Glasgow
March 23	121985	Henry Greener & Co., Sunderland
March 26	122093-4	G. V. de Luca, London
March 26	122096	Boulton & Mills, Stourbridge
March 28	122274	F. & C. Osler, Birmingham
March 28	122279-91	Edward J. Shaw & Co., Walsall

Date	Rd. No.	Manufacturer or Registrar
March 30	122393	Sowerby's Ellison Glass Works Ltd, Gateshead-on-Tyne
April 2	122519	Sowerby's Ellison Glass Works Ltd, Gateshead-on-Tyne
April 2	122581	Pilkington Bros, St Helens, Lancashire
April 5	122790	John Henry Downing, Birmingham
April 10	123198	George Davidson & Co., Gateshead-on-Tyne
April 25	124116-8	Pilkington Bros, St Helens, Lancashire
May 8	124835	Richard Vann, Birmingham
May 14	125323	William Davis, Birmingham
May 31	126315	F. & C. Osler, Birmingham
June 1	126688	Boulton & Mills, Stourbridge
June 5	126694	George Davidson & Co, Gateshead-on-Tyne
June 8	126869	Percival, Vickers & Co. Ltd, Manchester
June 11	126940	Sowerby's Ellison Glass Works Ltd, Gateshead-on-Tyne
June 22	127515	Matthew Turnbull, Sunderland
June 22	127516	Matthew Turnbull, Sunderland
July 17	128882	Henry Greener & Co., Sunderland
July 17	128883	Henry Greener & Co., Sunderland
July 17	128884	Henry Greener & Co., Sunderland
July 20	129295-6	Alfred Arculus, Birmingham
July 31	129933	Edward Moore, South Shields
Aug. 13	130641	George Davidson & Co., Gateshead-on-Tyne
Aug. 13	130642	George Davidson & Co., Gateshead-on-Tyne
Aug. 13	130643	George Davidson & Co., Gateshead-on-Tyne
Aug. 23	131653	Stuart & Sons, Stourbridge
Aug. 31	132189	Edward Moore, South Shields
Sept. 11	133053	Sowerby's Ellison Glass Works Ltd, Gateshead-on-Tyne
Sept. 18	133560	Edward Moore, South Shields
Sept. 24	133909	Sowerby's Ellison Glass Works Ltd, Gateshead-on-Tyne
Oct. 1	134350	William J. Blenko, London
Oct. 5	134907	Percival, Vickers & Co. Ltd, Manchester
Oct. 5	134908	Molineaux, Webb & Co. Ltd, Manchester
Oct. 28	136980	Stevens & Williams, Stourbridge
Nov. 4	137288	Stevens & Williams, Stourbridge
Nov. 14	138051	Henry Greener & Co., Sunderland
Nov. 26	139101	Pilkington Bros., St Helens, Lancashire
Dec. 4	139589	Edward Moore, South Shields
Dec. 6	139808	Sowerby's Ellison Glass Works Ltd, Gateshead-on-Tyne

DATE	RD. NO.	MANUFACTURER OR REGISTRAR
Dec. 6	139809	Sowerby's Ellison Glass Works Ltd, Gateshead-on-Tyne
Dec. 24	141068	Edward Moore, South Shields
Dec. 27	141080	Sowerby's Ellison Glass Works Ltd, Gateshead-on-Tyne
Dec. 27	141128	F. & C. Osler, Birmingham
1890		
Jan. 18	142433	Boulton & Mills, Stourbridge
Jan. 18	142434	Henry Derbyshire (glass merchant), Manchester
Jan. 22	142675	Sowerby's Ellison Glass Works Ltd, Gateshead-on-Tyne
Jan. 28	142985	Burtles, Tate & Co., Manchester
Jan. 28	143153	Molineaux, Webb & Co. Ltd, Manchester
Feb. 11	143884	Matthew Turnbull, Sunderland
Feb. 25	144779	Molineaux, Webb & Co. Ltd, Manchester
Feb. 28	145008	Matthew Turnbull, Sunderland
March 11	145580	Henry Greener & Co., Sunderland
March 14	145813	A. & R. Cochran, Glasgow
April 30	148661	Burtles, Tate & Co., Manchester
May 14	149468	John Walsh Walsh, Birmingham
May 14	149470	Schindler & Co., London
May 22	149959	James Bridger, London
May 24	150045-6	Kempton & Sons, London
June 3	150277	Henry Greener & Co., Sunderland
June 5	150401	Henry Greener & Co., Sunderland
June 7	150532	Chance Bros. & Co. Ltd, Birmingham
June 10	150597	Chance Bros. & Co. Ltd, Birmingham
July 1	151657	Stevens & Williams, Stourbridge
Aug. 2	153858	George Davidson & Co., Gateshead-on-Tyne
Aug. 20	154744-5	J. H. Davey & Co., Upper Edmonton
Sept. 2	155744	John Walsh Walsh, Birmingham
Sept. 10	156417	J. H. Davey & Co., Upper Edmonton
Oct. 9	158841	Schindler & Co., London
Oct. 15	158948	Molineaux, Webb & Co. Ltd, Manchester
Oct. 15	158967	Schindler & Co., London
Oct. 16	159189	Percival, Vickers & Co. Ltd, Manchester
Nov. 3	160244	Henry Greener & Co., Sunderland
Dec. 16	163075	Henry Greener & Co., Sunderland
Dec. 17	163179	James Marshall, Stourbridge

DATE	RD. NO.	MANUFACTURER OR REGISTRAR
1891		
Jan. 12	164521	Molineaux, Webb & Co. Ltd, Manchester
Jan. 13	164606-7	Stone, Fawdry & Stone, Birmingham
Jan. 14	164670	John Walsh Walsh, Birmingham
Jan. 20	165012	John Walsh Walsh, Birmingham
Jan. 30	165559	Sowerby's Ellison Glass Works Ltd, Gateshead-on-Tyne
Feb. 10	166178	Burtles, Tate & Co., Manchester
Feb. 12	166347	A. & R. Cochran, Glasgow
March 5	167516	Thomas Webb & Sons Ltd, Stourbridge
March 13	168130	Percival, Vickers & Co. Ltd, Manchester
March 24	168686	James Hateley & Co., Birmingham
April 2	169054	Alfred Arculus, Birmingham
April 9	169410	Matthew Turnbull, Sunderland
April 25	170363	A. & R. Cochran, Glasgow
April 30	170658	Stevens & Williams, Stourbridge
May 29	172125	John Walsh Walsh, Birmingham
June 11	172810	John Walsh Walsh, Birmingham
June 18	173044	Percival, Vickers & Co. Ltd, Manchester
June 18	173059	Sowerby and Company, Newcastle-on-Tyne
July 23	175031	Boulton & Mills, Stourbridge
Aug. 4	175802	Thomas Webb & Sons Ltd, Stourbridge
Aug. 10	176239	Henry Greener & Co., Sunderland
Aug. 15	176566	George Davidson & Co., Gateshead-on-Tyne
Aug. 28	177399	Boulton & Mills, Stourbridge
Sept. 2	177733	John Walsh Walsh, Birmingham
Sept. 9	178174	Thomas Webb & Sons Ltd, Stourbridge
Sept. 16	178653	Thomas Webb & Sons Ltd, Stourbridge
Sept. 29	179709	J. & W. B. Smith, London
Oct. 27	181572	Stevens & Williams, Stourbridge
Oct. 29	181922	John Walsh Walsh, Birmingham
Oct. 30	182002	Henry Greener & Co., Sunderland
Nov. 3	182180	Webb, Shaw & Co. Ltd, Stourbridge
Nov. 3	182181	Webb, Shaw & Co. Ltd, Stourbridge
Nov. 20	183415-7	John Walsh Walsh, Birmingham
Dec. 4	184359	Stone, Fawdry & Stone, Birmingham
Dec. 7	184501	John Walsh Walsh, Birmingham
Dec. 8	184548	John Walsh Walsh, Birmingham

Date	Rd. No.	Manufacturer or Registrar
1892		
Jan. 7	185911	Thomas Webb & Sons Ltd, Stourbridge
Jan. 12	186137	John Walsh Walsh, Birmingham
Jan. 14	186286	Richard Wilkes, Dudley, Worcestershire
Jan. 15	186382	Boulton & Mills, Stourbridge
Jan. 21	186546	John Walsh Walsh, Birmingham
Jan. 21	186567	John Walsh Walsh, Birmingham
Jan. 25	186770	Thomas Webb & Sons Ltd, Stourbridge
March 10	188944-5	Alfred Arculus, Birmingham
March 15	189247	Percival, Vickers & Co. Ltd, Manchester
March 16	189324	Sowerby's Ellison Glass Works Ltd, Gateshead-on-Tyne
March 16	189344	Percival, Vickers & Co. Ltd, Manchester
April 2	190428	Boulton & Mills, Stourbridge
April 5	190543	J. & J. Price, Birmingham
April 21	191254	Pilkington Bros., St Helens, Lancashire
May 3	191886	Webb, Shaw & Co. Ltd, Stourbridge
May 4	191932	Boulton & Mills, Stourbridge
May 10	192298	Robinson, Skinner & Co., Warrington, Lancashire
May 16	192595	Thomas Webb & Sons Ltd, Stourbridge
May 20	192807	Thomas Webb & Sons Ltd, Stourbridge
May 21	192876	Percival, Vickers & Co., Ltd, Manchester
June 1	193365	George Davidson & Co., Gateshead-on-Tyne
June 9	193694	Percival, Vickers & Co. Ltd, Manchester
June 9	193695	Percival, Vickers & Co. Ltd, Manchester
June 14	193821	Percival, Vickers & Co. Ltd, Manchester
June 25	194616	Chance Bros. & Co. Ltd, Birmingham
June 27	194638	Percival, Vickers & Co. Ltd, Manchester
July 15	195482	J. & W. B. Smith, London
July 26	196009	S. Reich & Co., London
Aug. 10	196641	Henry Greener & Co., Sunderland
Aug. 12	196748-9	Pilkington Bros, St Helens, Lancashire
Sept. 20	199109	H. G. Richardson, Stourbridge
Sept. 23	199384	Woodall & Son, London
Oct. 11	200505	Boulton & Mills, Stourbridge
Oct. 21	201225	Molineaux, Webb & Co. Ltd, Manchester
Nov. 25	203135	John Walsh Walsh, Birmingham

Date	Rd. No.	Manufacturer or Registrar
1893		
Jan. 17	205994	Boulton & Mills, Stourbridge
Jan. 18	206025	Webb Bros. Ltd, Manchester
Jan. 18	206026	Webb Bros. Ltd, Manchester
Jan. 27	206612	Thomas Webb & Sons Ltd, Stourbridge
Feb. 4	207065	Webb, Shaw & Co. Ltd, Stourbridge
Feb. 7	207120	Wood Bros. & Co., Barnsley, Yorkshire
Feb. 20	207909	George Davidson & Co., Gateshead-on-Tyne
March 1	208367	Matthew Turnbull, Sunderland
March 17	209414	Molineaux, Webb & Co. Ltd, Manchester
March 20	209493	Stevens & Williams, Stourbridge
April 10	210371	Henry Greener & Co., Sunderland
April 15	210704	Stone, Fawdry & Stone, Birmingham
April 15	210719	Stone, Fawdry & Stone, Birmingham
April 17	210755	Thomas Webb & Sons Ltd, Stourbridge
May 3	211617	Percival, Vickers & Co. Ltd, Manchester
May 6	211778	John Walsh Walsh, Birmingham
May 17	212315	Pilkington Bros, St Helens, Lancashire
May 25	212684	George Davidson & Co., Gateshead-on-Tyne
May 29	212730	Thomas Webb & Sons Ltd, Stourbridge
June 9	213324	Pilkington Bros, St Helens, Lancashire
June 10	213374	Matthew Turnbull, Sunderland
June 10	213381	Percival, Vickers & Co. Ltd, Manchester
June 21	213768	Stone, Fawdry & Stone, Birmingham
July 15	215082	Sowerby's Ellison Glass Works Ltd, Gateshead-on-Tyne
July 18	215154	Henry Greener & Co., Sunderland
Aug. 3	216088	Burtles, Tate & Co., Manchester
Aug. 3	216157	H.G. Richardson & Sons, Stourbridge
Aug. 16	216779-80	H.G. Richardson & Sons, Stourbridge
Aug. 25	217199	Sowerby's Ellison Glass Works Ltd, Gateshead-on-Tyne
Aug. 25	217202	H.G. Richardson & Sons, Stourbridge
Sept. 4	217651	Molineaux, Webb & Co. Ltd, Manchester
Sept. 6	217749	Henry Greener & Co., Sunderland
Sept. 6	217752	George Davidson & Co., Gateshead-on-Tyne
Sept. 9	217900	H.G. Richardson & Sons, Stourbridge
Sept. 11	218085	Thomas Webb & Sons Ltd, Stourbridge
Sept. 12	218103	Stevens & Williams, Stourbridge

DATE	RD. NO.	MANUFACTURER OR REGISTRAR
Sept. 20	218710	Henry Greener & Co., Sunderland
Oct. 3	219565	John Ford & Co., Edinburgh
Oct. 4	219638	Matthew Turnbull, Sunderland
Oct. 14	220471	Molineaux, Webb & Co. Ltd, Manchester
Oct. 14	220472	Molineaux, Webb & Co. Ltd, Manchester
Oct. 14	220473	Molineaux, Webb & Co. Ltd, Manchester
Oct. 19	220863	Stevens & Williams, Stourbridge
Oct. 27	221354	Boulton & Mills, Stourbridge
Nov. 8	222032	J. & J. Price, Birmingham
Nov. 8	222033	J. & J. Price, Birmingham
Dec. 5	223362	John Ford & Co., Edinburgh
Dec. 11	223742	Henry Greener & Co., Sunderland
Dec. 19	224171	George Davidson & Co., Gateshead-on-Tyne
Dec. 28	224603	Stevens & Williams, Stourbridge
1894		
Feb. 3	226750	Stevens & Williams, Stourbridge
April 3	230031	Jules Lang & Co., London
April 7	230286	John Ford & Co., Edinburgh
April 26	231387	Thomas Webb & Sons Ltd, Stourbridge
May 22	232529	Jules Lang & Co., London
May 30	233062	Matthew Turnbull, Sunderland
June 11	233766	Percival, Vickers & Co. Ltd, Manchester
June 11	233768	Molineaux, Webb & Co. Ltd, Manchester
June 14	234231	Henry Greener & Co., Sunderland
July 11	235779	Edmund Coaney & Co., Birmingham
July 12	235824	Boulton & Mills, Stourbridge
Aug. 1	237038	George Davidson & Co., Gateshead-on-Tyne
Aug. 23	238352	Sowerby & Company, Newcastle-on-Tyne
Aug. 23	238908	Wood Bros. & Co., Barnsley, Yorkshire
Sept. 27	240865	A. & R. Cochran, Glasgow
Oct. 10	241930	Henry Greener & Co., Sunderland
Oct. 27	243177	Edward J. Shaw & Co., Walsall
Nov. 1	243452	Chance Bros. & Co. Ltd, Birmingham
Nov. 23	245141	John Walsh Walsh, Birmingham
Dec. 10	245720	Matthew Turnbull, Sunderland

DESIGN REGISTRATIONS

Date	Rd. No.	Manufacturer or Registrar
1895		
Jan. 2	247064	Alfred Arculus, Birmingham
Jan. 4	247225	Alfred Arculus, Birmingham
Jan. 12	247617	Alfred Arculus, Birmingham
Jan. 17	247921	De Grelle, Houdret & Co., London
Jan. 30	248671	Thomas Webb & Sons Ltd, Stourbridge
Feb. 7	249104	John Shaw, Sheffield
Feb. 14	249450	Boulton & Mills, Stourbridge
Feb. 14	249451	Boulton & Mills, Stourbridge
Feb. 20	249824	Schindler & Co., London
Feb. 27	250254	Webb, Shaw & Co., Stourbridge
March 2	250515	Matthew Turnbull, Sunderland
March 12	251168	Alfred Arculus, Birmingham
March 15	251393	Molineaux, Webb & Co. Ltd, Manchester
March 23	251816	John Walsh Walsh, Birmingham
April 10	252968	Mills, Walker & Co. Ltd, Stourbridge
April 29	253934	John Walsh Walsh, Birmingham
April 29	253935	John Walsh Walsh, Birmingham
May 1	254027	George Davidson & Co., Gateshead-on-Tyne
May 7	254406	Percival, Vickers & Co. Ltd, Manchester
June 11	256117	De Grelle, Houdret & Co., London
June 20	256562-5	Jules Lang & Co., London
July 15	258147	John Walsh Walsh, Birmingham
July 15	258156	Henry Greener & Co., Sunderland
Sept. 4	261065	H.G. Richardson & Sons, Stourbridge
Sept. 4	261066	H.G. Richardson & Sons, Stourbridge
Sept. 7	261292	Schindler & Co., London
Sept. 16	262018	Henry Greener & Co., Sunderland
Oct. 24	264500	Jules Lang & Co., London
Oct. 29	264751	John Walsh Walsh, Birmingham
Nov. 1	264997	John Walsh Walsh, Birmingham
Nov. 1	265003	Jules Lang & Co., London
Nov. 14	265716	G. C. Fowler & M. B. Fowler, Brockley, Kent
Dec. 2	266768	Eunson & Scurr, Sunderland
Dec. 4	266897	Pilkington Bros. Ltd, St Helens, Lancashire
Dec. 20	267931-2	Eunson & Scurr, Sunderland
Dec. 27	268126	Jules Lang & Co., London

Date	Rd. No.	Manufacturer or Registrar
1896		
Jan. 3	268576-8	Jules Lang & Co., London
Jan. 13	268968	Percival, Vickers & Co. Ltd, Manchester
Jan. 15	269113	Molineaux, Webb & Co. Ltd, Manchester
Jan. 15	269119	Hearn Wright & Co., London
Jan. 16	269203	Jules Lang & Co., London
Jan. 27	269927	Thomas Webb & Sons Ltd, Stourbridge
Jan. 27	269928	Thomas Webb & Sons Ltd, Stourbridge
Jan. 27	269929	Thomas Webb & Sons Ltd, Stourbridge
Feb. 7	270546	Jules Lang & Co., London
Feb. 12	270831	Jules Lang & Co., London
Feb. 21	271422	John Walsh Walsh, Birmingham
Feb. 24	271540	John Walsh Walsh, Birmingham
Feb. 26	271700	Molineaux, Webb & Co. Ltd, Manchester
March 13	272672	Edmund Coaney & Co., Birmingham
March 25	273414	John Walsh Walsh, Birmingham
April 1	273840	Davies & Stewart, Birmingham
April 11	274253	Edward John Shaw, Birmingham
April 21	274732	Jules Lang & Co., London
April 24	274887	John Walsh Walsh, Birmingham
April 24	274888	John Walsh Walsh, Birmingham
April 24	274889	John Walsh Walsh, Birmingham
April 27	275000-3	Edward John Shaw, Birmingham
May 7	275802	Percival, Vickers & Co. Ltd, Manchester
May 18	276415-8	Edward John Shaw, Birmingham
June 1	276977	Henry Greener & Co., Sunderland
June 4	277168	Jules Lang & Co., London
June 23	278273	Arthur Thomas Woodall, London
July 30	280525	Eunson & Scurr, Sunderland
Aug. 1	280695	John Walsh Walsh, Birmingham
Aug. 25	282113-4	Schindler & Co., London
Aug. 31	282607	John Walsh Walsh, Birmingham
Aug. 31	282608	John Walsh Walsh, Birmingham
Sept. 10	283577	Thomas Webb & Sons Ltd, Stourbridge
Sept. 23	284639	Henry Greener & Co., Sunderland
Sept. 23	284640	The Baccarat Glass Company, London
Oct. 2	285342	George Davidson & Co., Gateshead-on-Tyne

DATE	RD. NO.	MANUFACTURER OR REGISTRAR
Nov. 2	287472	H.G. Richardson & Sons, Stourbridge
Nov. 4	287653	Percival, Vickers & Co. Ltd, Manchester
Dec. 11	290039	Jules Lang & Co., London
Dec. 15	290299	William Ramsey, London
1897		
Jan. 8	291659	H.G. Richardson & Sons, Stourbridge
Jan. 8	291662	Eunson & Scurr, Sunderland
Jan. 23	292506	Percival, Vickers & Co. Ltd, Manchester
Jan. 3	293210-3	John Walsh Walsh, Birmingham
March 6	295260	Wood Bros & Co., Barnsley, Yorkshire
March 15	295653-4	John Walsh Walsh, Birmingham
March 23	296071	F. & C. Osler, Birmingham & London
March 27	296418-20	Alfred Arculus, Birmingham
April 17	297595	Chance Bros. & Co. Ltd, Birmingham
April 21	297675	Chance Bros. & Co. Ltd, Birmingham
May 22	299383	Schindler & Co., London
May 28	299712	John Walsh Walsh, Birmingham
July 8	301224	Schindler & Co., London
July 13	301443	Jules Lang, London
July 23	302034	Jules Lang, London
Aug. 18	303519	George Davidson & Co., Gateshead-on-Tyne
Sept. 3	304505	Henry Greener & Co., Sunderland
Sept. 20	305840	Percival, Vickers & Co. Ltd, Manchester
Dec. 16	310924-5	Scotney & Earnshaw, London
1898		
Jan. 5	311867	Edward John Shaw, Birmingham
Feb. 18	314494	Percival, Vickers & Co. Ltd, Manchester
March 4	315340	John Walsh Walsh, Birmingham
March 18	316068	Pilkington Bros Ltd, St Helens, Lancashire
March 24	316413	Burtles, Tate & Co., Manchester
March 29	316611	Percival, Vickers & Co. Ltd, Manchester
April 15	317331	Jules Lang, London
April 18	317448	H.G. Richardson & Sons, Stourbridge
April 25	317767	William Breffit, Castleford, Yorkshire
May 6	318345	H.G. Richardson & Sons, Stourbridge

Date	Rd. No.	Manufacturer or Registrar
May 19	319151	Percival, Vickers & Co. Ltd, Manchester
May 24	319400	Alfred Arculus, Birmingham
May 24	319604	James Stevens & Sons, Birmingham
June 10	320124	George Davidson & Co., Gateshead-on-Tyne
July 8	321667	Alfred Arculus, Birmingham
July 15	322001	Alfred Arculus, Birmingham
July 20	322177	John Walsh Walsh, Birmingham
Aug. 9	323288	John Walsh Walsh, Birmingham
Aug. 9	323289	John Walsh Walsh, Birmingham
Aug. 20	323997	Percival, Vickers & Co. Ltd, Manchester
Aug. 23	324169	Alfred Arculus, Birmingham
Sept. 7	325071	Jules Lang, London
Sept. 9	325194	Henry Greener & Co., Sunderland
Sept. 15	325539	Henry Greener & Co., Sunderland
Sept. 16	325615	Alfred Arculus, Birmingham
Oct. 18	327603	Schindler & Co., London
Nov. 3	328530	James Stevens & Sons, Birmingham
Nov. 3	328531	James Stevens & Sons, Birmingham
Nov. 4	328630	Webb, Shaw & Co. Ltd, Stourbridge
Nov. 4	328631	Webb, Shaw & Co. Ltd, Stourbridge
Nov. 4	328632	Webb, Shaw & Co. Ltd, Stourbridge
Dec. 13	330770	John Walsh Walsh, Birmingham
Dec. 13	330771	John Walsh Walsh, Birmingham
Dec. 19	331189	H.G. Richardson & Sons, Stourbridge
1899		
Jan. 21	332563	Alfred Arculus, Birmingham
Jan. 21	332564	John Walsh Walsh, Birmingham
Jan. 21	332565	John Walsh Walsh, Birmingham
Feb. 4	333324	Thomas Webb & Sons Ltd, Stourbridge
Feb. 16	333851	John Walsh Walsh, Birmingham
Feb. 16	333852	John Walsh Walsh, Birmingham
Feb. 18	333944	John Walsh Walsh, Birmingham
March 2	334659	The York Glass Company Ltd, York
March 9	334962	Jules Lang, London
March 23	335692	A. Ruch & Co., London
March 27	335854	La Société Anonyme des Glaces de Charleroi, Roux, Belgium

Date	Rd. No.	Manufacturer or Registrar
April 1	336112	Schindler & Co., London
April 6	336261	Burtles, Tate & Co., Manchester
April 12	336510	Percival, Vickers & Co. Ltd, Manchester
April 18	336752	John Walsh Walsh, Birmingham
April 22	336967-8	Jules Lang, London
May 2	337607-8	Jules Lang, London
May 20	338590	Molineaux, Webb & Co. Ltd, Manchester
June 8	339343	Burtles, Tate & Co., Manchester
June 9	339402	Webb, Shaw & Co. Ltd, Stourbridge
June 9	339403	Webb, Shaw & Co. Ltd, Stourbridge
July 5	340825	George Davidson & Co., Gateshead-on-Tyne
Aug. 11	343063	Henry Greener & Co., Sunderland
Dec. 4	350115	Thomas Webb & Corbett Ltd, Stourbridge
1900		
Jan. 5	351372	Burtles, Tate & Co., Manchester
Jan. 20	352198	Molineaux, Webb & Co. Ltd, Manchester
Feb. 16	353374	John Walsh Walsh, Birmingham
March 24	355194	F. & C. Osler, Birmingham
March 26	355232	John Ford & Co., Edinburgh
June 13	358727	George Sowerby Ltd, Newcastle-on-Tyne
July 13	360167	George Davidson & Co., Gateshead-on-Tyne
July 14	360332	Henry Greener & Co., Sunderland
Aug. 3	361366	Percival, Vickers & Co. Ltd, Manchester
Aug. 8	361580	Jules Lang, London
Aug. 31	362643	Jules Lang, London
Sept. 1	362682	Thomas Webb & Sons Ltd, Stourbridge
Sept. 8	363130	George Sowerby Ltd, Newcastle-on-Tyne
Sept. 18	363606-8	Jules Lang, London
Nov. 20	366502	Stevens & Williams, Stourbridge
Dec. 3	367054	Thomas Webb & Sons Ltd, Stourbridge

GLOSSARY

ANNEALING To temper glass by controlled and gradual cooling after manufacture.

BATCH The mixture of chemicals used in a single glass-melting operation.

BLANC-DE-LAIT The name given to their opalescent pressed glass by Sowerby's of Gateshead in 1880. Appears milky by reflected light and shows many blue and golden tints by transmitted light.

CHAIR Term used for a seat with long flat arms which is occupied by the leading member of the team of glassmakers. Also used to describe a group of men who work together in the production of glass.

COLLAR In glass pressing, a term applied to the metal ring at the top of the mould which prevents the glass being pressed out of the mould and also shapes the upper rim of the article.

CRUCIBLE The melting pot for glass.

CRYSTAL GLASS A general term for lead-potash glass.

CULLET Broken glass of any kind that is suitable for re-melting.

FIRE-POLISHING Reheating the surface of the glass to soften it and so produce a smooth polished finish. Removes mould marks and gives greater brilliance.

FLINT GLASS A term commonly used for any kind of colourless glass.

FOUND The period, often at night, during which the furnace is kept at a high temperature to melt the glass.

GADGET A spring-clip tool, mounted on an iron rod, used to hold the foot of a glass while the body part is being shaped by the glassmaker, or to hold a glass while subjecting it to the heat of the glory-hole for fire-polishing.

GATHER The blob of glass taken up from the pot of molten glass on the end of a blow iron or pontil rod.

GATHERER The member of the pressing team who collects the gather and brings it to the press.

GLASS HOUSE The building in which the glass-melting furnaces stand, and in which the actual handling of the molten glass takes place.

GLORY-HOLE A glassmaker's supplementary furnace, used for finishing the glass by fire-polishing.

LEAD GLASS Glass made with oxide of lead as the flux, which gives the metal the appearance of natural rock crystal; often called flint glass, though flint has rarely been used in the batch.

LEHR Sometimes written leer or lear. The tunnel in which the glass is annealed to prevent strain on cooling.

MELTER The member of the pressing team who takes the article from the mould and fire-polishes it.

METAL A semi-technical term, commonly used for glass in the molten state, and less frequently for glass when cold.

MIXER A worker who weighs and mixes glass-making materials in a mechanical mixer or by hand.

MOULD The receptacle into which the molten glass is pressed to give it form.

MOVE A piece-work term in the glass house. Glassmakers, when on piece-work, agree to make a certain number of articles per move for an agreed price.

OPAL In pressed glass, the name given to opaque glass coloured white and first used by the firm of Sowerby of Gateshead to refer to their white Vitro-Porcelain introduced in 1877. The name was adopted by other leading manufacturers for the same type of glass. Not to be confused with Sowerby's Blanc-de-Lait, which was opalescent.

PONTIL Also written as pontie, ponty, puntee or punty. An iron rod used for holding glassware during manufacture.

PONTIL MARK The rough piece of glass on the underside of glasses and goblets where the pontil was attached during making, and then broken off. Seldom appears on pressed glass unless very early.

POT The fireclay crucible in which the founding of the glass takes place.

PRESSED GLASS Glassware shaped in a press-mould.

PRESSER The member of the pressing team who actually presses the article in the mould.

QUARRY A name given in glazing to a pane of glass, usually diamond- or lozenge-shaped.

SERVITOR Chief assistant in a team or chair.

SLAG GLASS Specifically bottle glass. So named because of the addition of blast furnace slag to the batch for cheapness. The word 'slag' is often erroneously used when referring to the opaque coloured glass known as Vitro-Porcelain.

SODA-LIME GLASS A common batch mixture for glass which has as its principal ingredients soda, lime and silica. The formula was discovered in 1864 by William Leighton in America. Lighter in weight than lead glass, nearly as clear, and much cheaper to make, lime glass produced a great expansion in the pressed glass industry in the late 19th century.

STICKER-UP The boy who holds the glass article on an iron and heats it afresh after being pressed by holding it in the glory-hole.

TAKER-IN The boy who takes the glass, immediately it is made, and places it in the annealing lehr or kiln.

TEASER OR FOUNDER An operator who maintains the correct furnace temperature for feeding the batch into the furnace pot.

TURN A working period in the glasshouse, originally of six hours.

VITRO-PORCELAIN The name given to an opaque coloured glass produced by the pressing technique, and first used by Sowerby's of Gateshead in 1877. The body resembles that of china or porcelain.

WHITE GLASS Transparent colourless glass.

NOTES AND SOURCES

1 A *History of the Trade and Manufactures of the Tyne, Wear and Tees*, 1863

2 *Pottery Gazette*, 1 December 1881, p. 1061

3 Harry J. Powell, *The Principles of Glass-Making*, 1883

4 Catalogue for the Great Exhibition of the Industry of All Nations, 1851

5 British Parliamentary Papers, Children's Employment Commission (1862), fourth report, HMSO, 1865, p. 239

6 *Pottery Gazette*, 1 August 1888, Fancy Trades Supplement, p. 10

7 The works were known as the Ellison Glass Works, not the Ellison Street Glass Works – and were situated in East Street, Gateshead.

8 *Newcastle Daily Chronicle*, 21 October 1882

9 *Pottery Gazette*, April 1878, p. 182

10 *Pottery Gazette*, November 1877, p. 75

11 Patent no. 2156, 28 November 1878

12 *Pottery Gazette*, 1 January 1880, p. 23

13 *Pottery Gazette*, 1 May 1880, p. 280

14 *Newcastle Daily Chronicle*, 21 October 1882

15 *Pottery Gazette*, 1 December 1888, pp. 1118-19

16 *Pottery Gazette*, 1 June 1888, p. 546

17 Patent no. 4505, 15 October 1881

18 *Pottery Gazette*, 1 November 1881, p. 953

19 Sebastian Evans, 'Glass Manufactures, Staining, and Painting' in *The Practical Mechanic's Journal: Record of the Great Exhibition*, 1862, pp. 407-8

20 *Pottery Gazette*, 2 August 1886, p. 954

21 *Pottery Gazette*, 2 June 1884, p. 645

22 *Pottery Gazette*, 1 November 1900, p. 1229

23 Claude L. Fraser, *Pressed Glass: A Short History of Geo. Davidson & Co. Ltd., 1867-1948*, n.d., p. 5

24 *Pottery Gazette*, 1 February 1881, p. 139

25 *Pottery Gazette*, 1 April 1881, p. 327

26 *Pottery Gazette*, 1 October 1881, p. 866

27 *Pottery Gazette*, 1 December 1884, p. 1351

28 Advertisement in the *Pottery Gazette*, 1 December 1884, Supplement, p. 1403

29 *Pottery Gazette*, 1 March 1887, Fancy Trades Supplement, p. 9

30 *Pottery Gazette*, 1 April 1889, Fancy Trades Supplement, p. xix

31 Patent no. 2641, 7 December 1889

32 *Pottery Gazette*, 1 March 1889, Fancy Trades Supplement, p. 3

33 *Pottery Gazette*, 1 April, 1890, Fancy Trades Supplement, p. 3

34 *Pottery Gazette*, 1 October 1890, Fancy Trades Supplement, p. 3

35 *Pottery Gazette*, 1 April 1895, Fancy Trades Supplement, p. 3

36 *Pottery Gazette*, 1 October 1896, p. 813

37 *Pottery Gazette*, 1 October 1896, p. 813

38 *Pottery Gazette*, 1 September 1879, p. 326

39 Advertisement in the *Pottery Gazette*, 1 July 1881, Supplement, p. 565

40 *Pottery Gazette*, 1 January 1880, p. 23

41 *Pottery Gazette*, 1 April 1887, Fancy Trades Supplement, p. 9

42 *Pottery Gazette*, 1 August 1889, Fancy Trades Supplement, p. xix

43 *Pottery Gazette*, 1 November 1887, Supplement, p. 1094

44 *Pottery Gazette*, 2 November 1896, p. 952

45 *Pottery Gazette*, 1 March 1894, Fancy Trades Supplement, p. 3

46 *Gateshead and Tyneside Echo*, 2 January 1880, p. 2

47 British Parliamentary Papers, Children's Employment Commission (1862), fourth report, HMSO, 1865, p. 238

48 Report presented to Parliament 1870 by the Hon. T. J. Thurlow on the International

Exhibition of Domestic Economy, held at Amsterdam in 1869

49 International Exhibition, Sydney, Australia, 4 December 1879

50 Patent no. 4821, 17 April 1887

51 Patent no. 4822, 3 May 1887

52 *Pottery Gazette*, 1 November 1888, Fancy Trades Supplement, p. 3

53 *Pottery Gazette*, 1 December 1888, Fancy Trades Supplement, p. 3

54 *Pottery Gazette*, 1 May 1893, Fancy Trades Supplement, p. 3

55 I am indebted to Roger Dodsworth of the Broadfield House Glass Museum, West Midlands, for details of this letter

56 *Pottery Gazette*, 1 April 1884, p. 403

57 *Glass*, February 1927

58 *Pottery Gazette*, 1 January 1891, Fancy Trades Supplement, p. 4

59 *Pottery Gazette*, 1 June 1892, Fancy Trades Supplement, p. 3

60 *Pottery Gazette*, 1 January 1894, Fancy Trades Supplement, p. 3

61 *Pottery Gazette*, 1 July 1881, p. 593

62 *Pottery Gazette*, 1 December 1884, p. 1358

63 *Pottery Gazette*, 1 February 1890, Fancy Trades Supplement, p. 3

64 *Pottery Gazette*, 1 April 1898, Fancy Trades Supplement, p. 461

65 *Pottery Gazette*, 1 September 1880, p. 558

BIBLIOGRAPHY

Angus-Butterworth, L.M., *British Table and Ornamental Glass*, Leonard Hill, 1956

Aslin, Elizabeth, *The Aesthetic Movement: Prelude to Art Nouveau*, Elek, 1969, Ferndale Editions, 1981

British Parliamentary Papers, *Industrial Revolution, Children's Employment*, fourth report of the commissioners, HMSO, 1865

Buckley, Francis, 'Old Lancashire Glasshouses' in *Journal of the Society of Glass Technology*, 1929

Crane, Walter, *An Alphabet of Old Friends*, George Routledge & Sons, 1874

Crane, Walter, *Aladdin*, George Routledge & Sons, 1875

Crane, Walter, *Baby's Own Alphabet*, George Routledge & Sons, 1875

Crane, Walter, *The Baby's Opera*, George Routledge & Sons, 1877

Dodsworth, Roger, 'The Manchester Glass Industry', Glass Circle paper no. 4, 18 March 1980

Evans, Sebastian, 'Glass Manufactures' in R. Mallett ed., *The Practical Mechanic's Journal*, 1862

Fairbairn's Book of Crests, fourth edition, T. C. & E. C. Jack, 1905

Fraser, Claude L., *Pressed Glass: A Short History of Geo. Davidson & Co. Ltd., 1867-1948*, privately printed, n.d.

Girouard, Mark, *Sweetness and Light: The 'Queen Anne' Movement, 1860-1900*, Oxford University Press, 1977

'Glass-Making on Wearside', part 1 of *The Glass Industry of Tyne and Wear*, Tyne and Wear County Council, 1979

Godden, Geoffrey A., *Antique Glass and China Under £5*, Arthur Barker, 1966

Hagar's Directory of the County of Durham, 1851

Hughes, G. Bernard, *English Glass for the Collector 1660-1860*, Lutterworth Press, 1958

Jarves, Deming, *Reminiscences of Glass Making*, Eastburn's Press, Boston, 1854

Kelly's Post Office Directory of Durham, 1858

Konody, P. G., *The Art of Walter Crane*, George Bell & Sons, 1902

Lattimore, Colin R., *English 19th-Century Press-Moulded Glass*, Barrie & Jenkins, 1979

Lee, Ruth Webb, *The History of the Boston & Sandwich Glass Company*, privately printed, 1947

Morris, Barbara, *Victorian Table Glass and Ornaments*, Barrie & Jenkins, 1978

Morris, Barbara, 'Aspects of English Pressed Glass', paper read to the Glass Circle, 17 May 1979

Pellatt, Apsley, *Curiosities of Glass Making*, 1849

Pigot's Manchester Directory, 1830-3

Pilbin, Preston, 'The Influence of Local Geography on the Glass Industry of Tyneside', *Journal of the Tyneside Geographical Society of Newcastle-upon-Tyne*, no. 1, vol. 1, October 1936

Powell, Harry J., *The Principles of Glass-Making*, George Bell & Sons, 1883

Powell, Harry J., *Glass-Making in England*, Cambridge University Press, 1923

Ridley, Ursula, 'The History of Glass-Making on Tyneside', Circle of Glass Collectors, paper no. 122, January 1961

Robson's Birmingham and Sheffield Directory, 1839

Slater's Northern Counties Directory, 1854-5

The Tyneside, Newcastle and District: An Epitome of Results and Manual of Commerce, Historical Publishing Co., 1889

Wakefield, Hugh, *Nineteenth Century British Glass*, rev. ed., Faber & Faber, 1982

Ward's North of England Directory, 1852-3

Ward's Northumberland and Durham Directory, 1850

Webber, Norman W., *Collecting Glass*, David & Charles, 1972

Whelan's History, Topography and Directory of Northumberland, 1855-6

Wills, Geoffrey, *Victorian Glass*, G. Bell & Sons, 1976

Numbers in italics refer to plates

206